FIELD & TUER,
——— THE ———
LEADENHALL PRESS

Andrew W. Tuer.

Portrait published in *The British Printer,* Vol. VI, No. 34, 1893.

FIELD & TUER,
—THE—
LEADENHALL PRESS

A Checklist
with an
Appreciation of
Andrew White Tuer

BY
MATTHEW McLENNAN YOUNG

Oak Knoll Press
The British Library
2010

First Edition 2010

Published by
Oak Knoll Press
310 Delaware Street
New Castle, DE 19720
www.oakknoll.com

and

The British Library
96 Euston Road
London NW1 2DB
www.bl.uk/publishing

© 2010 Matthew McLennan Young. All rights reserved.

ISBN: 978-1-58456-280-1 (USA)
ISBN: 978-0-7123-5807-1 (UK)

Design & Typography: Matthew McLennan Young
Publishing Director: Laura R. Williams

No part of this book may be reproduced in any manner without the express written consent of the publisher, except in cases of brief excerpts in critical reviews and articles. All inquiries should be addressed to: Oak Knoll Press, 310 Delaware Street, New Castle, DE 19720.

∞ Printed in the United States of America on acid-free paper meeting the requirements of ANSI/NISO Z39.48–1992 (Permanence of Paper)

Cataloguing-in-Publication Data

A CIP Record for this book is available from
The Library of Congress and The British Library

Contents

Acknowledgments
vii

Introduction
1

Andrew White Tuer
5

A Checklist of Field & Tuer and The Leadenhall Press
35

A Selection of Examples in Color, 1869–1905
after page 104

Appendix A: Checklist of Andrew W. Tuer
105

Appendix B: Ephemera
109

Appendic C: Series
119

Appendix D: Collections
123

Bibliography
127

Index
129

abcdefghijklmnopqrstuvwxyz
abcdefghijklmnopqrstuvwxyz
abcdefghijklmrstvwxyz
abcdefghikmrstuvyz
abcdefgikopxyz
abcdefghijklxyz
ABCD LE'DN-HALL PR'SS HXYZ

abcdefghijklmnowxyz
ABEGRSTVW

abcdefghirstuwyz
ABCDSTYZ
abcdefghijkmnowxyz

aabcdeefghijklmnnopxyz
※ 1234567890 ※

Types from
The Leadenhall Press,
50, Leadenhall Street, London, E.C.

Acknowledgments

I could not have completed this book without the encouragement and advice of those who agreed to read the manuscript. Mark Samuels Lasner has been an inspiration, as well as an advisor and friend. David McKitterick commented from his perspective as a librarian, print historian, and longtime member of the editorial board of *The Book Collector*, and he put me in touch with the Bury family. Clare Lorenz, J. P. T. Bury's daughter, lent cheerful encouragement and graciously sent photographs of books, letters, and memorabilia. Richard Landon, Director of the Thomas Fisher Rare Book Library, University of Toronto, offered expert advice as a fellow Leadenhall Press admirer and sent a copy of the lists compiled by booksellers Ian Hodgkins and Susan Biltcliffe, the basis for my research into the Leadenhall Press job numbers. My proofreader, Nora Lin, caught many errors and inconsistencies, and Laura Williams, my editor at Oak Knoll Press, provided guidance and suggestions that have significantly improved the end result.

My research was advanced in 2008 by an Everett Helm Visiting Fellowship grant from the Lilly Library at Indiana University to examine their outstanding collection. Director Breon Mitchell, Curator of Books Joel Silver, and the entire staff were supportive before, during, and after my visit. I am grateful for the assistance of librarians at the British Library, Princeton University, The New York Public Library, the University of Toronto, the Grolier Club, the Houghton Library (Harvard), and Winterthur Library. I would also like to thank the librarians and photographers at other institutions who patiently handled my requests for information, digital images, and photocopies, especially those at the National Library of Scotland, the Bodleian Library, Trinity College Dublin, Cambridge University, the Clark Library (UCLA), the Woodson Research Center (Fondren Library, Rice University), the Harry Ransom Center (University of Texas at Austin), and Newcastle University.

Finally, thanks to my wife, Valerie, for unfailing enthusiasm and patience.

Introduction

"In the eighties the publishing house of Field & Tuer was showing a dexterity and invention that must have shocked the established Trade... theirs is a strangely unrecounted history."

—Francis Meynell, *Modern Books and Writers*[1]

Andrew White Tuer was among the most active and innovative printers and publishers of the late nineteenth century. However, no comprehensive bibliographic study of Field & Tuer and the Leadenhall Press had been completed when Francis Meynell and Desmond Flower included Joseph Crawhall's *Olde ffrendes wyth newe Faces* in their selection of "One hundred books chosen to illustrate the renascence of book design in England" for a 1951 exhibition in London. Even today, even among scholars of Victorian culture, there is often only a vague notion of the firm and its output.

Some years ago, I bought a plain-looking oblong volume with the running title: *The Book of Delightful and Strange Designs, Being One Hundred Facsimile Illustrations of the Art of the Japanese Stencil-cutter to which the Gentle Reader is Introduced by one Andrew W. Tuer, F.S.A. Who Knows Nothing at All About It.* My initial interest was in the inscription it bore, from Gleeson White to the Oxford historian Frederick York Powell, but that quickly became secondary. The book contains title pages and introductions in English, French, and German, an original Japanese stencil cut as a frontispiece, and reproductions on plates of 104 designs in white on bold black ground. Clearly, Andrew Tuer must have been a curious fellow, and my own curiosity was aroused. As I found other Leadenhall Press titles, I became increasingly captivated by the variety of the subject matter, design, and production. In the spirit of Andrew Tuer, I set out to research a subject about which I knew nothing at all. This book is the result.

I have been able to identify nearly 450 publications bearing the Field & Tuer and Leadenhall Press imprints (not including the various special issues, later editions, and ephemera), yet there seems almost to have been a conspiracy against the press among some printing historians. In Sawyer and Darton's 1927 two-volume work *English Books 1475–1900: A Signpost for Collectors*, there is but a single reference to Andrew Tuer as "director of a press that does not deserve oblivion." Little has been written about the Leadenhall Press since, apart from a few paragraphs and reproduced title pages in a 1931 piece on Victorian typography by A. F. Johnson in *The Monotype Recorder*[2] and a very informative 1987 article in *The Book Collector* by the historian J. P. T. Bury, who was related to Andrew Tuer by marriage and was Mrs. Tuer's godson.[3] Bury prepared a tentative table of the numbers of books

---

1. *Modern Books and Writers: The Catalogue of an Exhibition held at Seven Albemarle Street, April to September, 1951.* (Cambridge: Published for the National Book League by the Cambridge University Press, 1951). p. 33.
2. A. F. Johnson, "Old-Face Types in the Victorian Age," *The Monotype Recorder*, Sept.–Dec. 1931, pp. 5–14.
3. J. P. T. Bury, "Andrew W. Tuer and the Leadenhall Press," *The Book Collector*, Summer 1987, pp. 225–241.

published by the Leadenhall Press in each year from 1879 to 1905, totaling 317 by his reckoning. He also wrote an article about Andrew Tuer's bookplates, which was published posthumously in the March, 1888 issue of *The Bookplate Journal*. Where Tuer is mentioned in histories of printing, it is generally in the context of chapbook reprints and use of old style type, but in fact he published books of all descriptions on all subjects, from popular shilling series titles to elaborate limited editions, as well as two important and long-running journals, *The Paper & Printing Trades Journal* and *The Printers' International Specimen Exchange*.

There are several reasons for this oversight. The chief obstacle to research has been a lack of records. The Leadenhall Press stopped publishing shortly after Tuer's death, continuing as a print shop and closing in 1927. The archives were destroyed by Companies House in 1972. Only with the availability of research resources on the World Wide Web could I have imagined taking on this project. The fact that Tuer's contributions were largely forgotten soon after his death can be attributed, in part, to his own playful sense of humor. His tendency not to take himself too seriously may have led others, mistakenly, to do likewise. Probably the Leadenhall list did not include enough authors and illustrators whose reputations have stood the test of time, and the wide variety of publications makes a brief summary so difficult as to be pointless. (I once had two booksellers at the same book fair tell me they didn't have any Leadenhall Press books: one because he didn't deal in private presses, and the other because he carried *only* fine press books.)

But perhaps there *was* a conspiracy of sorts among historians of the nineties, satirized by Max Beerbohm in his essay "1880." Looking backward from the lofty present of 1896, he wrote, "To give an accurate and exhaustive account of that period would need a far less brilliant pen than mine." With a straighter face, Holbrook Jackson, in his 1913 book *The Eighteen Nineties*, casually dismissed decades of publishing thus: "suddenly, with few obvious preliminaries, we found ourselves in the midst of the Golden Age of what may be termed subjective printing." The movement of the "Book Beautiful," in defining itself, rejected wholesale the printing of the recent past, and most chroniclers of the period have perpetuated the notion of discontinuity.

Yet there were printers working in the seventies and eighties whose contributions are worthy of note. William Peterson, in *The Kelmscott Press, a History of William Morris's Typographical Adventure*, cites the publications of Rev. C. H. O. Daniel and Joseph Cundall, wondering, "Did Morris ever see them? We do not know, because he was silent about the Victorian books he considered worthy of admiration, but certainly Cundall, like Pickering, belongs to a very small group of nineteenth-century publisher-designers whose work may have influenced Morris. Likewise, it would be fascinating to discover whether Morris was aware of the books published and printed by Andrew Tuer, whose Leadenhall Press ('Ye Leadenhalle Presse' was the quaint version) in London issued many lively, amusing exercises in pastiche."

Almost certainly Morris was well aware of Tuer and his press. Tuer had been a committee member and exhibitor at the 1877 Caxton Celebration of the 400th anniversary of printing in England, and by the mid 1880s, Leadenhall Press trade titles were selling in the tens of thousands, while the limited edition productions were being widely praised. William Harcourt Hooper designed several bookplates for Tuer before becoming Kelmscott's principal woodcutter, and the frontispiece illustration to the 1885 Leadenhall Press first edition of *Songs of the North* was by Morris's close friend Edward Burne-Jones. In 1890, Morris wrote to Tuer declining an offer to publish a lecture because it was given without notes.[4] Not long after the founding of the Kelmscott Press, Arthur Gaskin was producing illustrations for Morris while his wife, Georgie Cave France (whose work, as a member of the Birmingham Group, Morris also knew), was doing the same for Tuer.

While Morris may not have approved of Tuer's playful approach to book design, the best of the Leadenhall Press publications provided a standard that the designers and printers of the 1890s no doubt studied in developing their own ideas. I hope this study will generate additional interest and research, and contribute to a more complete understanding of Andrew Tuer and his contributions to the development of printing in England in the second half of the nineteenth century.

---

4. Norman Kelvin, *The Collected Letters of William Morris, Vol. 3: 1889–1892* (Princeton University Press, 1995), p. 243.

Bookplate design by William Harcourt Hooper.

Andrew White Tuer

Tuer . . . was like a joyous juggler tossing into the air his miscellaneous elements of design and unerringly retrieving them in all sorts of postures.
—Dr. John Johnson, Printer to Oxford University[1]

One Joseph Tuer came to Tyne and Wear from Westmoreland in the late 18th century, establishing himself in the Deptford glassworks firm of White, Young and Tuer. He married Elizabeth Dixon, daughter of shipowner Hugh Dixon, in 1802. Some years later, Elizabeth's much younger sister, Ophelia, married Andrew White, a successful businessman, Sunderland's first mayor, and member of Parliament from 1837–41. The Whites were to become the most important people in Andrew Tuer's early life.

Joseph and Elizabeth's son, Joseph Robertson Tuer, became a partner in the drapery firm of Jopling and Tuer, and in 1836 he married Jane White Taft, Andrew White's niece. Their first child, also named Joseph, was born in September 1837. A second son, born on Christmas Eve 1838, was named Andrew White, after Jane's favorite uncle. A daughter, Jane, was born in 1840 but did not survive. Tragically, the boys' mother died in 1841, and by 1848 their father was also dead, leaving the orphaned boys in the guardianship of Andrew and Ophelia White. The 1851 census shows Joseph and Andrew, ages 13 and 12, boarding at Rev. William Bowman's Gainford Academy (later attended by Arthur Stanley Jefferson, who became famous as Stan Laurel). Andrew was also educated at Dr. Bruce's Percy Street Academy in Newcastle-upon-Tyne, and then at York. Records have not been found identifying which school in York, but it may have been Archbishop Holgate's, a Church of England school known for strength in the sciences and technologies, the sort of training evident in Andrew's later activities. His guardian intended him for the ministry, but when Andrew White died in 1856, young Tuer went up to London and enrolled as a medical student at Guy's Hospital. That did not suit him either, and after a brief period in a merchant's office, at age 22 he was in business as a wholesale stationer, living with his widowed aunt Ann (Taft) Hubie and her family in Stepney. In 1862, he co-founded the partnership of Field & Tuer, "printers of forms, lithographers, and wholesale manufacturing stationers," at 136 Minories.

Born around 1830 in St. James, Westminster, Abraham Field was a stationer's apprentice at the age of 21 and an established producer of registers and log-books in Nicholas Lane by the time he met Andrew Tuer. By 1881, he and his wife, Mary, and four children were living at 8 Buckland Villas, St. John's Parish, Hampstead. Not much else is known of Field or his part in the business; perhaps he managed daily financial affairs and the general printing work that remained an important foundation of the firm's revenues, but he appears to have had little or no role in the

---

1. "The Development of Printing, other than Book-Printing," a paper given at Oxford, 1936.

publishing enterprise. In 1877, he was a subscriber in the formation of the Frongoch Slate Quarry in Tewyn, Merionteth, so he had at least one outside business interest.[2] Within a decade, Andrew Tuer's entrepreneurial spirit and creative energy had taken the company in an entirely new direction, and he soon became the public face and driving spirit of the business.

Printing had been a hobby of Tuer's, and he soon added ornamental printing to the list of Field & Tuer's services. His education in chemistry also led to the invention of Stickphast Paste, a clean, white product that quickly became a popular and highly profitable alternative to the gums and animal-based glues in use at the time. The manufacturing side of the business included carbonic and manifold papers, an ink powder for home mixing, and the introduction, in 1883, of the *Author's Paper Pad*, a block of ruled, detachable sheets "of unusual but not painful smoothness," adhered along one edge to a base of thick blotting paper, with an eye hole for securing after detaching. Sometime after, a holder was made available for use in railway carriages.

The pad was later advertised as the *Author's Hairless Paper Pad*, to the delight of "The Baron de Book-Worms" of *Punch*, who recommended it to Mr. Gladstone as "*The Hairless Author's Paper Pad*," the "knee-plus ultra" of portable writing accessories. Tuer was happy to feature the *Punch* inversion in subsequent advertising. His knack for marketing was noted by advertising expert Thomas Russell in a 1919 lecture at the London School of Economics: "It is given to few men to write a good advertisement in fewer words than the three into which Mr. Andrew W. Tuer thus condensed the story of a famous product: 'Stickphast Paste Sticks'."[3]

Courtesy, Lilly Library, Indiana University, Bloomington, IN.

Members of the firm patented various devices for the book trades over the years. In 1868, Field & Tuer obtained a patent (No. 3125) for an advertising display with ribs to which strips printed on both sides were attached, allowing more than one notice to be presented. When viewed at an angle, the strips "which are towards the observer have all the appearance of having become united

---

2. *North Wales Chronicle*, April 14, 1877.
3. Thomas Russell. *Commercial Advertising. Six Lectures at the London School of Economics and Political Science* (London & New York, G. P. Putnam's Sons, Ltd., 1919), p. 18. Russell was President of the Incorporated Society of Advertisement Consultants and occasional Advertising Manager of *The Times*.

or joined together so as to present to the eye of the observer complete letters, words, or illustrations." Tuer also invented and patented a "Duplex Process" for printing headline type over text, with the text continuing uninterrupted in reverse within the larger black letters. An advertisement demonstrating the effect appeared in *The Graphic* of May 10, 1879.

Commercial success allowed Andrew Tuer the freedom not only to advance his professional ambitions, but also to develop his personal life. On October 10, 1867, he and Thomasine Louisa Louttit, daughter of Samuel John and Thomasine Louttit, were married at St. Mary's Church, Bromley St. Leonard. Samuel was Controller of Accounts in the tea office at Her Majesty's Custom House, and as the Louttits were living in Stepney when Andrew was boarding nearby with his aunt and starting in business, it seems likely the couple met at that time. Thomasine and Andrew shared a love of music; he was a talented pianist and a fine tenor, while she possessed a rich contralto voice and, through training by Madame Charlotte Sainton-Dolby, became well known as an amateur opera singer, remaining active into her seventies. In a review of an otherwise unimpressive 1885 concert by the Handel Society, the *Monthly Musical Record* reported, "Of the principal solo vocalists . . . we would only mention Mrs. Tuer; she has a fine voice, and sang the 'David' music with much taste and intelligence." A surviving scrapbook[4] shows that she performed before royalty at charity events and, on one occasion, with Henry Irving and Ellen Terry. Thomasine also became an avid bridge player, no doubt leading to the publication by the press of two books on bridge, in 1902 and 1905. Andrew maintained close relationships with the Louttit family throughout his life, and two of Louisa's brothers, Samuel and Duncan, are listed as subscribers in the formation of the Leadenhall Press, Limited, in 1892. The couple did not have children of their own, but in addition to their various interests and pursuits, by all accounts they entertained frequently and led a full social and cultural life.

In 1868, Field & Tuer moved to larger quarters at 50 Leadenhall Street and the adjoining Sugar Loaf Court, where the manufacturing part of the business was situated. With the expansion, the firm began printing pamphlets and books on a regular basis, some for private publication, others with established publishers such as Sampson Low, Trübner & Co., and Simpkin, Marshall & Co., who later became a regular distributing partner for the Leadenhall Press. Even before the move, Field & Tuer had printed and co-published (with Goddard & Son of Hull) *Clayton's Annual Register of Shipping and Port Charges for Great Britain* (1865). The first book in their own right that I have identified appeared in 1869: *Uncle, Can You Find a Rhyme for Orange?*, an illustrated collection of doggerel (most likely by Tuer, who indulged in word games throughout his life) containing excruciating rhymes for "orange," the best of which are "porringe" and "door hinge." Another early co-publication (with

---

4. In the possession of the Bury family.

the author) was Samuel Palmer's *St. Pancras; Being Antiquarian, Topographical, and Biographical Memoranda* (1870), an early indication of Tuer's interest in publications about London history that eventually formed a significant part of the catalogue. Within a few years, continued growth in business prompted the partners to tear down the old building and construct modern facilities with considerably more space.

Tuer was interested in both the preservation of fine hand-press work and the artistic use of new technology. With typography and book production in a generally deplorable state at the time, Tuer took it upon himself not only to improve the output of his own shop, but also to encourage higher standards in the trade as a whole. In 1872, he launched and edited *The Paper & Printing Trades Journal*, published by Field & Tuer under the imprint Ye Leadenhalle Workes. The introduction described the quarterly as "A Medium of Intercommunication Between Stationers, Printers, Publishers and Booksellers and the Manufacturers." Initially circulated gratis, in 1874 a charge of one shilling was imposed for four issues consisting of half advertising and half news, reviews, articles about new products and devices, tables, directories, jokes, and critiques of work sent in for evaluation. Well received, The journal was eventually sold in 1891 to John Southward.[5]

Courtesy, Lilly Library, Indiana University, Bloomington, IN.

One indication of Tuer's publishing ambitions was a privately printed memento for the Caxton Celebration of the 400th anniversary of the introduction of printing into England, held in June 1877 in South Kensington.[6] With a cover title in Old English type, *1477. In Honour of William Caxton this Pamphlet is Gratuitously Circulated. A.D. 1877*, it was a reprint of *Some Rules for the Conduct of Life*, a Corporation of London publication presented to apprentices upon achieving the Freedom of the City of London. The special issue featured letterpress printing on specially prepared paper and a binding of

Courtesy, Lilly Library, Indiana University, Bloomington, IN.

5. Author of works on printing, including: *Practical Printing* (London: Powell 1882).
6. Possibly sponsored by William Blades, an organizer of the Caxton Celebration Exhibition. See note, page 40.

half vellum parchment ruled in gilt over buff boards stamped in black. According to the catalogue of the Caxton Celebration,[7] Field & Tuer (and Tuer personally) lent for exhibition American paper money, antique facsimile and modern printing, periodicals, initial letters and ornaments, type founders' specimen sheets (including Isaac Moore and William Caslon), and Edmund Fry's *Pantographia* (1799).[8]

Tuer was in charge of cataloguing examples of steam and commercial printing for the exhibition, as part of a committee that included R. Bagster, William Clowes, Francis Fry, Alexander Macmillan, Henry Stevens, Elliot Stock, George Unwin, and other notables. Prior to the event, he issued an invitation, reported in the February 17, 1877, issue of *Publishers' Weekly*: "The enterprising proprietors of the *Paper & Printing Trades Journal*, Messrs. Field & Tuer, have undertaken to collect specimens of American as well as colonial printing, and they request us to state that they will be glad to receive small assortments of every description of first-class letterpress printing . . . It is their intention to exhibit the specimens of printing in large guard-books." A volume comprised of samples from 28 American printers was indeed exhibited.

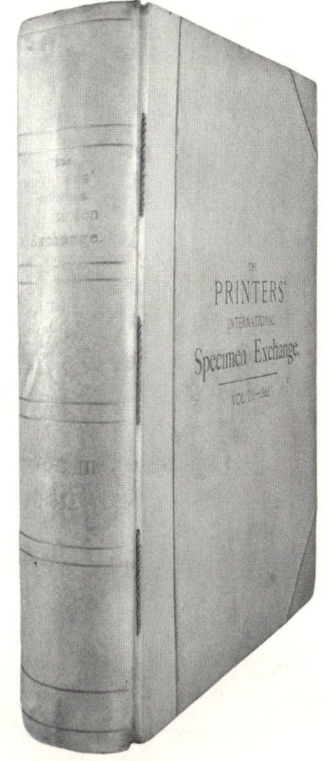

In September of 1879, Thomas Hailing, proprietor of the Oxford Printing Works in Cheltenham and publisher of the small but influential *Hailing's Circular*, wrote a letter to the editor of *The Paper & Printing Trades Journal* proposing an organized exchange of specimens among printers "interested in improving the style and quality of their work." The plan, as developed by Hailing and Tuer, was for printers and their employees, both at home and abroad, to send in multiple examples of their work and receive back a set of all specimens accepted, at the subscription cost of a shilling (bound sets for 5 shillings additional). In September 1880, Field & Tuer introduced *The Printers' International Specimen Exchange*, edited by Tuer. The initial set of rules appeared in *Hailing's Circular*:[9]

1. The Subscription to the *Printers' International Specimen Exchange* is One Shilling per annum.
2. Members must be practical letterpress or lithographic printers. Managers of printing offices, compositors, press men, etc., are eligible.
3. The specimens produced for the *Specimen Exchange* must be from the hands of the subscriber or his workmen; trade work, of course, cannot be admitted.

---

7. George Bullen, *Caxton Celebration 1877. Catalogue of the Loan Collection of Antiquities, Curiosities, and Appliances Connected with the Art of Printing* (London: Trübner and Co., 1877).
8. At the 1884 Health Exhibition, the Leadenhall Press demonstrated a 200-year-old wooden printing press.
9. "Specimen Exchange." *Hailing's Circular*, Vol. I, No. 6, Summer 1880, p. 37.

4. Two hundred copies of each half-yearly job must be sent, carriage paid, addressed to the Editor of *The Paper and Printing Trades Journal*, 50 Leadenhall Street, London, E.C.
5. The first English specimens in each year are to be sent in (carriage paid) any time before the 15th of June, and the second any time before the end of November; but American and Colonial specimens are to be posted (packed between boards) a fortnight earlier. Subscriptions may be remitted in postage stamps of any denomination.
6. For the protection of subscribers, the Editor reserves the right of rejecting specimens which he may consider unsuitable, but notices of rejection will be given privately.

John Ruskin, on hearing of the enterprise, wrote to Tuer, "I assure you again how gladly I hear of an association of printers who will sometimes issue work in a form worthy of their own craft, and showing to the uttermost the best of which it is capable . . . I have the most entire sympathy with your objects, but believe that people *will* have bad paper nowadays, bad printing nowadays, and bad painting nowadays, and nothing else."[10]

Tuer's determination to remedy that state of affairs met with unexpected success. The initial call for submissions resulted in 230 subscribers and 178 submissions, far surpassing expectations, and publication was changed from semiannual to annual. Among the contributors to the early volumes were Aird & Coghill of Glasgow, J. Davy & Sons (the Dryden Press), J. F. Earhart of Columbus, Ohio, A. V. Haight of Poughkeepsie, New York, A. R. Mowbray & Son, R. Oxley & Son, Smith & Ritchie of Edinburgh, John Springer of Iowa City, and Unwin Bros. (the Gresham Press). At its peak, the *Specimen Exchange* contained over 400 specimens from as far away as Russia, South America, and China. By 1886, Tuer was able to boast in the preface, "Contributors . . . will no doubt be gratified to learn that their productions have come directly under the notice of the Queen, Her Majesty having been graciously pleased to accept and acknowledge a copy of the latest volume."

While many of the submissions perpetuated the "artistic" typography and overly ornate borders of the period, some are surprisingly attractive and innovative (not least those by employees of the Leadenhall Press). In his introduction to Volume III, Tuer answered criticism from some quarters that the publication included inferior examples by saying that the *Specimen Exchange* was not a competition, and that while bad work would always be rejected, "it is doubtful if a better or more valuable means of advancing typographical education could be devised than the opportunity thus afforded to printers of all degrees of skill to study the productions of their *confrères*." By this method, he argued, those with less opportunity for advancement would be inspired, gradual improvement in the work of individual printers would become evident over succeeding volumes, and the level of quality in the trade as a whole would be raised.

---

10. Extract published in the introduction to *The Printers' International Specimen Exchange, Vol. I*, 1880. Reprinted in *Igdrasil*, November 1890, Vol. I, p. 66, and *Ruskiniana*, Part II, 1890, p. 94.

Robert Hilton, an editor at *The Paper & Printing Trades Journal*, coordinated the submissions to the *Specimen Exchange*, but he was a great admirer of German and American printing and may have clashed with Tuer over the editorial tone of the publication and selection of specimens.[11] Hilton, in collaboration with George W. Jones of Raithby, Lawrence & Co., began a new journal, *The British Printer*, for British Typographia in 1887, and Tuer turned publication of the *Specimen Exchange* over to the new enterprise beginning with Volume IX (1888). In 1893, *The British Printer* ran a profile of Tuer in which his contributions as the first publisher of the *Specimen Exchange* were understated as "appreciation and liberal support." The last volume, a much slimmer version of its former self, appeared in 1898.

By the early 1880s, the Tuers were living in Kensington at No. 20 Notting Hill Square (renamed Campden Hill Square in 1893 at Tuer's suggestion),[12] and Andrew could indulge his passion for collecting, which over the years included type specimens, early children's books, specimen covers to novels, 18th century advertising, bank notes, engravings and woodcuts, paintings and drawings, bookplates, china and silver, Christmas cards and valentines, hornbooks, lottery tickets, ornamental alphabets, miniature books and bookcases, silhouettes and samplers, clocks, fashion plates, and trade cards. Tuer contributed to scholarship in a number of areas. His collection of hornbooks was a landmark (as we shall see), and in an 1896 article about samplers in *The Studio*, Gleeson White wrote:

> It is a matter of surprise that the making of samplers, so common in bygone times, has not been revived in these days of "Arts and Crafts." As an object for collecting it has found votaries; foremost among whom is, most probably, Mr. Andrew Tuer, from whose superb collection the examples here reproduced, with one exception, are taken. Mr. Tuer is a most faithful devotee of the past, and his collections number so many different subjects that probably he may deem this to be one of his least important; yet, notwithstanding the attractions of the others, it cannot be considered as the least interesting.[13]

The couple and their collections eventually moved two doors down to No. 18, which Tuer had rebuilt in 1887-88 to designs by J. T. Newman that were out of character with the neighborhood. Newman himself later declared the house hideous, suggesting that the design was more Tuer's idea than his own. (The overly tall house has since been restored to the more conservative proportions of its neighbors.) The Tuers also owned a tennis court near St. Mary Abbott's Church in Kensington, which Walter Crane, who lived in nearby Holland Street, rented from time to time. Friends and neighbors included Andrew Lang, Wilfrid and Alice Meynell, and *Punch* cartoonists Phil May, Linley Sambourne, and Charles Keene.

---

11. Graham Hudson, "Artistic Printing: a Re-evaluation," *Journal of the Printing Historical Society*, New Series, 9, Spring 2006, pp. 31–63.
12. "Dear Mr. Tuer. Exactly at 6 pm we changed Notting Hill Squ. into Campden Hill Squ! Accept my congratulations on the success of your agitation! Yours ever, W. F. Blake." (Andrew White Tuer letters, MS 137, courtesy Woodson Research Center, Fondren Library, Rice University.)
13. Gleeson White, "The Sampler, an appreciation and a plea for its revival," *The Studio*, Winter Number 1896-7, p. 58.

In 1890, Tuer wrote an article titled "The Art of Silhouetting" for *The English Illustrated Magazine.* The opening read, "Will the day ever come when the Iron Duke will be popularly remembered by the Wellington boot, or the great Sir Robert Peel by the double-barrelled nicknames he contributed to his country's police? Certain it is that M. Etienne de Silhouette, the great financial minister of France, has his immortality altogether away from money bags, and is familiar by name only because that name was affixed to the shadow portraits which had their heyday in the days of his decline."

THE ART OF SILHOUETTING.

By ANDREW W. TUER.

WILL the day ever come when the Iron Duke will be popularly remembered by the Wellington boot, or the great Sir Robert Peel by the double-barrelled nicknames he contributed to his country's police? Certain it is that M. Etienne de Silhouette, the great financial minister of France, has his immortality altogether away from money bags, and is familiar by name only because that name was affixed to the shadow portraits which had their heyday in the days of his decline.

It happened this way. M. de Silhouette may have been a heaven-born minister, but in that case he was a bit before his date. The date was 1709. Destined for public life, he visited England to study her polity; and in this he succeeded so well that, when by his merit and the power of Madame Pompadour he was made Comptroller General, in 1757, he began to reform French finance on English models. Whether it was the reform or the Anglicism matters not, but for one or the other reason M. de Silhouette became the favourite butt of French public life. All that was shabby, mean, and perhaps a little ridiculous, began to be spoken of as *à la Silhouette*. Amongst these things was the bare outline likeness, which began about then to be produced both in France and England, and to which the name was attached.

Not that silhouetting was a discovery of the eighteenth century; in fact, and naturally, it was older than the Christian era. Portraiture is, after all, an art to which love is under long obligation; and it is fitting that this first rudimentary portraiture was, according to tradition, achieved by an Etrurian maiden, the daughter of a potter, who traced on the wall the shadow of her swain. That was 776 B.C. The first artists in monochrome—Crates of Sicyon, Philocles of Egypt, and Cleanthes of Corinth—the Doultons, and Mortlocks, and Walter Cranes of their day—practised the art which then went by the name of skiagraphy.

AUGUSTIN AMANT CONSTANCE FIDÈLE EDOUART.

Germany, no less than France and England, shared in the modern revival of silhouetting. In 1780 a German follower of Lavater wrote a volume in which he claimed the shadow portrait as a specimen of true art when compared with the "daub

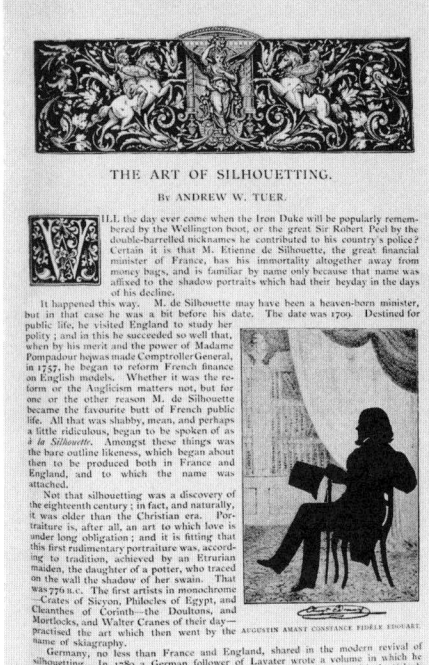

The experience and publicity gained during the Caxton Celebration apparently gave Tuer the confidence to take the next step toward becoming a noted publisher, as he introduced a new imprint. In 1877, *Histoire du Bonhomme Misère*, a series of 6 engravings in folio by Alphonse Legros, was published by R. Gueraut in an edition of 60 copies, "the engravings printed by Field & Tuer at the Leadenhall Press." The following year, Bickers & Son published *Ballads of Schiller No. 1*, by the Rev. Frederick Harford, which carried the colophon "Imprinted by Field & Tuer, at the Leadenhall Press."

Finally, in July 1879, the Leadenhall Press made a splash, so to speak, with its first book, Tuer's own *Luxurious Bathing*, a whimsical treatise on the joys of hygiene, illustrated with twelve landscape etchings and initials by Sutton Sharpe. Field & Tuer's ambitions were clear, in part from the Scribner & Welford imprint on the title page as American agents, a relationship that lasted into the twentieth century. As for design and production, the book was a large oblong folio printed in red and black, the regular edition was limited to 250 copies at three guineas, with a special edition of twenty-five copies on Japanese paper at seven guineas. *The University Magazine* had this to say in its review: "But to have a dip into the present folio is luxury indeed for anyone whose eye loves to appreciate flawless typography and paper, even surpassing that of the rare volumes produced before the age of shoddy. Messrs. Field and Tuer proceed on the traditional plan of the old craftsmen—that of doing first-rate work, and becoming gradually known for it, rather than by specious advertisement, which is a modern snare."[14]

14. *The University Magazine, a Literary and Philosophic Review*, Vol. IV, July-December, 1879, pp. 508-9.

The second edition, issued the following year in a smaller size with etchings by Tristram Ellis, had an addendum: "Since going to press the author's attention has been drawn—not over-courteously perhaps—to the sweeping denunciation in this sketch of the habitual use of scented soaps; but after a careful examination and trial of various kinds, one alone—Pears' transparent soap—may in his opinion be safely indicated as a pure detergent in every way suitable for Luxurious Bathing." (Not coincidentally, perhaps, the Leadenhall Press printed a number of advertisements for Pears' Soap over the years.

The next book to appear, in 1880, was *Journals and Journalism: With a Guide for Literary Beginners* by John Oldcastle, pseudonym of Wilfrid Meynell. The Meynells were close friends of the Tuers, who took an interest in the development of the press. Wilfrid acted as something of a literary advisor, while Alice, writing as "Francis Phillimore," contributed a preface to *Dickens Memento* (1884). Wilfrid provided prefaces to the four titles in *The Leadenhall Press Sixteenpenny Series: Illustrated Gleanings from the Classics* (1885–1888), and later he edited *The Child Set in the Midst: by Modern Poets* (1892).

In 1881, the elegant *On a Raft, and Through the Desert*, by Tristram J. Ellis, was published in two volumes with thirty-eight etchings on copper by the author,

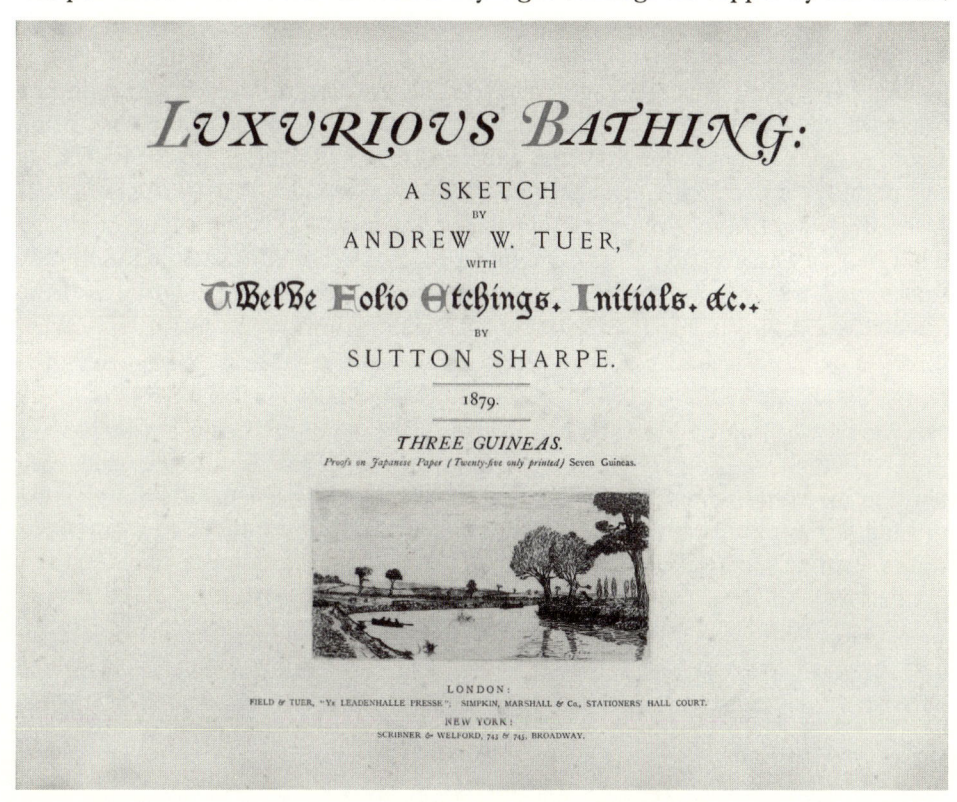

Title page of the first edition, with initials in red.

followed by Tuer's first important work as an author. The two-volume *Bartolozzi and His Works* (1882) was issued in three editions of increasingly elaborate production and included a biographical account, information on how to date impressions and identify deceptions, and a list of over 2,000 engravings. An anonymous review in the *Athenaeum* of September 23, 1882 stated that Bartolozzi's techniques in certain transcriptions from Guercino were line engravings rather than etchings, as Tuer had defined them. Tuer promptly wrote to leading engravers, etchers, and art critics for their opinions, all of whom (except John Ruskin, who was out of the country) supported his position to one degree or another, but in the end the *Athenaeum* would publish neither a letter nor an advertisement in rebuttal. Tuer took his revenge in his introduction to the catalogue of the first Bartolozzi exhibition, held in 1883, which recounted the events and argued his point at length. He then assembled the review, thirty-seven letters, other clippings, and the catalogue in a vellum-bound scrapbook titled in gilt, *The Guercino Etchings Dispute*, and inserted a note on which he scribbled, "Accepted by the *Athenaeum* & then declined . . . A.W. T."[15] The relevant passage from the catalogue introduction appeared in the second edition of *Bartolozzi and His Works* (1885), which also quoted from an odd letter Ruskin wrote to Tuer in December 1882: "The Bartolozzi has reached me safely but I have no time to acknowledge books sent to me out of my line. I see it is rising in price, and when I come to it, with your good leave will return it, as it is of no use to me."

Tuer admired Ruskin and had referred to his writings in *Bartolozzi*, and despite the curtness of the response, he continued to send along an occasional book and smooth sheets of paper for drawing, which were acknowledged cordially. During this period, coincidentally or otherwise, both men produced facsimile reprints of *Dame Wiggins of Lee and her Seven Wonderful Cats*, a book of children's verse originally published in 1823. Ruskin's version appeared in 1885 with additional verses by Ruskin and new illustrations by Kate Greenaway. Tuer subsequently located the original wood blocks and (as related in his introduction) wrote to Ruskin, asking if he would mind if the Leadenhall Press issued another edition, and received the reply: "I shall be entirely glad that the public should be further interested in or more generally possessed of the old designs." Tuer's edition came out in 1887 as the first of the *Leadenhall Press Series of Forgotten Picture Books for Children*, each with illustrations from original Dean & Munday blocks[16] with sheets hand-colored in the original fashion by assigning a different color to each of six girls who passed the sheets from one to another.

In his introduction, Tuer acknowledged his luck in finding the blocks and referred to what journalist (and friend) George Augustus Sala termed his "omnivorous drag-net" for old type, woodcuts, initials, head- and tailpieces, and engravings. Such decorations were often the basis for facsimile reprints, but incidental ornaments

---

15. *The Guercino Etchings Dispute* scrapbook is in the collection of the Winterthur Library, Winterthur, Delaware. For a list of correspondents, see Appendix D: Collections and Resources.
16. Tuer's introduction traced the publication history, identifying the printers as Dean & Munday rather than A. K. Newman & Co. of the Minerva Press, which had bought 1,000 copies and substituted their imprint.

appeared in many Leadenhall Press publications over the years, giving them both a reference to the past and a signature appearance. Many of these cuts appeared in *London Cries* (1883) and *Old London Street Cries and the Cries of To-day* (1885), with illustrations by Thomas Rowlandson and George Cruikshank, and in *1,000 Quaint Cuts from Books of Other Days* (1886), described as "a selection of pictorial initial letters & curious designs & ornaments from original wooden blocks belonging to the Leadenhall Press."

Tuer was a notable contributor to the revival of letterpress printing, not only through *The Printers' International Specimen Exchange*, but also through contributions to the 1877 Caxton Exhibition, the 1884 International Health Exhibition, and the 1885 Inventions Exhibition, in addition to examples of his own publications. The Leadenhall Press established a reputation for distinctive typography, described in the 1893 profile of Tuer in *The British Printer*: "Originality, quaintness, and fertility of invention are apparent in almost everything issued from the Leadenhall Press, so that it is possible to recognize its productions by their typographical peculiarities without reference to the imprint." Tuer was well suited to carry forward the revival of

Souvenir card from the 1884 Health Exhibition. (Courtesy, the Bury family.)

Caslon Old Face by Charles Whittingham (the younger) of the Chiswick Press and publisher William Pickering in the eighteen forties. *Luxurious Bathing* and *On a Raft, and Through the Desert* were set in Caslon, while the title page and preliminaries of *The Printers' International Specimen Exchange* were in Caslon and Lyons capitals.

Most of the Leadenhall books were set in Old Style, but the type founders employed by the press produced some unique variations on 18th century fonts, including an old style of their own, outlines created by cutting away the interior of letters, and a roughed-up "antique" face. Stanley Morison wrote of Tuer in 1928: "Alone in his generation, he possessed and used a set of open outline capitals of old-style design like those to be found in the specimen books of Wilson (1780) and Caslon (1795). This letter . . . seems to have been the only fount obtaining regular use in English books between Tuer's generation and our own."[17] A few books were set in modern

---

17. Stanley Morison. "Decorative Types," *The Fleuron*, no. 6, 1928.

styles, and the less serious books and job printing often featured ornamental faces for titles and initials. For one Vellum-Parchment series book, *Are We to Read ?SDRAWKCAB*, the lettering for the key word in the title was cut in and set in reversed sans serif. In the mid 1880s, the press began issuing *A New Shilling Book of Alphabets*, "ancient and modern, plain and fanciful ... selected from those in everyday use at the Leadenhall Press." Ruari McLean has noted, "Tuer tended to affect 'Ye Olde' styles, often in deliberate fun, but he had a real feeling for type ... The Leadenhall Press style is shown at its best in the various entertaining books illustrated by Joseph Crawhall which Tuer produced, and in John Ashton's *A History of English Lotteries*, 1893."[18]

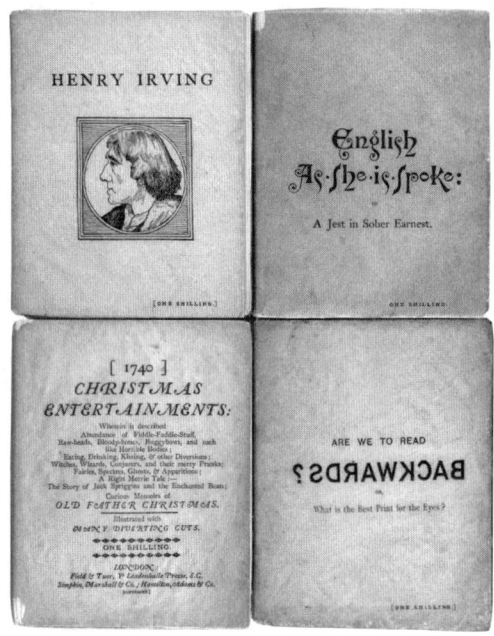

Four titles from the Vellum-Parchment Series of Miscellaneous Literature. (*Henry Irving* and *Are We to Read ?SDRAWKCAB* courtesy Lilly Library, Indiana University, Bloomington, IN.)

Joseph Crawhall II (1821-96) was a wood engraver who had illustrated a number of books published in his native Newcastle-upon-Tyne, and he and Tuer had a mutual friend in Charles Keene, who may have introduced the two. Crawhall's illustrative style, sense of humor, and interest in North country ballads fit perfectly with Tuer's lively personality, antiquarian tastes, and background. Theodore L. De Vinne (to whom Tuer sent presentation copies of *Olde Tayles Newlye Relayted* and other books)[19] wrote in 1902:

> The late Andrew Tuer of London considered [chap-books] as valuable exhibits of the uneducated taste for books and republished a few with all their features of quaintness ... Words need not be wasted on the great silliness of the matter and the manner of the early chap-book, but it is not at all out of place here to say that its crude typography, as illustrated by Tuer, justly may be considered as the real beginning of the revival of bold and black printing, which was afterward developed on other lines by William Morris and his disciples.[20]

The collaboration began in 1883 with a series of seventeen old ballads printed on handmade paper in parts and bound in three collections: *Olde Tayles Newlye*

18. Ruari McLean, *Victorian Book Design and Colour Printing*, second edition (London: Faber & Faber, 1972).
19. *The Library of the Late Theodore Low De Vinne* (The Anderson Galleries, 1920).
20. Theodore L. De Vinne, "The Chap-book and Its Outgrowths," *The Literary Collector: an Illustrated Monthly Magazine of Book-Lore and Bibliography*, November 1902, p. 1.

Relayted, *Crawhall's Chap-book Chaplets*, and *Olde ffrendes wyth newe Faces*, the last two with hand-colored illustrations. Advertisements for *Olde ffrendes wyth newe Faces* read, "Reproductions in facsimile of a large collection of the crudely printed and humorously illustrated pamphlets that were hawked about the country by chapmen of a bygone age. The illustrations will provoke smiles from the gravest." The publishing history of *Olde Tayles Newlye Relayted* is unclear. The book does not appear in Field & Tuer lists or the *Publishers' Circular*, and the title page bears only the Leadenhall Press imprint, while the title pages of other two collections list Field & Tuer and three distribution partners, consistent with the individual parts. The project may not have gone quite as planned; on January 7, 1885, Crawhall wrote to Tuer, "After the questionable success of our joint venture, do you think you'll care to trouble [with] *Izaak Walton's Wallet Booke*?"[21] Tuer did, putting a great deal of care into the production of Crawhall's next book. The delightful *Izaak Walton: His Wallet Booke* was issued later in 1885 in a regular edition and a limited edition of 100 copies in vellum, the woodcuts hand-colored, with small cloth pockets at the front for "Baccy," "Hookes and I's," "Tyme flies," "More Baccy," and "Fysshe Tales I Believe" – and a very large one at the back for "Fysshe Stories I Don't Believe."

Crawhall's cuts adorned the children's books *Old Aunt Elspa's ABC* and *Old Aunt Elspa's Spelling Bee* (Elspa was his nickname for his beloved daughter Elspeth), and his work appeared in several other books. He also designed Christmas cards, valentines, and invitations for Tuer, and the two men carried on a lively correspondence. In 1884, Crawhall enlisted an agent to bid for Tuer on some early

21. Letter from Crawhall to Tuer in the possession of the Bury family.

copperplates in the sale at auction of books, prints, furniture, and other items that had passed down from the great Newcastle engraver Thomas Bewick to his last surviving daughter.[22] The bid was not successful, but Tuer afterward did publish *Bewick Memento*, including the catalogue of the sale with prices realized, illustrated with a dozen cuts from original blocks (not all by Bewick).

Crawhall and Tuer enjoyed an informal competition, contributing a steady stream of jokes for illustration by Charles Keene, whose wit did not match his artistic talent. (Tuer also sent ideas to his friend George Du Maurier). M. H. Spielman wrote of these amateur humorists in *The History of "Punch"*:

> The chief of these no doubt is Mr. Joseph Crawhall, of Newcastle, whose devoted service to his friend Charles Keene was an important factor in the artist's *Punch*-life. From his other friends, Mr. Birket Foster and Mr. Andrew Tuer, Keene was in receipt of a great number of jokes—from the latter they came almost as regularly as the weekly paper. It was also from Mr. Tuer that he received, among many others, that happy thought, so happily realised, of the gentleman who one day paid an unaccustomed visit to his stables to give an order, and asking his coachman's child, "Well, my little man, do you know who I am?" received for answer, "Yes, you're the man who rides in our carriage."[23]

Humor delighted Tuer, and it became an important part of the Leadenhall list; hence such titles as *"Never Hit a Man Named Sullivan," History of the Decline and Fall of the British Empire, Slip-shod English in Polite Society, Tennis Cuts and Quips*, and Andrew Lang's *How to Fail in Literature*. One of the most successful authors published by the firm was the Frenchman Paul Blouët, who, as "Max O'Rell," wrote sharp-eyed observations about English society from the French point of view. His first book for Tuer, *John Bull and His Island*, published in 1883, sold more than 200,000 copies by 1898. His second, *John Bull's Womankind (Les filles de John Bull)*, came out in 1884, preceded by a pamphlet with the same title and a parenthetical subtitle, "Suggestions for an alteration in the law of copyright in the titles of books, called forth by the piracy of the title originally proposed for the translation of Max O'Rell's work: *Les Filles de John Bull*." In the text, Tuer pointed out that "in order to secure the title of one book it is necessary to write another—and here it is," recommending that the laws be changed to allow registration of a title six months before the actual publication of a book. In addition to his interest in copyright law, Tuer was a strong proponent of the royalty system.

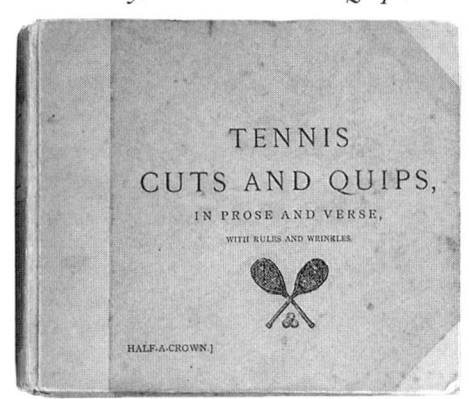

22. Letters from Crawhall to Tuer at the Lilly Library, Indiana University, Bloomington, IN.
23. M. H. Spielman, *The History of "Punch"* (Cassell and Co., 1895), p. 147.

In 1885, the press accepted and published *On the Stage—and Off*, the first book by the young Jerome K. Jerome. The aspiring author had unsuccessfully offered his manuscript to several other London publishers, including Sampson Low, Marston & Co., where Mr. Marston told him that, while he didn't want to be discouraging, the work was "simply rubbish."[24] Jerome went on to publish four books with the Press, the last in 1893. In *My Life and Times*, recalling the success of his second book, *The Idle Thoughts of an Idle Fellow*, Jerome wrote, "The books sold like hot cakes, as the saying is. Tuer always had clever ideas. He gave it a light yellow cover that stood out well upon the bookstalls. He called each thousand copies an 'edition' and, before the end of the year, was advertising the twenty-third. I was getting a royalty of twopence-halfpenny a copy; and dreamed of a fur coat."

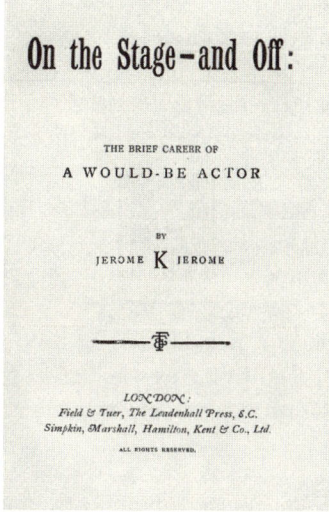

Some humorous and satirical books (perhaps by Tuer and his friends) were issued under whimsical pseudonyms, including "POOF," "Puck," "Cylinder," "Goosestep," and "Alere Flammam" (the title of an Edmund Gosse poem in the first issue of *The Yellow Book* and *In Russet and Silver*). Only a few identities are known, one being the writer of *Gladstone Government: a Chapter of Contemporary History* by "Teufelsdröckh Junior," actually Edward Abbott Parry, later a distinguished judge and author. *History of the Decline and Fall of the British Empire*, by "Edwarda Gibbon," was the work of barrister Charles J. Stone, and the American humorist Oliver Bell Bunce was behind "Censor," author of *Don't: A Manual of Mistakes & Improprieties More or Less Prevalent in Conduct & Speech*. (This American view of manners was so popular that Tuer issued a parody from the English perspective, *You Shouldn't* by "Brother Bob," combining New York pretension with Wild West etiquette.) *Humours and Oddities of the London Police Courts* is credited on the title page as being illustrated and edited by "Dogberry," whose true identity has yet to be discovered.[25]

Tuer was the anonymous author of *The Kaukneigh Awlminek, 1883. Edited by 'Enery 'Arris*, and later *"Thenks awf'lly!" Sketched in Cockney and Hung on Twelve Pegs* (1890). He was fascinated with cockney dialect and maintained that Dickens and other writers had not kept up with changes over the years. In *Old London Street Cries and the Cries of To-day* (1885), he offered his version of cockney pronunciations of the new London Inner Circle Railway stations, including "Glawster Rowd," "I street Kenzint'un," "Nottin' Ill Gite," "Queen's Rowd Bizewater," "Biker Street," "King's Krauss," and "Bishergit, S'n Jimes-iz Pawk," and "Emma Smith" (Hammersmith),

---

24. Quoted in "Personal Gossip About Writers," *The Author*, Vol. III. No. 1, January 15, 1891, p. 10.
25. A copy in the British Library has a monogram "TK" in pencil below "Dogberry" on the title page, and one illustration is initialed "J.C.K." A satirical police report, "Dogberry's Diary," appeared in *Punch*, June 2, 1888.

which, Tuer explained, "while not a main line station, may be cited here simply as a good example of Cockney, for 'Arry and 'Arriet are quite incapable of any other verbal rendering." George Augustus Sala, writing in the *Illustrated London News*, took issue with Tuer's ideas: "On the whole, the *Kaukneigh Awlminek* seems to consist in pretty equal proportions of the vocabulary of Tim Bobbin, Josh Billings, Joe Scoap, the 'Fonetik Nuz,' and the 'Marowsky' language: the whole corrected by a German Ph.D. The editor has the hardihood to correct Charles Dickens's Cockney orthography."[26] One who thought Tuer was on the right track was George Bernard Shaw, who later wrote in "Notes to *Captain Brassbound's Conversion*," "Some time in the eighties the late Andrew Tuer called attention in the *Pall Mall Gazette* to several peculiarities of modern cockney, and to the obsolescence of the Dickens dialect that was still being copied from book to book by authors who never dreamt of using their ears, much less of training them to listen."

While Shaw apparently admired Tuer's observations about cockney dialect, he made it clear on more than one occasion that he did not think especially highly of Tuer's publications in comparison to those of William Morris. Shaw's strict ideas about typography and design originated with Morris, a fellow socialist and good friend, and Shaw seems to have begrudged Tuer his commercial and critical successes. Lamenting the taste of the average buyer of books, he wrote, "if you offered him his choice of a Kelmscott Press book and a Leadenhall Press one, he would reject William Morris and accept Andrew Tuer, whose taste he would honestly believe superior to Jenson's."[27] Of course, Morris's books were hardly intended for the average buyer, while Tuer published for many different audiences at prices ranging from sixpence to several guineas. While Kelmscott represents a high point in book design, the Leadenhall Press was setting a singular example for both popular and fine press publishing more than a decade earlier.

Tuer was a businessman and an inventor in addition to being a designer and printer, and he was more open-minded than Morris or Shaw concerning what constituted a well-designed book. Although best known for "antiquarian" printing, the press also had a reputation for innovation and for publishing well-printed, attractive books at reasonable prices. Designers were not credited and are, for the most part, unknown (except where an illustrator contributed a cover design). It would be interesting to learn who was responsible for some of the anonymous designs, such as the geometric leaf pattern that graces *Tree Gossip*, or the artwork for the two books by John Lascelles that formed the "Sun and Serpent Series," a design that would not have seemed out of place in the avant-garde of the 1920s.

---

26. George Augustus Sala. *Living London: Being Echoes Re-echoed* Remington, 1883. pp. 490-491. "A selected republication of the 'Echoes of the Week' and 'The Playhouses' which, with the signature of 'G.A.S.,' appeared in the course of the year 1882 in the columns of the *Illustrated London News*."

27. "The Author's View," *Caxton Magazine*, January 1902. Reprinted as *Bernard Shaw on Modern Typography* (Cleveland: Horace Carr at The Printing Press, 1915).

Many Leadenhall books were plain and unremarkable, but where subject matter warranted, even some of the least expensive were attractively designed and well printed. The Leadenhall Press Sixteenpenny Series, edited by Wilfrid Meynell, included illustrations from original eighteenth and early nineteenth century copper-plate engravings, while the Vellum-Parchment Shilling Series of Miscellaneous Literature titles were bound in vegetable parchment over flexible boards and had attractive decorations. Experiments included books printed in colored ink, on colored paper, or both. *The Henry Irving Dream of Eugene Aram* (1888), illustrated by F. Drummond Niblett, featured text and illustrations blocked in "Mephistophelian sanguine on a black ground" (as an advertisement in the *Publishers' Circular* accurately described it). One mystery novel, *Mrs. Greet's Story of the Golden Owl* (1892–3), was printed on brown paper with illustrations by Ambrose Dudley on light gray plates, with a gold embossed owl in place of the words "Golden Owl" on the title page. Harold Boulton's *Songs Sung and Unsung* was printed in two parts and bound *dos-à-dos*. There was the occasional failure when a binding material or ink was not successful: the Vellum-Parchment Shilling Series second edition of *The Story of a Nursery Rhyme*, for instance, was advertised as "printed throughout in a new shade of blue ink." I assumed that the ink must have faded over time, but a review in *The Bookseller* of August 4, 1883, noted, "Some of the pages look as if the ink had been washed off after printing . . . the illustrations, so far as they are visible, seem to be very well drawn."

An illustration from Thomson's *The Seasons*, a Leadenhall Press Sixteenpenny Series title.

The press employed women and girls, and their skills are reflected in the designs of a number of books, several of them bound in patterned cloth: *Rus in Urbe* (1886) and *Our Grandmothers' Gowns* (1884) in floral cloth with paper labels and ribbon ties; the privately printed *Diary J. A. H. M.* (1886), in Japanese-style velvet with printed silk endpapers; and *Views of English Society by a little girl of eleven* (1886), which has an unusual sewn turn-in construction designed by the author, Mabel, who also drew the illustrations. In her last chapter, "How to Get a Book Printed," and an addendum, Mabel offers some observations of Andrew Tuer that are worth quoting at length. She tells (not unlike Jerome K. Jerome) of disappointing visits to surly or unresponsive publishers, manuscript in hand and Cummings, the family maid, in tow, and of finally arriving at the Leadenhall offices:

> I found myself in the presence of a gentleman who reminded me of an amiable curate we once had; he spoke naturally, not just in set speeches as the other publisher had done. He wore a clerical waistcoat, and had on one of those bendey sort of collars, which I suppose are made of india-rubber and slip on over the head, for I have never been able to discover how they fasten. He was very brisk, and had such keen eyes that I think they looked straight through the cover of a book and saved him the trouble of opening it. He seemed to know all about mine in a minute. He made a few remarks about it, and even went so far as to say I was a clever little girl, and . . . explained to me that instead of my paying him, as I expected to do, he was going to pay me.

She then recounts her proposal of the binding design to Tuer:

> I took it to my publisher and told him if he liked it, and would give me sufficient time, I would make them all. I supposed he would want twenty or perhaps even as many as thirty. He looked very quizzical and asked if I would undertake to make two or three thousand. At first I thought he was making fun of me, but I found he was quite in earnest, so I could only shake my head and tell him that was quite impossible. I feared I should have to put up with those uninteresting cloth things with gilt letters, just like other people's books, but the dark-eyed young man helped me out of the difficulty by saying there were lots of little girls in his factory who had to earn their bread-and-butter, and that they could make the covers quite as well as I could if I would leave the one I had made as a pattern for them to copy.

One other book that features work by women's hands was *The Follies & Fashions of Our Grandfathers* (1886–7), which has embroidered silk labels on the cover and spine, floral-patterned cloth endpapers, and a cloth bookmark with the title of the book embroidered on both sides. This work is also an example of Tuer's affection for limited editions. The "Demy octavo" has thirty-seven plates hand-tinted and heightened with gold and silver. The "Large Paper crown quarto," 250 copies only at three guineas each, has the earliest impressions, extra carefully tinted and heightened. The "Special Large Paper" edition was printed on brown paper and

limited to three copies at ten guineas each. In his introduction (printed in red), Tuer explained, "It seems that the British Museum has the legal right—a right always rigorously enforced—of demanding one of the most expensive copies of any book published. The writer has suffered before, and he takes this opportunity of getting even. He had intended to print only one copy on brown paper, but, before going to press, elected to have an edition of three—the first copy for the British Museum, the second for himself to take home and chuckle over when out of sorts, and the third for anyone who likes to pay for it."

Quads for Authors, Editors, & Devils (1884), a collection of printers' jokes culled from almost twelve years of *The Paper & Printing Trades Journal,* is a work in which two editions form a third. The primary issue is a midget folio (royal 304mo) bound in vellum with silk ties, described in the prospectus as "printed in pearl type on hand-made bank-note paper . . . a facsimile in size, paper, type, and binding of Peele's *Tale of Troy* in verse, published in 1604." A duodecimo "enlarged edition" was issued with a vellum parchment wrapper. The combined issue, *Quads within Quads*, is a vellum-bound enlarged edition with extra pages at the back, which are glued together to form a block and hollowed out to house the midget folio. The prospectus described *Quads within Quads* as "A book and a box, or rather two books and a box, and yet after all not a box at all, but a book and only one book." Stamped in gilt beneath the title on the cover is the warning: "In unlocking this Forme see that the QUADS do not drop out." Finally, twelve special copies of each edition were printed on vellum.

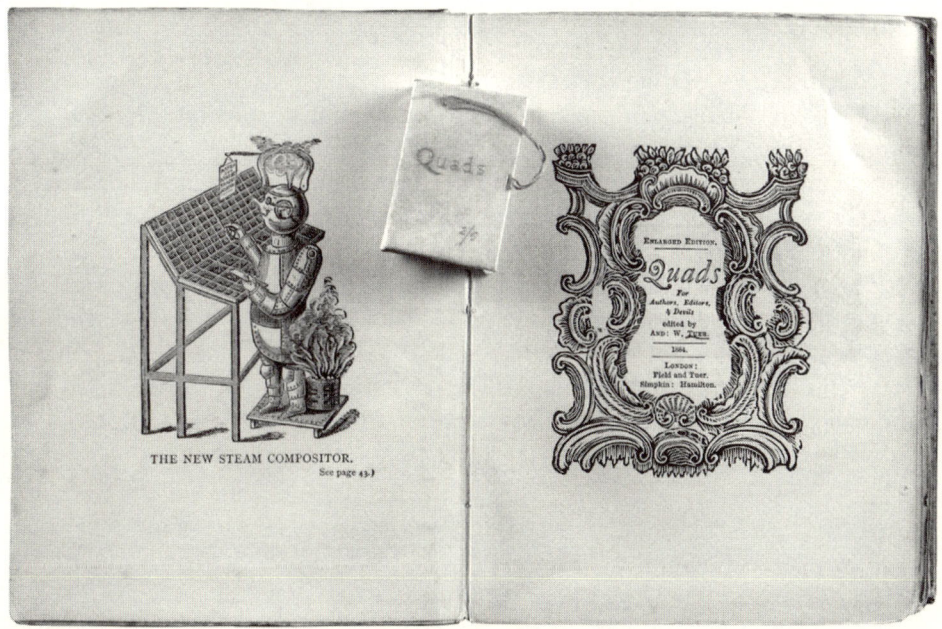

Quads within Quads: the "midget folio" fits in a compartment at the back of the "enlarged edition."

Another work with compartments is Tuer's two-volume *History of the Horn-Book* (1896), dedicated by command to Her Majesty the Queen-Empress. The volumes are bound in vellum, with the title inside a hornbook-shaped device stamped in gilt on the cover, leather labels on the spine, and seven facsimile hornbooks and battledores in the shaped compartments at the front of each volume.[28] Along with photographs of hornbooks, illustrations and decorations were provided by many artists, including Joseph Crawhall, Georgie Cave France, C. M. Gere, Charles H. M. Kerr, John Leighton, Celia Levetus, Kate Light, William Luker Jr., Phil May, Percy McQuoid, Linley Sambourne, Walter J. West, and R. I. Williams. As noted by Tuer, *The Studio* magazine held a competition for illustrations intended for the book (with Walter Crane as a judge); the winners were (1) Celia Levetus, (2) Kate Light, and (3) Georgie France. The work is not only one of the most impressive Leadenhall Press productions, it was the first important work on the subject, and it remains the primary resource for information.[29] The significance of Tuer's achievement is evident in his preface:

> At the Caxton Exhibition in London in 1877 were four horn-books, and at the Loan Exhibition of the Worshipful Company of Horners, held at the (London) Mansion House in October 1882, when special efforts were made to bring together as many as possible, the total number shown was eight. That something like one hundred and fifty are noted herein is due to the power of the fourth estate. Unaided by the Press, the writer would never have heard of a quarter of them. So many horn-books having turned up, others are perhaps lurking in out-of-the-way places. May the reader become possessed of some! And in return for the good wish, perhaps he will send me an account of his spoils.

Tuer added, "The writer has pestered countless people for information about the horn-book. Mr. Gladstone's reply was unexpected, but to the point; he said that he knew nothing at all about it." After receiving a presentation copy, Gladstone responded, "I thank you very much for your highly interesting gift. It has already disabled me from repeating the confession which I formerly made, with perfect truth, but I hope not in the terms given in the preface, for they seem to convey disparagement; and it is a gross and vulgar error to disparage that which one does not know." *History of the Horn-Book* was greeted with widespread praise and did indeed produce reports of other examples; a second edition, issued in 1897 in one volume with three facsimile hornbooks, included a new chapter discussing twenty additional specimens. Both editions were out of print by the end of 1897.[30]

---

28. *The Academy* reported that members of the Society of Antiquaries had expressed concern that the facsimiles might be sold as originals, but Tuer explained that they had been marked in such a way that they could always be identified.
29. "*The History of the Horn-Book* was undoubtedly Tuer's magnum opus . . . It has never been superseded." Leslie Shepard, *The History of the Horn Book: a Bibliographical Essay* (Cambridge: Rampant Lions Press for the Broadsheet King, 1977).
30. "Books of the Day" in the *Liverpool Mercury*, Dec. 1, 1897.

Tuer sometimes accepted manuscripts submitted by friends or well-connected acquaintances, a practice that was no doubt responsible for the publication of books that proved unpopular and are largely forgotten. The American painter and poet Atherton Furlong suffered a characteristically condescending review from Oscar Wilde in "A Bevy of Poets" in the *Pall Mall Gazette* of March 27, 1885:

> This Spring the little singers are out before the little sparrows and have already begun chirruping. Here are four volumes already, and who knows how many more will be given to us before the laburnums blossom? The best-bound volume must, of course, have precedence. It is called *Echoes of Memory*, by Atherton Furlong, and is cased in creamy vellum and tied with ribbons of yellow silk. Mr. Furlong's charm is the unsullied sweetness of his simplicity . . . Mr. Furlong must not be discouraged. Perhaps he will write poetry some day.

When titles failed to sell, Field & Tuer made way for new ones by placing remainders at auction. An advertisement in the *Athenaeum* of February 6, 1886, announced, "Messrs. Hodgson will sell by Auction, at their Rooms, 115, Chancery-lane, W.C., on Wednesday, February 10, at 1 o'clock, several thousand volumes of Recent Popular Works." All were Leadenhall Press titles, including 800 copies of *Lord Beaconsfield on the Constitution*, 3,200 of *Holy Blue!*, and 1,800 of *Sermons in Sentences*.

The Leadenhall Press list includes only a few authors collected today for their literary importance, but many were prominent in their time, and some interesting names pop up. Wilde's poem, "A Night Vision," appeared in *A Book of Jousts* in 1888, and the collection *The Child Set in the Midst: by Modern Poets* (1892), edited by Wilfrid Meynell, marked the first appearance of Francis Thompson's poetry in book form, along with poems by Robert Buchanan, Austin Dobson, George Meredith, Coventry Patmore, Dante Gabriel Rossetti, Katherine Tynan, and earlier poets. Also published in the early nineties were *Spicilegium Poeticum*, by Manley Hopkins, father of Gerard Manley Hopkins, and *The Shadow of Death*, by Count Eric Stanislaus Stenbock. In addition to *How to Fail in Literature*, Andrew Lang wrote an introduction for the Leadenhall Press edition of Charles Lamb's *Beauty and the Beast*.

Tuer, as noted by Jerome K. Jerome, was a clever marketer. On May 10, 1893, Grant Allen wrote, "My dear Mr. Tuer, I forward herewith by book post, registered, the completed manuscript of our projected shocker 'Michael's Crag.' . . . I shall be curious to see what the typographical resources of

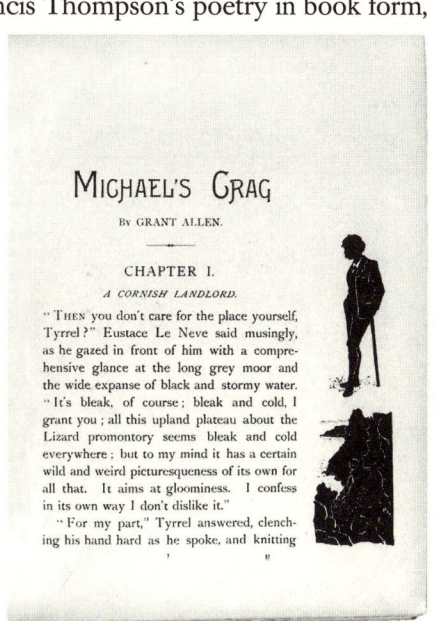

Illustrated with marginal silhouettes.

the Leadenhall Press will do for our venture."[31] In a manner worthy of Stephen King today, Tuer expanded the title of this story of mystery and insanity to *Mr. Grant Allen's New Story "Michael's Crag"* on the cover, spine, and title page in capitals. An ornamental face was used to introduce the first chapter, and the text was set in Caslon with wide margins to accommodate the 350 silhouette illustrations provided by Francis Carruthers Gould and Alec Carruthers Gould. The only misstep was that none of the drawings was used to decorate the plain, gray cloth binding.

A different promotional ploy backfired when, in 1891, Tuer printed 10,000 copies of a shilling book, *Guess the Title of This Story! £100 for the Person who does!!* The frontispiece was a clue, as was the opening sentence, "I have only one eye but I was born with two." The outcome was reported in *The Literary World* on July 22, 1892: "The prize of one hundred pounds . . . has not been gained. More than one-half the competitors thought that the word 'eye' had something to do with it; and they were so far right, the desired phrase being 'An Eye and an I.' Mr. Andrew Tuer is the author, and now that the prize is withdrawn, he has scored out 'one shilling' on the cover and has substituted the lower price of sixpence, with 'satis superque' printed underneath!"

Women were well represented, including several known for their activism and advocacy for women's rights. As early as 1873, Field & Tuer published *The Life of Christ, and Its Bearing on the Doctrines of Communism*, by Sarah Maud Heckford.[32] In the 1880s, the Leadenhall Press issued Emily Pfeiffer's *Flying Leaves from East and West* and *Sonnets, Revised and Enlarged Edition*, as well as the mystic Anna Bonus Kingsford's *The Perfect Way; or, The Finding of Christ* (1882). Lady Florence Dixie, ardent feminist, agnostic, adventurer, and younger sister of the infamous Marquess of Queensberry, published five books of fiction and poetry with the Leadenhall Press, all of them written or begun many years earlier (some poems written in her teens) and issued after Andrew Tuer's death in 1900, suggesting that the publication of Lady Dixie's works may have been a pet project of Thomasine's, although I have not located any correspondence to that effect. Titles such as *Isola, or the Disinherited: A Revolt for Woman and all the Disinherited* and *The Story of Ijain, or, the Evolution of a Mind* give some idea of Lady Dixie's passionate style. The Press also published *Through England on a Side Saddle*, the diary of Celia Fiennes, who traveled on horseback throughout England over a period of nearly two decades at the end of the 17th century.

Women were also important to the Leadenhall Press children's publications, not all of which were reprints of old tales. Lady Jane Wilde contributed a story, "The Child's Dream," to *The Bairns' Annual* for 1885–6, edited by Alice Corkran, and writers such as Gwendoline Davidson *(Kitten's Goblins, A Story of Stops)* and Louise Blennerhassett Poirez *(Eight Tales of Fairyland)* contributed to the growing popularity

---

31. Andrew White Tuer letters, MS 137, courtesy Woodson Research Center, Fondren Library, Rice University. The *Michael's Crag* manuscript is in the Grant Allen collection at Penn State University Special Collections Library.
32. Heckford was a philanthropist and traveler whose writings included *A Lady Trader in the Transvaal* (London: Sampson Low, 1882) and *The Story of an East London Hospital* (London: Macmillan, 1904).

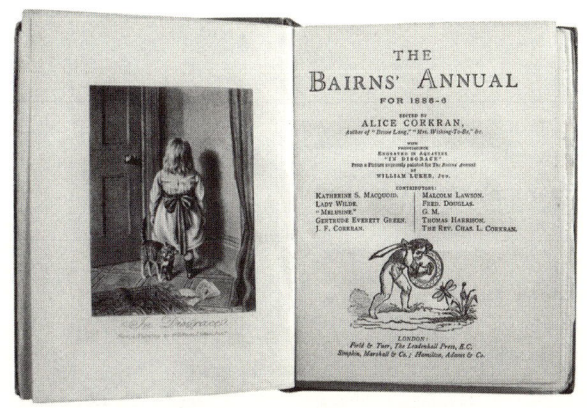

of fairy tales. *Prince Pertinax*, by Mrs. George Hooper, was given an elaborate production with illustrations, title page vignette, head- and tailpieces, and historiated initials by Margaret Hooper and Margery May, printed separately in sepia and mounted. The book was bound in half sheep over blue-gray boards and housed in a folding box.

The non-fiction side of the Leadenhall list included books on history, politics, diplomacy, business and trade, archaeology, travel, religion, art, nature, songs, sports, genealogy, food and drink, social customs, collecting, and even one or two on scientific subjects. John Ashton wrote or edited notable books on a variety of subjects: *Men, Maidens and Manners a Hundred Years Ago*, *Real Sailor-Songs*, *A History of English Lotteries*, and *A righte Merrie Christmasse!!!: The Story of Christ-tide*. Louis Fagan, of the British Museum's Department of Prints and Drawings, researched and compiled *Collectors' Marks* (1883), which categorized and reproduced in facsimile 671 examples of book ownership marks, with names, dates, and other details.[33] Archibald Ross Colquhoun, a civil engineer, *London Times* correspondent, and diplomat, wrote six important books about the Far East, Southeast Asia, and Africa, including *English Policy in the Far East*, *The Truth about Tonquin*, and *Matabeleland: the War, and Our Position in South Africa*. The distinguished Egyptologist W. M. Flinders Petrie set new standards for scientific archaeology in his studies, *The Pyramids and Temples of Gizeh*, *A Season in Egypt 1887*, and *Hawara, Biahmu, and Arsinoe*. The botanist Francis George Heath penned *Tree Gossip*, which was given one of the most attractive of the trade binding designs and typographic treatments.

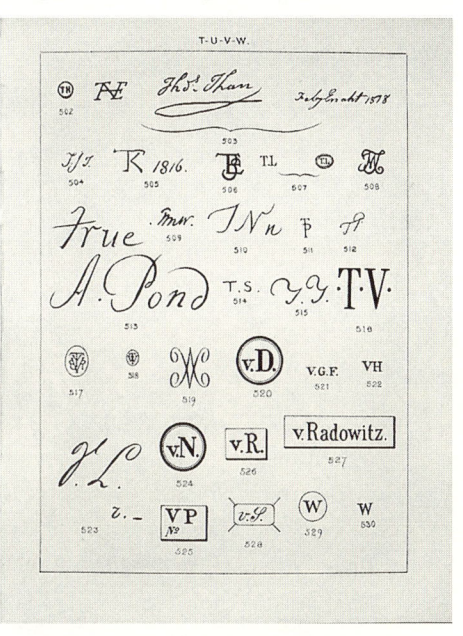

A page from Louis Fagan's *Collectors' Marks*.

---

33. Fagan's book is the basis for the 1918 Laryngoscope Press book of the same title, edited and expanded by Milton Einstein and Max Goldstein to include 205 additional marks (reissued in 2007 by Martino Publishing).

From the vantage point of more than a century, the significance and appeal of the Leadenhall Press catalogue is due more to its illustrators than its authors. The firm's reputation for quality attracted many of the best artists of the day, and the company also printed etchings and engravings for other publishers. A list of notable names closely associated with the press would include Joseph Crawhall II, Edwin J. Ellis, Tristram J. Ellis, Georgie Evelyn Cave France (Mrs. Arthur Gaskin), William Luker Jr., and Phil May. The first edition of *Songs of the North* (1885) featured the frontispiece "A Jacobite Lament" by Burne-Jones, and included artwork by Jemima (Mrs. Hugh) Blackburn, Charles Keene, Cecil Lawson, J. H. Lorimer, Albert Moore, Noel Paton, John Pettie, George Reid, Frederick Sandys, J. M. Whistler, and others.

"Proud Maisie" by Frederick Sandys, an illustration for *Songs of the North*.

Louis Wain contributed characteristic drawings of cats for Jerome K. Jerome's *Novel Notes*, and Randolph Caldecott illustrated a children's tale, *The Owls of Olynn Belfry*. Interesting work was also produced by Ambrose Dudley for, among other books, *A Life's Reminiscences of Scotland Yard* by Detective Inspector Andrew Lansdowne. (Dudley also drew two of Tuer's bookplates.) Kenneth Skeaping, a versatile artist, illustrated several books, including two of Jerome K. Jerome's: the illustrated edition of *On the Stage—and Off*, and *Told after Supper*.

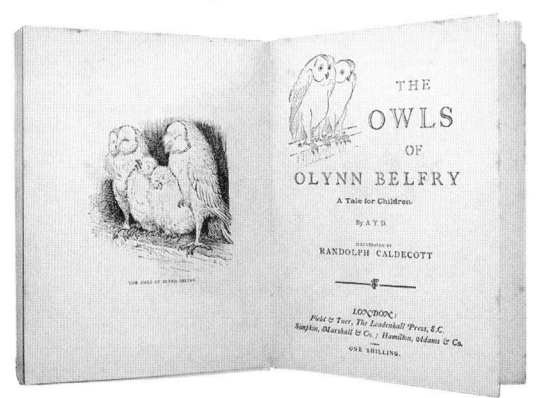

Using her married name, Mrs. Arthur Gaskin, Georgie Cave France followed up *History of the Horn-Book* with her own *Horn-Book Jingles*, consisting of 74 leaves of full-page illustrations incorporating hand-lettered rhymes. She also designed a bookplate for Tuer that appeared in the *Ex Libris Journal* in 1894. As members of the influential Birmingham Group, the Gaskins contributed illustrations to the 1895 Cornish Brothers publication of *Good King Wenceslas*, which featured an introduction by William Morris. They both had long and successful careers as illustrators and, later, as jewelry makers.

Edwin John Ellis, with John Butler Yeats, had formed "The Brotherhood," a group of artists heavily influenced by William Blake. With W. B. Yeats, he edited a three-volume work on Blake (Bernard Quaritch, 1893) and contributed poems to the two Rhymers' Club books. For the Leadenhall Press, he illustrated *Shakespeare's Play of Antony & Cleopatra*, *The Winter's Tale*, *The Story of a Nursery Rhyme*, and his own sonnets for *When Is Your Birthday?*

Tristram J. Ellis, who illustrated the second edition of *Luxurious Bathing* and his own *On a Raft, and Through the Desert*, later executed *Six Etchings of Well-known Views in Kensington Gardens*. He and Edwin Ellis (no kinship has been found) collaborated on designs and etchings for *Some Well-known "Sugar'd Sonnets" by William Shakespeare*, the special edition of which featured proofs on satin.

William Luker's illustrations for W. J. Loftie's *Kensington Picturesque and Historical* (1888), and *London City* (1891), and Percy Fitzgerald's *London City Suburbs, as They Are To-day* (1893), give a wonderful sense of the city and its surroundings. The latter two are dedicated by command to Her Majesty the Queen. A different aspect of London was depicted in *Phil May's Gutter-snipes* and *Phil May's ABC*. Tuer and May shared a fascination with and affection for cockney street life, and were not above including a joke at their own expense, in the form of two rascals making irreverent drawings on a wall and the pavement below, captioned, "ANDROO TUER IS A PUDDENED" and "FILL MAY IS A PHOOL." The dedication in *Gutter-snipes* is a delightful double portrait of the artist and his publisher.

Not every negotiation with a noted author or artist was successful. Some who were approached by Tuer declined, while others who offered their work were rejected. As mentioned in the Introduction, Tuer offered to publish a lecture by William Morris, who explained that the talk was given extemporaneously. Sir Hubert von Herkomer, Slade Professor at Oxford, wrote to Tuer in June 1891: "After your kind suggestion to publish my next lecture, I thought it over and felt that I ought to give my old friends the Macmillans my *first* lecture to publish."[34] Tuer asked Robert Browning to write a book on Kensington, but eventually turned to W. J. Loftie for *Kensington Picturesque & Historical* (1888). George Du Maurier turned him down, and correspondence between Tuer and Kate Greenaway in 1885[35] did not result in a project. The art critic Harry Quilter sent a chapter of his new work, *Sententiae Artis*,

---

34. Letter in private collection.
35. Letters in the Kate Greenaway Collection, Rare Book Room, Detroit Public Library.

to Tuer in February of 1886, writing, "I must ask you however to let me know as soon as you can, as I have got rather a special introduction to another publishing house."[36] Tuer apparently chose not to act, and the book was published by William Isbister. Marie Corelli, whose ne'er-do-well half-brother, Eric Mackay, had two books of poetry published by the Leadenhall Press with her support, twice proposed projects of her own that never materialized, one called "Cigarette Papers by a Non-Smoker" and another describing a visit to the Oberammergau Passion Play.

Tuer was interested in publishing the memoirs of at least one American celebrity. A letter dated June 11, 1887, from Buffalo Bill's Wild West Co., reads, "Gentlemen– We have arranged for the publication of Co. Cody's Biography. If any hitch should occur, we will give you a call."[37] It is not clear if Tuer offered to publish a book by the author of the following note, dated January 2, 1890, but I include it for the pleasure of imagining Tuer's letter: "Dear Sir, In reply to your esteemed favour of the 31st ult: I would be very grateful if you would let me know how you successfully entered our exhibition without a ticket or paying. You will be conferring a great favour on me by giving this information, and I will treat your reply with the respectful consideration your kindness deserves. Sincerely yours, P. T. Barnum."[38]

An embarrassing situation arose when, in late 1889 or early 1890, Field & Tuer accepted a manuscript brought to them by an American journalist, Sheridan Ford, acting on behalf of J. M. Whistler. Whistler was, indeed, initially working with Ford to publish material relating to the artist's unsuccessful lawsuit against John Ruskin, but a dispute over Ford's role led the artist to end the relationship. Ford did not bother to inform the publishers of this turn of events, allowing the project to proceed. Alerted to a notice in the *Pall Mall Gazette,* Field & Tuer wrote a letter to Whistler's solicitors on March 25 that was reproduced in *The Gentle Art of Making Enemies* (Heinemann, 1890):

> We have seen the paragraph in yesterday's *Pall Mall Gazette* relating to the publication of Mr. Whistler's letters. You may like to know that we recently put into type for a certain person a series of Mr. Whistler's letters and other matter, taking it for granted that Mr. Whistler had given permission. Quite recently, however, and fortunately in time to stop the work being printed, we were told that Mr. Whistler objected to his letters being published. We then sent for the person in question, and told him that until he obtained Mr. Whistler's sanction we declined to proceed further with the work, which, we may tell you, is finished and cast ready for printing, and the type distributed. From the time of this interview we have not seen or heard from the person in question, and there the matter rests.

Tuer subsequently met with Whistler to discuss the matter and, in a personal letter dated March 27,[39] explained that Ford had, at the last minute, asked the publishers

---

36. Courtesy, Lilly Library, Indiana University, Bloomington, IN.
37. Andrew White Tuer letters, MS 137, courtesy Woodson Research Center, Fondren Library, Rice University.
38. Andrew White Tuer letters, MS 137, courtesy Woodson Research Center, Fondren Library, Rice University.
39. Correspondence of James McNeill Whistler, University of Glasgow Library.

to leave final settlement to him and not to communicate with Whistler. In the letter, Tuer mentioned that he had retained copies of all correspondence with Ford, but those records, if they survive, have not been located.

❦

Abraham Field retired from the business in 1890 and died in 1891. As previously noted, *The Paper and Printing Trades Journal* was sold to John Southward, and on February 9 of the following year the firm was incorporated as "The Leadenhall Press, Limited." ("Field & Tuer" had already been dropped from the imprint on some books as early as 1888.) The first Directors were Andrew Tuer (Managing Director), Samuel H. Louttit, and James Millington. Four others, including Duncan Louttit, received one share each as subscribers. The list of company activities included: newspaper proprietors, printers, booksellers, stationers, typefounders, paper, ink and paste manufacturers, designers and draughtsmen, lithographers, stereotypers, electrotypers, photolithographers, engravers, die sinkers, bookbinders, and advertising agents. At the same time, Stickphast was incorporated as "Fixol & Stickphast, Limited."

Some of the firm's best books were published in the nineties, not least among them Tuer's *History of the Horn-Book* and the book that first caught my eye, *The Book of Delightful and Strange Designs*. A reviewer in the December 1892 issue of *The Bookworm* wrote:

> Mr. Andrew W. Tuer . . . has found time to issue a book on a subject concerning which he candidly admits knowing "nothing at all." This is probably the first time that our versatile confrere has ever admitted ignorance on any subject under the sun, and this fact alone is sufficient to give the book an individuality all its own. But "The Book of Delightful and Strange Designs, Being One Hundred Facsimile Illustrations of the Art of the Japanese Stencil-cutter" (Leadenhall Press, E.C.), does not need any extraneous help to its appreciation by the lover of

The Book of Delightful and Strange Designs: the title page spread, with original stencil plate.

the beautiful. That "provokingly incorruptible and absolutely necessary person, the gentle reader," to whom Mr. Tuer dedicates this book, must be indeed a "capricious and never-to-be-understood" person if he fails to appreciate this astonishing array of quaint designs, scarcely two of which have the remotest similarity with one another.

The output of the press gradually declined after the incorporation, due in part to higher quality and increased competition in the market: ironically enough, a direct result of Tuer's influence and achievements during the eighties. Emerging publishers such as J. M. Dent, William Heinemann, John Lane, Elkin Mathews, and Sir Algernon Methuen, were attracting writers and illustrators (some had published with Tuer) for whom the Leadenhall Press must have represented recent history rather than the future.

With a new business model and management structure, Tuer was devoting more attention to personal projects. *History of the Horn-Book* and the other books he wrote or edited during the nineties must have taken much of his time. He became a Fellow of the Society of Antiquaries in 1890, and he was also a member of the Ex Libris Society, the Society of Authors and the Arts Club. In 1899, he was appointed a director of Kelly & Co., the publisher of *Kelly's Post Office Directory*. He was a regular correspondent to the *Times, Notes and Queries*, the *Athenaeum*, the *Pall Mall Gazette*, and other periodicals on all manner of subjects, from "missing word" competitions to the musical key produced by skaters on the ice in Kensington Gardens ("G as nearly as I could judge, but corrected to G sharp when, half an hour later, I got to a piano"),[40] from proposing an exhibition of clocks to describing the printing technique by which perpetrators of fraudulent charity appeals were reproducing the look of typewritten letters.

Tuer was also pursuing a new interest, the decorative art of shagreen (the prepared skin of certain sharks or dogfish). In an 1893 contribution to *Notes and Queries*, he wrote, "In recent interesting and not unsuccessful experiments, I fastened a skin on to a flat stone, and the surface was ground with fine sand and water, an operation involving many hours of arm-aching but vicarious labour . . . A file gives a smooth edge, and then comes a final polishing. Shagreen makes lovely panels for bookbinding." He began comparing results with the young Arts & Crafts artist John Paul Cooper[41] and, in 1899, was able to report in *Notes and Queries*, "at the Exhibition of the Artful and Crafty ones now being held in the New Gallery, Regent Street, I am showing a little box, the lid of which I have covered outside with pearl-grey, and inside with light-blue shagreen. Mr. J. P. Cooper is exhibiting some prettily designed boxes covered with the same beautiful material."

Unfortunately, he did not live long enough to perfect his techniques for use in book binding. Having suffered an illness a couple of years previously from

---

40. Letter to the *Pall Mall Gazette*, January 25, 1892.
41. For more on the relationship between Tuer and Cooper, see: N. Natasha Kuzmanovic. *John Paul Cooper, Designer and Craftsman of the Arts and Crafts Movement*. Sutton Publishing, 1999.

which he never fully recovered,[42] Andrew Tuer was suddenly taken ill and, within four days, died of pleurisy on February 24, 1900. He was buried in Kensal Green Cemetery, leaving an estate of £72,176 to Thomasine, with bequests to several of the Leadenhall Press staff.

Fondly recalled by many after he died, the obituaries captured much of the personality Tuer expressed through the Leadenhall Press and his many activities. The *Athenaeum* described Tuer as "ingenious and resourceful" and "one of the kindliest and most hospitable of men." *Publishers' Weekly* wrote, "Mr. Tuer was actively engaged to the last, so that the announcement of his death came with a shock to his friends. A man of energy and ideas, he had many interests, but through them all he remained loyal to books, and especially to books connected with the subjects which he may be said to have made his own." *The Times* called him a "widely known and versatile man . . . of uncommonly varied knowledge in literary and artistic byways." The *Pall Mall Gazette* of Monday, March 5, offered the following tribute:

> London Publishing is the poorer in high spirits and humour by the death of Mr. Andrew Tuer. In all his doings he was mirthful; and he gave readers several very excellent books. His *History of the Horn-Book* was really valuable; his *Bartolozzi and His Works* is of great use to all collectors; and his two medleys from old children's books are full of entertainment. His *Book of Delightful and Strange Designs,* a collection of Japanese stencils, is something more—a treasure to all decorative artists. Mr. Tuer was the inventor of Stickphast Paste and the *Hairless Paper Pad*; he provided the late Charles Keene with many good jokes for *Punch*; and he was among the first to see beauty in old samplers.

A sale of Tuer's collection of early children's books and hornbooks, held at the Sotheby, Wilkinson & Hodge gallery in July of that year, raised just over £602. The names of the buyers included: Maggs, Dobell, Spencer, Sotheran, Parsons, Currie, Shepherd, Burman, Quaritch, Tregaskis, Edwards, Matthews, Hocklieve, Darton, Baron, Barton, Ellis, Ferris, Sabin, Dobell, and Walford.[43] Thomasine apparently took an interest in the press for at least a few years, judging from the books published after 1900, but neither she nor the managers could maintain the publishing side of the business for long. The last original books appeared in 1905, although the most popular titles continued to be reissued in cheap editions, and a scattering of publications appeared as job work. At some point, the Leadenhall Press and Fixol & Stickphast were moved to 24-27 Garden Row, Southwark, S.E., where the press continued on as "catalogue & prospectus printers, circular and form letter specialists and addressing experts."[44]

---

42. Note of Tuer's death in *Ex Libris Journal*, Vol. X Part 3, March 1900.
43. From an annotated copy of *Catalogue of the Well-Known Collection of Children's Books of the XVIIth, XVIIIth and XIXth Centuries, and the Valuable Series of Horn-Books, of the late A. W. Tuer, Esq. F.S.A. &c. July 17, 1900* (London: Sotheby, Wilkinson & Hodge, 1900) at the Grolier Club, inscribed "Gift of Sotheby, W. & H." .
44. From ad in *Estimate of the Numbers Engaged in the Trades and Professions in the United Kingdom and Colonies* (London, The Leadenhall Press, Ltd., 1919).

After Thomasine's death in 1927, the Leadenhall Press, Ltd., was dissolved. Fixol and Stickphast continued on for many years, becoming part of a larger company in 1960. The estate's executors ordered a second auction, held at Sotheby & Co. on June 27, 1927. Included were presentation and office copies of Leadenhall Press books (many with correspondence and original drawings), autograph letters, prints, proofs, books and periodicals from Tuer's library, and collections of type specimens, valentines, silhouettes, lotteries, ballads, bookplates, bank notes, and miniature books. The items that were sold at the two auctions are widely scattered, and while some have found their way to institutional collections (see Appendix D), the whereabouts of many is unknown.

I leave the last word to John Johnson, printer and collector of ephemera, from his J. M. Dent Memorial Lecture delivered on October 27, 1933. In discussing how, if the craft is good, the goals of publisher and printer converge to mirror the living world, he gave the following example:

> Last week, for instance, I was turning over my file of nearly two hundred years' advertisements of stationery and kindred material when my eyes were suddenly arrested by a small group of advertisements of Stickphast paste in the year 1894. My first thought was surprise that Stickphast was a good forty years old. My second thought was one of pleased association. For the Leadenhall Press and Messrs. Field & Tuer have always fascinated me with their fantasies, and I said to myself that no one could have printed those particular advertisements except the Leadenhall Press. Then my eyes fell to the foot, where I saw the familiar name.[45]

---

45. John Johnson, *The Printer, His Customers and His Men* (London & Toronto: J. M. Dent, 1933), p. 55.

Checklist of Field & Tuer and The Leadenhall Press

The following list includes all publications I have been able to identify that bear one of three imprints: "Field & Tuer," "Field & Tuer, the Leadenhall Press E.C.," and "The Leadenhall Press, Ltd." While there is some overlap, the imprints correspond roughly with the periods 1862–78, 1879–92, and 1892–1927. Publishing and book printing began in 1869, blossomed between 1877 and 1879, and ended in 1905. Ephemeral printings are covered in Appendix B.

I have not included publications advertised but unverified. Trade notices for two copyright pamphlets I have been unable to locate are noted in the listings for the books they were intended to protect. I have also not included the *Book of Japanese Designs* (printed in Japan), listed at 3s 6d from 1883 to 1885. I have not found this book, but it was almost certainly a special import unique in the Field & Tuer lists.

No library holds every title, and the scarcest are widely scattered. I have physically examined at least one copy of the majority, primarily at the British Library, the Lilly Library (Indiana University), The New York Public Library, Princeton University, and in private collections. Additional research was done at the Grolier Club Library (New York), the University of Delaware, the University of Toronto, the Houghton Library (Harvard), and Winterthur Library in Winterthur, Delaware. When physical examination was impractical, and for additional detail, I relied on photographs, photocopies, and descriptions of copies in the original bindings provided by the following libraries: the Bodleian, Bristol University, the British Library, Cambridge University, Clark Library (UCLA), Georg-August-Universität Göttingen, Harry Ransom Center (University of Texas), The Huntington, Johns Hopkins, Michigan State University, the National Library of Australia, the National Library of Scotland, Newcastle University, Trinity College Dublin, and Yale University. I have also reviewed digitized versions of many books for additional confirmation.

The listings follow chronological order. Information appears as follows:
1. Checklist number;
2. Author (where applicable);
3. Title;
4. Edition (where more than one);
5. Publishing imprint;
6. Month (where available) and year of publication;
7. Job number (where none given, either not present or same as first edition);
8. Numbered page total (only for significantly different editions);
9. Height in centimeters (both dimensions for oblong format);
10. Price (where known);
11. Binding and cover design (where not specified, the material is paper);
12. Noteworthy aspects of content, production, and publication;
13. Location of examples of special note or scarcity.

Company records do not survive, and the presence of a year on the title page seems arbitrary. Years and months of publication were confirmed in most cases from listings in the biweekly *Publishers' Circular* and the annual *English Catalogue of Books*. For titles not recorded there, I turned to *The Bookseller*, *New Catalogue of British Literature* for 1896, Bertram Dobell's *Catalogue of Books Printed for Private Circulation* (London: Published by the Author, 1906), and other publications as noted. Within a given year, titles for which the month is not known are listed after those with months identified.

I have ignored the firm's practice of calling each subsequent printing an "edition," but I have included later editions of note as sub-listings, except in five cases. Certain editions of Tuer's *Luxurious Bathing* and *Bartolozzi and His Works,* John Oldcastle's *Journals and Journalism with a Guide for Literary Beginners*, *The Story of a Nursery Rhyme*, and Jerome K. Jerome's *On the Stage—and Off* I judged to be so different in form or content as to warrant a separate entry. I have included the names (slightly abbreviated) of all publishers listed on title pages, as it seemed the best way to record the history of relationships with other publishing houses.

Publisher's job numbers were given with the imprint in several ways; for consistency I have used the most common form of a period between the prefix letter and the number (T.4,567). These numbers seem to represent the order of opening of accounts rather than the order of printing or publication. The prefix letters may have identified the type of job or the person who originated the project; the vast majority begin with "T," while some begin with other letters and a few have no letter at all. I have noted those instances where no job number appears. I have been unable to locate some pamphlets in the original covers, so there may be a few job numbers I have not yet discovered.

I have given locations of some copies of special interest, and I have noted cases in which only one or two (or no) examples were found. The words "University" and/or "Library" have been dropped for some locations: Bodleian, Bristol, Glasgow, Lilly, Newberry, Newcastle, Princeton, Wellcome. For others, the following abbreviations are used: BL (British Library), CL (City of London Libraries), GAU (Georg-August-Universität Göttingen), HRC (Harry Ransom Center), ISH (International Institute of Social History, Amsterdam), NLS (National Library of Scotland), NLZ (National Library of New Zealand), NYHS (New York Historical Society), NYPL (New York Public Library), SLA (State Library of South Australia), TCD (Trinity College Dublin), and UL (University of London).

1863.1   EMMA COLE. *Respectfully Inscribed to Mr. G. Ridler, Second Master of the Merchant Seamen's Orphan Asylum.* Field & Tuer, printers. [1863]. No job number. 24 cm. Single sheet, printed on one side. Poem printed within an ornamental border, dated at end: 4th January, 1860. "By Emma Cole; as a token of gratitude for his kindness to her only son, George William Cole. (Copy located: BL, with MS. dated 1863.)

1865.1 *Ledger.* Field & Tuer. [ca. 1862–1867]. 19 cm. Price unknown. Half leather, "Ledger" in gilt on spine. Label of Field & Tuer, Manufacturing Stationers, on front pastedown. Blank ruled forms. (Copy reported, but not seen.)

1865.2 *Log Book, Containing a Record of the Proceedings on Board the ___ from the Port of ___ , etc.* "Published by Field & Tuer, Printers of Forms, Lithographers, and Wholesale Manufacturing Stationers, 136 Minories. [ca. 1865]. No job number. 31 cm. Price unknown. Brown leather spine, dark blue-green card covers, white label reading: "Log Book of the Ship ___ From ___ To ___ Commencing ___ Ending ___ Kept by ___." Forms. (Copy located: BL.)

1865.3 *Cargo Book.* Published by Field & Tuer. [1865]. 26 cm. Price unknown. Blank forms. (Copy located: BL, lacking original covers.)

1865.4 H. W. CLAYTON. *Clayton's Annual Register of Shipping and Port Charges for Great Britain, the Islands of Jersey, Guernsey, Alderney, &c.,* H. W. Clayton; Field & Tuer; Goddard & Son. 1865. No job number. 23 cm. Price unknown. Blue cloth, title, date, and border in blind. Possibly the only issue.

Note: republished as a photocopy by the National Museums & Galleries on Merseyside in 2002.

1867.1 "A LADY." *Housekeeping Made Easy.*

a. First edition: Field & Tuer. [1867]. 19 cm. 1s. "A simplified method of keeping accounts . . ." Introductory advice, with blank forms.

b. Second edition: Field & Tuer, the Leadenhall Press; Simpkin, Marshall; Hamilton, Adams. [1886]. 1s. Republication with revised imprint. (Advertised and possibly reissued in 1891 without "Field & Tuer," but not confirmed.)

1868.1 JOHN GAY, F.R.C.S. *On Varicose Disease of the Extremities and its Allied Disorder: Skin Discoloration, Induration, and Ulcer: Being the Lettsomian Lectures Delivered before the Medical Society of London in 1867.* John Churchill and Sons; Printed by Field & Tuer, 136 Minories (verso of t.p. and end of text). 1868. 23 cm. 5s. Green cloth with blind-stamped rules.

1869.1 *Uncle, Can You Find a Rhyme for Orange?* Field & Tuer; Simpkin & Marshall. 1869. No job number. Obl. 21.5 x 29 cm. Price unknown. Illustrated poems with rhymes for "orange," printed on rectos only. Black pebbled cloth, lettering and illustration of orange in gilt, rules in blind.

1869.2 WILLIAM LYON AND WALTER F. K. LYON. *Lyon of Ogil.* Field & Tuer, Printers. [1869]. 5,407. 29 cm. "Copy of a genealogical MS lent by Walter F. Lyon, Esq." Ancestry of William Lyon of Scotland (10th laird of Ogil).

1869.3 "A WEST INDIAN." *Jamaica under the New Form of Government: A Series of Letters.* Field & Tuer; Simpkin, Marshall. [1869]. 21 cm. 1s. "With an appendix, containing an abstract of the last official report of Sir J. P. Grant." A series of letters reprinted from the *European Mail*. (Copies located: NLZ, SLA.)

1869.4   WILLIAM M. STOUT. *A Song of the Wind: An Original Recitation for the People. To which is added a speech on Minding Our Own Business.* Published by the author; printed by Field & Tuer. [1869]. {5,156 (number preceded by half bracket). 18 cm. 6d. Blue-green wrappers, lettering in black.

1870.1   JOHN DALY BESEMERES. *No Actress. A Stage Door-keeper's Story.* Effingham Wilson, Royal Exchange; printed by Field & Tuer. [Mar.] 1870. 5,243.[1] 16 cm. 3s 6d. Green cloth, title device and rules in gilt.

1870.2   CAPTAIN RICHARD WHITBOURNE. *Westward Hoe for Avalon in the New-Found-Land. As Described by Captain Richard Whitbourne of Ermouth, Devon, 1622.* Sampson Low; Field & Tuer. [Mar.] 1870. 5,243.[1] 18 cm. 5s. Brown cloth, beveled edges, lettering, pictorial device and rules in black. Edited and illustrated by T. [Thomas] Whitburn.

1870.3   SAMUEL PALMER. *St. Pancras; Being Antiquarian, Topographical, and Biographical Memoranda.* Samuel Palmer; Field & Tuer. [Apr.] 1870. No job number. 30 cm. 10s 6d. Red or brown cloth, decoration in blind, title and price in gilt on spine. Also seen in half burgundy calf with marbled paper boards. Frontis map.

1870.4   [CHARLES DICKENS]. *The Charles Dickens Sale. Catalogue (printed in facsimile) of the Beautiful Collection of Modern Pictures, Water-Colour Drawings, and Objects of Art, of the late Charles Dickens, with the whole of the Names of Purchasers and Enormous Prices Realised appended to each Lot, sold at their great Rooms, London, by Messrs. Christie, Manson, and Woods, on Saturday, July 9, 1870.* Field & Tuer; Simpkin, Marshall; Trübner. [July 1870]. 28 cm. 1s. Light brown printed wrappers. Facsimile of the original catalogue (printed by W. Clowes & Sons), with purchasers and prices. 47 other publishers (9 American) also listed. "Notice. — Field & Tuer have the sole concession of printing and publishing this Catalogue." Reprinted in *Dickens Memento* (checklist 1885.13.)

1871.1   JOHN GREEN [GEORGE HENRY TOWNSEND]. *Evans's Music and Supper Rooms, Covent-Garden. Selections and words of madrigals, glees, choruses, songs, &c., sung every evening in the above supper rooms, commencing at eight o'clock.* Field & Tuer. [ca. Sept. 1871].[2] A.1,704. 2 parts. 24 cm. "Ex. off. Field & Tuer" at bottom.

1871.2   JOSEPH SANDELL. *Memoranda of Art & Artists, Anecdotal and Biographical.* Simpkin, Marshall; Field & Tuer. [Sept.] 1871. A.1,718. 20 cm. 5s. Green sand grain cloth, titling and vignette in gilt.

1. Duplicate job number (checklist 1870.1 and 1870.2).
2. "The selections and words of the madrigals, glees, choruses, and songs, now sung every evening at Evans's, Covent Garden, are neatly printed by Field and Tuer, forming a book of 24 pages." — the *Daily News*, Oct. 4, 1871.

1871.3 *An Account of the Methods Whereby the Charity Schools Have Been Erected & Managed, and of the Encouragement Given to Them.* Field & Tuer. 1871. No job number. 40 cm. 6d. Pamphlet: Field & Tuer's Series of English Re-prints, no. 1. "London: Printed by Joseph Downing, in Bartholomew-Close, near West Smithfield, 1704. Reprinted from the original (forming the first of a series of English reprints)." (No others noted in this series.)

1872.1 REV. F. G. BLOMFIELD. *How Is the Gospel to Be Preached to the Poor?: An Answer to the Questions as to the Future Work of the Bishop of London's Fund, in a Letter to the Lord Bishop of London by the Rev. F. G. Blomfield, M.A.* "Not published"; Field & Tuer, printers. 1872. 21 cm. Price unknown. Pamphlet.

1872.2 L.v.H. [HENRI VAN LAUN]. *A Fusion of Parties in France, A.D. 1872. Adapted from the French of Monselet by L.V.H.* Printed by Field & Tuer. [1872]. 20 cm. Pamphlet. "Printed for private circulation only." Only 25 copies printed. In verse, adapted from the French of Charles Monselet (1825–1888). On cover: "Presented to ____ by J. L. Pfungst and Co." (wine merchants).

1872.3 ANDREW W. [WHITE] TUER [ed.]. *The Paper & Printing Trades Journal.* Printed & published for the proprietors by Field & Tuer, ye Leadenhalle Workes. Dec. 1872–1891.[3] 25 cm. 1s per annum (4s by 1891). Quarterly. (An *Index to the Paper & Printing Trades Journal,* numbers 1–32, compiled by Edwin R. Pearce, was published by Barnicott and Son, Taunton, 1881.)

1873.1 MRS. [SARAH MAUD] HECKFORD. *The Life of Christ, and Its Bearing on the Doctrines of Communism.* Field & Tuer; Simpkin, Marshall. [July] 1873. No job number. 20 cm. 2s 6d. Brown cloth, beveled edges, lettering in gilt and black, rules in black.

1873.2 GEORGE C. HOUNSELL [ed.]. *Flags and Signals of All Nations, by Hounsell Brothers, Flag Manufacturers to the Lords' Commissioners of the Admiralty.* Field & Tuer. [1873?]. No job number. 45 cm. Price unknown. Blue-green cloth, lettering and coat of arms in gilt. 188 chromolithographed and hand-tinted plates showing flags, standards, commercial codes, signals for pilots, and yacht club flags. "By Authority of the Lords Commissioners of the Admiralty."

1874.1 CAPT. R. T. STEVENS. *A Table of Distances in Nautical Miles between the Principal Ports of the United Kingdom, and Ports in the North Sea, Cattegat, Baltic Sea, and Gulfs of Finland and Bothnia.* Field & Tuer, ye Leadenhalle Workes. [ca. 1874-75].[4] B.2,646. Obl. 38 x 56 cm. Single sheet. 2s. Advertised in *The A B C Mariners' Guide* (1883.27). (Copy located: NLS.)

---

3. At dissolution of Field & Tuer in 1891, sold to John Southward. Last issue: no. 89, 1897.
4. The job number and imprint suggest that this chart was first issued around 1874. "Ye Leadenhalle Workes" appeared in the first issues of *The Paper & Printing Trades Journal,* and in *The Printers' Universal Book of Reference and Every-hour Office Companion. An Addendum to "The Printers', etc., Business Buide."* (London: J. Haddon, 1875), but I have not seen the imprint in that form after 1875.

1875.1   Carl Wilhelm C. Fuchs; Thomas William Danby [trans.]. *Practical Guide to the Determination of Minerals by the Blowpipe*. Field & Tuer; Simpkin, Marshall; Claxton, Remson & Haffelfinger. [Mar. 1875]. B.3,784. 23 cm. 5s. Brown cloth, lettering in gilt. With alternating blank pages. Translated and edited by T. W. Danby. (NYPL copy with typographic bookplate of George T. Hartshorn.)

1875.2   *Report of the Committee to the Half-Yearly Meeting of the Standing Committee of West India Planters and Merchants to Be Held on Thursday, 26th August, 1875.* Field & Tuer. [Aug.] 1875. 22 cm. Pamphlet. Printed for members.

1875.3   [West India Committee]. *West India Mails*. Field & Tuer. 1875. 3,147. Reprint of a letter from the West India Committee to the Postmaster General concerning the West India mails.

1876.1   A. F. Hill. *Secrets of the Sanctum: An Inside View of an Editor's Life*. Claxton, Remsen & Haffelfinger; Field & Tuer. [Jan.][5] 1876. T.2,092. 19 cm. Green cloth, title decoration in gilt and black. Advertised in *Ye Oldest Diarie of Englysshe Travell* (checklist 1884.2). First published in Philadelphia in 1875.

1876.2   Nevile Lubbock; W. H. Smith. *British Sugar and French Bounties*. Field & Tuer. [Feb. 1876 — *The Examiner*]. 21cm. 1s. Includes an Appendix, titled "Mr. Smith to Lord Tenterden" and signed: W. H. Smith.

1877.1   [Corporation of London]. *Some Rules for the Conduct of Life* (cover: *A.D. 1477. in Honour of William Caxton This Pamphlet Is Gratuitously Circulated. A.D. 1877.*) Printed by Field & Tuer. 1877. T.2,368. 21 cm. Price unknown.

a. Regular issue: Half gray ruled in dark gray, tan paper boards lettered in black. Reprint of the original edition published by H. Fenwick, London [1800?]. "A Citizen and Goldsmith deeply interested reproduces in this pamphlet the excellent Rules for the Conduct of Life presented by the Corporation of London to every apprentice on whom its freedom is conferred" (introduction).[6]

b. Special issue: Half parchment, buff boards ruled in gilt, lettering in black. Printed on specially prepared paper. (Lilly copy with the armorial bookplate of Iddesleigh.)

1877.2   Alphonse Legros. *Histoire du Bonhomme Misère*. R. Gueraut, Orris Villas, Hammersmith. The engravings printed by Field & Tuer at the Leadenhall Press. 1877. 36 cm. Price unknown. Vellum, lettering in red and black. ". . . avec six eaux-fortes par A. Legros." Each plate preceded by a letterpress leaf with title and quotation. 60 copies printed on Whatman paper, signed by Legros and initialed by Gueraut.

5. "Books Received" notice in *The Graphic*, Feb. 5, 1876. Reviewed in issue of Feb. 19.
6. One copy noted bears an inscription stating that the author (introduction) was "W. Blaydes," presumably William Blades, organizer of the Caxton Exhibition and author of *The Life and Typography of William Caxton* (London: Joseph Lilly, 1861).

1877.3 [R. Mawley]. *Pottery and Porcelain in 1876. An Art Student's Ramble through Some of the China Shops of London.* Field & Tuer. Privately Printed. 1877. 21 cm. (Copy located: Bodleian.)

1877.4 [Benjamin Standring]. *Epigrams: Original and Selected.* Simpkin, & Marshall; Printed by Field & Tuer. 1877. No job number. 17 cm. Price unknown. A collection of epigrams, some anonymous, some by Addison, Mrs. Barbauld, Coleridge, Herbert, Pope, Reid, J. Stewart, Swift, etc. Bodleian attributes editorial responsibility to Benjamin Standring (signature "B. S." on final epigram).

1878.1 *Sugar Bounties: Deputation of Proprietors and Merchants Interested in the Sugar Colonies to Sir Michael Hicks-Beach . . . on Wednesday, 8th May, 1878.* Field & Tuer, printers. [1878]. Pamphlet. (Copy located: ISH.)

1878.2 Angier Bros. *A Handbook of Freight Tables and Tonnage Schedules: Adapted for the Use of Steam-Ship: Brokers, Owners, Masters and Others, with Other Useful Information.* Field & Tuer, "ye Leadenhalle Presse." 1878. No job number. 25 cm. 3s 6d. Brown cloth spine, light gray covers, lettering and rules in black. Compiled by Angier Bros. Advertised at rear of *The A B C Mariners' Guide* (checklist 1883.27).

1878.3 ——. *Comparative Rates of Freight.* Field & Tuer. [ca. 1878]. Cloth 1s; leather 2s 6d. "Including the Mediterranean and Black Sea Freight Scale of 1863, and the Old Baltic Scale for Tallow and Wheat. Also a Comparative Table of Classification of Ships in the different Registers in vogue." Advertised at rear of *The A B C Mariners' Guide* (checklist 1883.27). (Not located.)

1878.4 Rev. Frederick K. Harford, M.A. *Ballads of Schiller No. 1. The Diver: with notes.* Bickers & Son; Imprinted by Field & Tuer, at the Leadenhall Press (colophon). 1878. No job number. 28 cm. Brown cloth spine, gray card covers, lettering and vignette in black. (The first appearance noted of the combined Field & Tuer/Leadenhall Press imprint.)

1878.5 Ω [Omega]. *Facta Non Verba. An Examination of the Figures and Statements Published as the Result of the Analyses of Professor Frankland, D.C.L., F.R.S, on the London Water Supply in 1876 and 1877.* Simpkin, Marshall; Field & Tuer. 1878. T.2,494. 23 cm. 1s.

1878.6 *The Port of Gibraltar.* Field & Tuer, Printers. [1878?]. 17 cm. Price unknown. Pamphlet.

1879.1 Andrew W. [White] Tuer. *Luxurious Bathing: A Sketch by Andrew W. Tuer with Twelve Folio Etchings, Initials, etc. by Sutton Sharpe.*

a. First edition: Field & Tuer, ye Leadenhalle Presse; Simpkin, Marshall; Scribner & Welford. [July] 1879. No job number. Obl. 36 x 46 cm. 250 copies, 3 guineas. Half vellum with gilt rules, parchment-covered boards, side-stitched, lettering in red and black, mounted etching. By Sutton Sharpe: vignette etchings, initials, and 12 folio landscape etchings, each preceded by a leaf with a quotation about water (quotations omitted from second edition).

b. Proof issue: 1879. Proofs on Japanese paper. 25 copies, 7 guineas.

Second edition: (see checklist 1880.1).

1879.2　JAMES L. OHLSON. *The British Sugar Industries and Foreign Export Bounties: A Summary of the Main Points of the Evidence Taken by the Select Committee of the House of Commons, Session 1879.* Field & Tuer. [1879]. 20 cm. Pamphlet. Introduction by James L. Ohlson. By direction of the West India Committee.

1880.1　ANDREW W. [WHITE] TUER. *Luxurious Bathing: (Second Edition) A Sketch by Andrew W. Tuer with Eight Etchings by Tristram Ellis.*

a. Second edition: Field & Tuer, ye Leadenhalle Presse; Scribner & Welford. [July] 1880. No job number. Obl. 16 x 24 cm. 5s. Half cream vellum, natural vellum-covered boards, lettering in black, side-stitched. Title vignette and 7 etchings by Tristram Ellis on white, cream, or light gray paper.

b. Proof edition: 100 copies, 10s 6d. On hand-made paper. Signed by the artist.

c. Proofs before letters: 20 copies, 21s. On Japanese laid paper. Signed.

d. Remarque proofs: 6 copies, £3 3s. On heavy Japanese laid paper. Signed.

1880.2　JOHN OLDCASTLE [WILFRID MEYNELL]. *Journals and Journalism: With a Guide for Literary Beginners.*

a. First edition: Field & Tuer, ye Leadenhalle Presse. [July] 1880. T.2,882. Obl. 15.5 x 14.5 cm. 1,000 copies, 3s 6d. Vellum, lettering in black, gilt rule, side-stitched. Facsimiles in the text. Slip tipped in at end: "Keep this book under a weight until thoroughly dry, otherwise the binding will warp."

b. Second edition: 1880. (Copies with different sets of publisher's ads noted.)

Note: A separate publication of the major part of the contents was issued in 1884 as *John Oldcastle's Guide for Literary Beginners* (see checklist 1884.11).

1880.3　ANDREW W. [WHITE] TUER [ed.]. *The Printers' International Specimen Exchange.* Office of The Paper and Printing Trades Journal; Field & Tuer "Ye Leadenhall Press." Volumes I–VIII: 1880–1887.[7] No job numbers. 30 cm. 1s. Annual, by subscription. "The volumes are, if desired, uniformly and artistically bound in half-vellum laced with catgut, and lettered back and side (old style) in gold, at a charge of 5s per volume." Edited and with an introduction by A. W. Tuer.

a. Vol. I, 1880: 178 contributors, no more than 230 copies.

b. Vol. II, 1881: 226 contributors, no more than 290 copies.

c. Vol. III, 1882: 283 contributors, no more than 350 copies.

d. Vol. IV, 1883: 344 specimens, no more than 400 copies.

---

7. Volumes IX–XVI, 1888–1898, were published by *The British Printer*. Vols. XV and XVI each covered two years.

        e. Vol. V, 1884: 347 contributors, no more than 400 copies.

        f. Vol. VI, 1885: 349 contributions, no more than 400 copies.

        g. Vol. VII, 1886: 351 contributors, no more than 450 copies.

        h. Vol. VIII, 1887: 375 contributors, no more than 450 copies

1881.1   [St. Bartholomew Rahere Almonry]. *Ye antiente fraternitie of ye Rahere Almoners, founded MCXXIII. Resuscitated MDCCCLXXXI. Ceremonies of opening and closing a Chapter. Approved and confirmed by the Grand Council of ye fraternitie April 4th, MDCCCLXXXI.* Field & Tuer, ye Leadenhalle Presse. [ca. May 1881]. F.1,962 (verso of t. p.), F.1,362 (last page). 15 cm. Printed for private circulation.

1881.2   ——. *Ye legende of ye anciente fraternitie of ye Rahere Almoners. Founded MCXXIII. Resuscitation of the ancient priory alms of St. Bartholomew the Great, London, A.D. MDCCCLXXXI. The lists of founders & members of Grand Council, and the rules and regulations of the St. Bartholomew Rahere Almonry, No. 1, holden at the Chapter House, Cloth Fair, London.* Field & Tuer, ye Leadenhalle Presse. [June 1881]. 22 cm. Printed for private circulation.

1881.3   Tristram J. Ellis. *On a Raft, and Through the Desert.*

        a. Regular edition: Field & Tuer, ye Leadenhalle Presse; Scribner & Welford. [June] 1881. T.2,926. 2 vols. 24 cm. £2 12s 6d. Vellum parchment, lettering in gilt with red circular lattice design. Map and 38 etchings on copper by the author. Vol. 1: *On a Raft*; Vol. 2: *Through the Desert.* "The Narrative of an Artist's Journey through Northern Syria and Kurdistan, by the Tigris to Mosul and Baghdad . . . across the Desert by the Euphrates and Palmyra to Damascus, over the Anti-Lebanon to Baalbek and to Beyrout."

        b. Large paper: 32 cm. 25 copies, 6 guineas. Full vellum, proof etchings taken from the copper-plates before steel facing, printed on hand-made paper. Signed by Tristram Ellis in both vols.

1881.4   "A Castillian." *The Conversion and Unification of the Spanish Debt.* Field & Tuer, ye Leadenhalle Presse. [ca. June 1881]. F.1,970. 27 cm. 6d. Pamphlet. "Amplification" at end signed: "A Castillian" and dated 25th May, 1881. (Copy located: Bristol, "2nd issue" imprinted on cover.)

1881.5   Rev. H. [Henry] Footman. *The Nature and Prevalence of Modern Unbelief. A Paper Read at a Clerical Meeting at Newbury.* Field & Tuer, ye Leadenhalle Presse; Hamilton, Adams. [July 1881]. T.3,000. 24 cm. 1s. Pamphlet.

1881.6   J. W. [James William] Gilbart-Smith. [Sir James Denham-Smith]. *My Ladye and Others: Poems: Satirical, Philosophical, & Arcadian.*

        a. First edition: Field & Tuer at ye Leadenhalle Presse. [Aug.] 1881. F.1,973. 21 cm. 10s 6d. White morocco grain paper-covered boards, lettering in sepia, sunflower design in green and yellow. Title page reads simply: "Poems." Text and ornaments printed in sepia.

b. Second edition: 1881. 20 cm. G.1,325. Dark olive cloth, lettering in black with gilt ornaments. With two additional poems not in the first edition, reprinted from *The Graphic*.

1881.7 "C. B." *The Story of a Nursery Rhyme*.

a. First edition: Field & Tuer, ye Leadenhalle Presse; Simpkin, Marshall; Hamilton, Adams. [Dec. 1881]. T.3,040. Obl. 16 x 23 cm. 2s 6d. Dark brown cloth spine, linen boards, lettering in black. Illustrated by Margaret Hooper.

[Second edition: see checklist 1883.8].

b. Third edition: With Scribner & Welford added as New York publishers. [1887]. 23 cm. Illustrated by Margaret Hooper.

1881.8 CAPTAIN R. T. STEVENS. *Table of Distances, to and from the Principal Commercial Seaports of the World: Shewing the Distances in Nautical Miles, Both Via the Capes and the Suez Canal, Including a Table of Distances in the Sea of Marmora, the Black Sea and the Sea of Azof.* Printed and published by Field & Tuer. [1881?].[8] No job number. Obl. 82 x 132 cm. Prices: 30s; mounted on linen 35s; mounted on linen, rollers, and varnished 40s. Advertised in *The A B C Mariners' Guide* (1883.27). (Copies located: BL, GAU.)

1882.1 ANDREW WHITE TUER. *Bartolozzi and His Works. A Biographical & Descriptive Account of the Life & Career of Francesco Bartolozzi, R.A.*

a. Regular edition: Field & Tuer, ye Leadenhalle Presse; Hamilton, Adams; Scribner & Welford. [Jan. 1882]. No job number. 2 vols. 29 cm. Thirteen illustrations, including title vignettes and frontis engravings printed in brown and repeated in red. 500 copies, 2 guineas. Full parchment, lettering and rules in gilt, side-stitched with yellow cord. Insert at front of Vol. II: "A few of the Principal Plates . . . can be obtained through the publishers at the rate of half-a-guinea, and on Large Paper (early impressions) at fifteen shillings each." "Dedicated by Gracious Permission to Her Majesty the Queen." (Private collection: presentation copy from Tuer to type founder James Figgins.)

b. Large paper issue: 2 vols. 30 cm. 100 copies, 3 guineas. Full vellum, side-stitched, maroon endpapers ruled in gilt. With duplicates of the plates printed in different colors, several on satin.

c. Collectors' edition: 4 vols. 34 cm. 50 copies, extra-illustrated, 15 guineas. Full vellum, side-stitched. Volumes I–IV at top and bottom of covers and on title pages as Vols. I, I-A, II, and II-A at bottom to correspond to two-volume

---

8. Likely year of publication from *Festschrift, herausgegeben von der Mathematischen Gesellschaft in Hamburg anlässlich ihres 200jährigen Jubelfestes 1890. Katalog der auf Hamburger Bibliotheken vorhandenen Litteratur aus der reinen und angewandten Mathematik und Physik* (Hamburg 1890). BL gives [1886?], later than *The A B C Mariners' Guide*, in which it is advertised.

edition. "Dedicated by command to Her Majesty the Queen."
Second edition, corrected and revised: (see checklist 1885.35).

1882.2 ———. *List of the Works of Bartolozzi (Arranged under Heads).* [Field & Tuer], [Jan. 1882]. 30 cm. "Accompanies: *Bartolozzi and His Works* by Andrew W. Tuer." Offprint with pagination 85–152, bound in vellum. "Thirty extra copies printed for British Museum and private collections."

1882.3 TRISTRAM J. [JAMES] ELLIS. *Six Etchings of Well-Known Views in Kensington Gardens, & Hyde Park, Etched on Copper from Nature.*

a. Prints: Field & Tuer, ye Leadenhalle Presse; Hamilton, Adams; the Artistic Stationery Co.; Scribner & Welford. January 25, 1882. Obl. 25 x 38 cm. £1 11s 6d in portfolio or 5s each print. Portfolio of six art prints with a descriptive account by W. J. Loftie. Proof etchings signed and dated August 1881: 1. Kensington Gardens, *the Palace*; 2. Kensington Gardens, *On the Long Water*; 3. Kensington Gardens, *the Broad Walk*; 4. Hyde Park, *the Albert Memorial (Twilight)*; 5. Hyde Park, *Rotten Row (Mid-day)*; 6. Hyde Park, *the Serpentine*. (Copy located: London Metropolitan Archives, Artist's proofs.)

b. Proofs (unsigned): 100 sets in portfolio, 5 guineas.

c. Artist's proofs (signed): 100 sets in portfolio, 6 guineas.

d. "Remarque" proofs (signed): 25 sets in portfolio, 10 guineas.

e. "Remarque" proofs, earliest, on satin (signed): 12 sets in portfolio, £21.

1882.4 [ANNA BONUS KINGSFORD AND EDWARD MAITLAND]. *The Perfect Way; or, The Finding of Christ.*

a. First edition: Field & Tuer, ye Leadenhalle Presse; Hamilton, Adams; Scribner & Welford. [Mar.] 1882. T.3,030. 342 pp. 23 cm. 12s 6d. Blue cloth, elaborate cover design stamped in black, spine lettered in gilt, star device in black on lower cover. Printed on light blue paper. "These Lectures were delivered in London, before a private audience, in the months of May, June, and July, 1881." Errata slip inserted after title page.

b. Second edition, revised and enlarged: Field & Tuer, the Leadenhall Press; George Redway; Simpkin, Marshall; Hamilton, Adams; Scribner & Welford. [Apr.] 1887. 397 pp.; 12s 6d.

c. Third revised edition: [May] 1890. 384 pp. 7s 6d.

1882.5 WILLIAM SHAKESPEARE. *Some Well-known "Sugar'd Sonnets" by William Shakespeare; Re-Sugar'd with Ornamental Borders Designed by Edwin J. Ellis, and Etched by Tristram J. Ellis.*

a. Regular edition: "Published by Henry Sotheran & Co.; Produced by Field & Tuer, ye Leadenhalle Presse." [Oct. 1882]. No job number. 23 cm. 750 copies, 15s. Half gray silk and marbled boards, paper label with lettering in gilt. Ten sonnets printed twice on leaves: once within a single-line border, once within an illustrated border. A gift book for 1882–1883.

b. Special edition: 25 copies, 5 guineas. Proofs on satin, window-mounted. Signed by Tristram Ellis.

1882.6 ROBERT HERRICK. *Selections from the Hesperides and Noble Numbers of Robert Herrick.* Sampson Low; Harper & Bros.; "Type from 'Ye Leadenhalle Presse' (Field & Tuer), London" (verso of t.p.). [Nov.] 1882. No job number. 31 cm. 42s. Pictorial tan cloth, elaborate cover design of gilt sun and yellow flowers, lettering in black and red. Illustrated by Edwin A. Abbey.

1882.7 [ANDREW WHITE TUER]. *The Kaukneigh Awlminek, 1883. Edited by 'Enery 'Arris, down't-tcher-now.* Field & Tuer, ye Leadenhalle Press; Hamilton, Adams; John Heywood; John Menzies. [ca. Nov. 1882].[9] No job number. 14 cm. 3d. Wrappers, lettering in black.

1882.8 M. A. [MADELINE ANNE] WALLACE-DUNLOP. *Glass in the Old World.* Field & Tuer, Ye Leadenhall Press; Scribner & Welford. [Nov. 1882]. T.3,054. 23 cm. 12s 6d. Brown cloth, lettering in gilt, decorative borders in black. With six plates, two printed in color.

1882.9 MARCO MINGHETTI. *The Masters of Raffaello (Raphael Sanzio).* Field & Tuer, Ye Leadenhall Press; Hamilton, Adams; Scribner & Welford. 1882. T.3,122. 23 cm. 100 copies. Price unknown. Translated by Louis Fagan. Vellum and parchment, ruled in gilt, lettering in black, spine side-stitched. (Lilly copy with Joseph Crawhall bookplate and signature, and presentation letter from Andrew Tuer stating that the book "was published five days ago and is already out of print.")

1882.10 JAMES STEVENS. *Ye Perfecte Historie Offe Ye Antiente Fraternitie Offe Ye Rahere Almoners... With an Account of the Life of Rahere... The Dissolution of the Almonry... A.D. 1534; and the Resuscitation of the Order, A.D. 1881.* Field & Tuer. Printed for private circulation only. [1882?]. 23 cm. 6d. Plain blue wrappers. Illustrated.

1882.11 AELEANOR TAYLOR. *Glimpses of the Great Jacobins; Being Examples of Their Speeches and Writings, Never Before Translated into English.* Cattell; "Field & Tuer, printers, Ye Leadenhall Press" (foot of p. 151). [1882]. F.1,741. 21 cm. Price unknown. Green cloth, decorative lettering and floral device in gilt. "To the unprejudiced reader" —p. [5] dated 4th March, 1882.

1883.1 [WINDSOR GALLERY]. *Catalogue of a Loan Collection of Engravings & Etchings by Francesco Bartolozzi, R.A., and Engravers of His School.* E. Barrington Nash; printed by Field & Tuer, ye Leadenhalle Presse; Simpkin, Marshall; Hamilton,

---

9. Year of publication often given as 1883, but reviewed by G. A. Sala in "Echoes of the Week," *Illustrated London News,* Nov. 1882, reprinted in *Living London: Being Echoes Re-echoed* (London: Remington, 1883), pp. 490-91.

Adams. [Jan.] 1883. T.3,158. Obl. 19 x 20 cm. 5,000 copies, 1s. Half vellum, brown paper boards, lettering in black. Introduction by Andrew W. Tuer. Frontis copperplate engraving. Exhibition at the Windsor Gallery, 26 Saville Row, 1883. (Lilly copy inscribed by Tuer.)

1883.2 ——. *Catalogue of the Second Exhibition (Loan Collection) of Engravings & Etchings by Francesco Bartolozzi, R.A., and Engravers of His School.* E. Barrington Nash; printed by Field & Tuer, ye Leadenhalle Presse. 1883. Obl. 19 x 20 cm. 1s. Half vellum, brown paper boards, ornamental lettering in black. Foreword by E. Barrington Nash. Frontis copperplate engraving in red.

1883.3 W. GORDON STABLES. *Tea: The Drink of Pleasure and of Health.* Field & Tuer, ye Leadenhalle Presse; Simpkin, Marshall; Hamilton, Adams. [Feb. 1883]. T.3,136. 15 cm. 5,000 copies, 1s. Vegetable parchment, lettering (the word "TEA" in oriental calligraphic lettering) and teapot illustration in black. Mounted frontis engraving after George Moreland.

Note: reprinted in facsimile by Pryor Publications (Whitstable) in 1990.

1883.4 JOSEPH CRAWHALL. *Olde Tayles Newlye Relayted: Enryched with All Ye Ancyente Embellyshmentes.* The Leadenhall Press. [Feb. 1883?][10] No job number. 30 cm. Price unknown. Olive green cloth, with lettering and decorations in red and black. Includes 14 of the 17 individually paginated ballads and tales that appear in *Crawhall's Chap-book Chaplets* (checklist 1883.15) and *Olde ffrendes wyth newe Faces* (checklist 1884.5), in varying combinations. Illustrations in black and white.

variant 1: *The Barkeshire Lady's Garland; The Babes in the Wood; John & Joan; Jemmy & Nancy of Yarmouth; The Taming of a Shrew; Blew Cap for Mee; George Barnewel; Ye Loving Ballad of Lorde Bateman; A True Relation of the Apparition of Mrs. Veal to Mrs. Bargrave; The Long Pack; The Sword-Dancers; Ducks & Green Peas; A Farce; Andrew Robinson Stoney Bowes Esquire; The Gloamin' Buchte.*

variant 2: Order of first six titles: *The Barkeshire Lady's Garland; The Babes in the Wood; Jemmy & Nancy of Yarmouth; The Taming of a Shrew; Blew Cap for Mee; John & Joan.*

variant 3: Omits *John & Joan*; includes *I Know What I Know* as third title.

variant 4: Omits *John & Joan*; includes *John Cunningham*.

variant 5: Omits *John & Joan* and *A True Relation of the Apparition of Mrs. Veal to Mrs. Bargrave*; includes *I Know What I Know* and *John Cunningham*.

---

10. Not in the *Publisher's Circular* or the *English Catalogue of Books*. The title pages of the individual parts bear the publishing imprint: "Field & Tuer. Simpkin, Marshall. Hamilton, Adams. Scribner & Welford" and the date 1883 in roman numerals. The colophon at the end of *The Glomm' Buchte* (the last part in every variant located) states: "Imprynted att ye Leadenhall Presse, London, by Field & Tuer, ande fynysshed thys XIV, daie of Februarie (being Sainct Valentyne hys daie) in the yere o thyncarnacon of Oure Lorde MDCCCLXXXIII." Copies of the separate parts survive, but they were not advertised or priced individually. I have chosen to list them as sub-entries under *Crawhall's Chap-book Chaplets* (checklist 1883.15) and *Olde ffrendes wyth newe Faces* (checklist 1884.5).

Note: This collection does not appear in the *Publishers' Circular* or the *English Catalogue of Books*, and it was not announced, advertised, or reviewed. Felver notes a copy purporting to be "one of 25 copies with woodcuts coloured by hand" but suggests that it was colored by an amateur (not seen).[11] Newberry copy with bookplate of T. L. DeVinne.

1883.5 [PEDRO CAROLINO]. *English as She Is Spoke: Or, a Jest in Sober Earnest.*[12]

a. First edition: Field & Tuer, ye Leadenhalle Presse; Simpkin, Marshall; Hamilton, Adams. [Mar. 1883]. T.3,202. 14 cm. 1s. Vegetable parchment over flexible boards, lettering in black. Vellum-Parchment Shilling Series of Miscellaneous Literature, no. I. With an introduction by James Millington. Extracts from *New Guide of the Conversation in Portuguese and English (O Novo Guia da Conversação em Portuguez e Inglez*, Paris, 1855), in which Pedro Carolino used a French-English dictionary to translate a Portuguese-French phrase book (by José da Fonseca, Paris, 1853) into English.

b. Special issue: Vellum, gilt lettering, printed on vellum. 6 copies, 1 guinea.[13]

Note: Published in America by Putnam's and Appleton, using Leadenhall sheets. Reprinted in facsimile by Hamish Hamilton/St. George's Press (London) in 1970 and Pryor Publications (Whitstable) in 1990.

1883.6 HENRY FOOTMAN. *Reasonable Apprehensions and Reassuring Hints: Being Papers Designed to Attract Attention to the Nature of Modern Unbelief, and to Meet Some of Its Fundamental Assumptions.* Field & Tuer, ye Leadenhalle Presse; Simpkin, Marshall; Hamilton, Adams.

a. First edition: [Apr.] 1883. T.3,145. 24 cm. 3s 6d.

b. New edition: [Dec. 1883]. 14 cm. 1s. Vegetable parchment over flexible boards, lettering in black. Vellum-Parchment Shilling Series of Miscellaneous Literature, no. VII.

c. Special issue: Vellum, gilt lettering, printed on vellum. 6 copies, 1 guinea.

1883.7 GEORGE LAMBERT, F.S.A. *St. Dunstan: A Paper Written to Be Read at Goldsmiths' Hall, but time not permitting it is most respectfully offered to the London and Middlesex Archaeological Society.* Field & Tuer, the Leadenhall Press. [June] 1883. 22 cm. Price unknown. Pamphlet. Dated June, 1883.

---

11. Charles S. Felver, *Joseph Crawhall The Newcastle Wood Engraver* (Newcastle upon Tyne: Frank Graham, 1973).

12. The phrase "English as she is spoke" was coined by Andrew Tuer, according to Millington, in a letter to Notes and Queries, 6th S . XI, June 13, 1885.

13. From *Recent Books and Something About Them*: "At the various times of publication of their Vellum-Parchment Series, Messrs. Field & Tuer, says the Academy, had six copies of each book printed on fine vellum. Two sets have been disposed of at one guinea per volume, and the remaining four sets of the following volumes—thirteen in all—are now offered for sale: *Reasonable Apprehensions and Reassuring Hints, Oldest Diarie of English Travell, Don't, You Shouldn't, Selected Texts from the 'Imitation of Christ,' Truth about Tonquin, Are we to Read Backwards?, Henry Irving, English as She is Spoke*, and ditto *Her Seconds' Part*; and in the Oblong Series, *Journalistic Jumbles, Oldcastle's Guide for Literary Beginners*, and *Decently and in Order*. Twelve copies have also been printed on vellum of that bibliographical curiosity, *Quads within Quads*: two guineas each."

1883.8   "C. B." *The Story of a Nursery Rhyme.*

[First edition: see checklist 1881.7].

a. Second edition: [July 1883]. T.3,200. 14 cm. 1s. Vegetable parchment over flexible boards, lettering in light blue. Vellum-Parchment Shilling Series of Miscellaneous Literature, no. II. Illustrated by Edwin J. Ellis and "printed throughout in a new shade of blue ink" that is very faint.

b. Special issue: Vellum, gilt lettering, printed on vellum. 6 copies, 1 guinea.

1883.9   WILLIAM ARCHER. *Henry Irving, Actor and Manager, a Critical Study.*

a. First edition: Field & Tuer, ye Leadenhalle Presse; Simpkin, Marshall; Hamilton, Adams. [Aug. 1883]. T.3,209. 14 cm. 1s. Vegetable parchment over flexible boards, lettering and portrait illustration (repeated as frontispiece) in black. Vellum-Parchment Shilling Series of Miscellaneous Literature, no. III.

b. Special issue: Vellum, gilt lettering, printed on vellum. 6 copies, 1 guinea.

c. New edition: [Aug.] 1885. 6d.

Note: Reprinted by the Scholarly Press (St. Clair Shores) in 1970.

1883.10   DR. JEREMY TAYLOR. *The Marriage Ring, or, the Mysteriousness & Duties of Marriage.* Field & Tuer, Ye Leadenhall Presse; Simpkin, Marshall; Hamilton, Adams. [Aug. 1883]. T.3,174. 18 cm. 2s 6d. Gray boards, title and rules in red with gilt ring below title. Introduction by F. A. Kerr.

1883.11   SIR W. M. [WILLIAM MATTHEW] FLINDERS PETRIE. *The Pyramids and Temples of Gizeh.*

a. First edition: Field & Tuer, the Leadenhall Press; Simpkin, Marshall; Hamilton, Adams; Scribner & Welford. [Sept. 1883]. T.3,224. 27 cm. 18s. Brown cloth, lettering in dark brown. Published "with the assistance of a vote of one hundred pounds from the government-grant committee of the Royal Society. 1883."

b. New and Revised edition: [Jan. 1885]. 25 cm. 6s.

1883.12   EDWIN JOHN ELLIS. *When Is Your Birthday? Or a Year of Good Wishes: A Set of Twelve Designs . . . With Sonnets by the Artist.* Field & Tuer, the Leadenhall Press. [Oct. 1883]. T.3,108. Sq. 22 cm. 21s. Gray paper boards, lettering and vignette in gilt, in loose gold-yellow suede covering stamped in gilt with ties, in outer folding box.

1883.13   LOUIS ALEXANDER FAGAN. *Collectors' Marks.* Field & Tuer, ye Leadenhalle Presse; Scribner & Welford. [Oct.] 1883. T.3,092. 20 cm. 21s. Full vellum, lettering and border in gilt. Facsimiles of book ownership marks, with index. Frontispiece portrait of Thomas Howard by the author.

Note: An expanded edition, edited by Milton Einstein and Max Goldstein, was published in 1918 by Laryngoscope Press. Part I reprinted Fagan's original entries, Part II was a Supplement to those entries, and Part III contained New Contributions. It was reissued in 2007 by Martino Publishing

1883.14 MRS. GEORGE [JANE M. WINNARD] HOOPER. *Prince Pertinax, a Fairy Tale.*

a. First edition: Field & Tuer, ye Leadenhalle Presse; Scribner & Welford. [Oct. 1883]. No job number. Obl. 22 x 28.5 cm. 21s. With 26 drawings in sepia by Margaret L. Hooper and Margery May. Illustrations, title vignette and historiated initials mounted on pages. Half brown sheep, blue-gray boards, lettering in gilt. In folding box with blue cloth sides, blue-gray boards, and paper label with gilt lettering. Originally published as *Prince Pertinax; or, The Blue Rose. A Fairy Tale* in serial form in the *Monthly Packet,* 1863.

b. Variant binding: Half dark brown cloth, blue-gray boards, lettering in black (reported but not seen).

1883.15 JOSEPH CRAWHALL [illust.]. *Crawhall's Chap-book Chaplets.* Field & Tuer; Simpkin, Marshall; Hamilton, Adams; Scribner & Welford. Imprynted at Ye Leadenhall Presse [at end of each part]. [Oct. 1883]; 1883 on title page, 1883-4 on spine. No job number. 8 parts in 1 vol. 30 cm. 25s. Half cream cloth, light gray boards with lettering in black on upper cover and spine, and hand-colored illustrations and decoration on lower cover, in plain dust jacket lettered on back. Reprints of eight ballads, each with hand-colored wrappers and individual pagination. As the illustrations herein are all hand coloured the issue is necessarily limited." –page facing t.p. Advertisement at rear announces *Olde ffrendes wyth newe Faces* in preparation. (Newcastle copy inscribed "Joseph Crawhall 23rd Oct. 1883 first copy" with bookplate, press cuttings, reviews, and letters. Private collection: presentation copy to Crawhall's daughter Elspeth, in dust jacket.)

a. Chaplet I. *The Barkeshire Lady's Garland.* 29 cm. Pictorial light blue-gray wrappers.

b. Chaplet II. *The Babes in the Wood.* 29 cm. Pictorial buff wrappers.

c. Chaplet III. *I Know What I Know.* 29 cm. Pictorial light lavender wrappers.

d. Chaplet IV. *Jemmy & Nancy of Yarmouth.* 29 cm. Pictorial light blue-gray wrappers.

e. Chaplet V. *The Taming of a Shrew.* 29 cm. Pictorial light gray wrappers.

f. Chaplet VI. *Blew Cap for Mee.* 29 cm. Pictorial buff or light gray wrappers.

g. Chaplet VII. *John & Joan.* 29 cm. Pictorial light blue-gray wrappers.

h. Chaplet VIII. *George Barnewel.* 29 cm. Pictorial light blue-gray wrappers. (Separate copy not located.)

Note: reprinted in facsimile by the Scolar Press (London) in 1976.

1883.16 *Christmas Entertainments: Wherein Is Described Abundance of Fiddle-Faddle-Stuff... Eating, Drinking, Kissing, & Other Diversions; Witches, Wizards,*

Conjurers... Fairies, Spectres, Ghosts, & Apparitions... The Story of Jack Spriggins and the Enchanted Bean; Curious Memoirs of Old Father Christmas.

a. First edition: Field & Tuer, ye Leadenhalle Presse; Simpkin, Marshall; Hamilton, Adams. [Oct. 1883]. T.3,218. 14 cm. 1s. Vegetable parchment over flexible boards, lettering and illustration in black. Vellum-Parchment Shilling Series of Miscellaneous Literature, no. IV. At head of title: "1740. New edition of *Round about our Coal Fire, or, Christmas Entertainments.* London: Printed for J. Roberts, 1740" with a second facsimile title page.

b. Special issue: Vellum, gilt lettering, printed on vellum. 6 copies, 1 guinea.

c. New edition: [Oct. 1884]. 14 cm. 6d.

Note: reprinted in facsimile by Pryor Publications (Whitstable) in 1991.

1883.17 WILLIAM ROSCOE. *The Butterfly's Ball and the Grasshopper's Feast.* Griffith & Farran; Field & Tuer, Ye Leadenhall Presse. [Oct.] 1883. No job number. 21.5 cm. 1s. Facsimile of 1808 edition published by J. Harris as part of "Harris's Cabinet." Gray wrappers, facsimiles of 1807 title page and adverts on covers.

1883.18 "A LADY" [CATHERINE ANN DORSET]. *The Peacock at Home. A Sequel to the Butterfly's Ball.* Griffith & Farran; Field & Tuer, Ye Leadenhall Presse. [Nov.] 1883. No job number. 21.5 cm. 1s. Facsimile of 1807 edition published by J. Harris as part of "Harris's Cabinet." With an introduction by Charles Welsh. Tan wrappers, facsimiles of 1807 title page and adverts on covers.

1883.19 "W. B." *The Elephant's Ball and Grand Fête Champetre: Intended as a Companion to Those Much Admired Pieces, the Butterfly's Ball, and the Peacock at Home.* Griffith & Farran; Field & Tuer, Ye Leadenhall Presse. [Nov.] 1883. No job number. 21.5 cm. 1s. Facsimile of 1807 edition published by J. Harris as part of "Harris's Cabinet." With an introduction by Charles Welsh. Gray wrappers, facsimiles of 1807 title page and adverts on covers.

1883.20 "A LADY" [CATHERINE ANN DORSET]. *The Lion's Masquerade. A Sequel to the Peacock at Home.* Griffith & Farran; Field & Tuer, Ye Leadenhall Presse. [Nov.] 1883. No job number. 21.5 cm. 1s. Facsimile of 1807 edition published by J. Harris as part of "Harris's Cabinet." Tan or gray wrappers, facsimiles of 1807 title page and adverts on covers.

1883.21 CHARLES WELSH [ed.]. *Harris's Cabinet. Numbers One to Four. The Butterfly's Ball; the Peacock at Home; the Elephant's Ball; the Lion's Masquerade: Reprinted from the Editions of 1807 & 1808.* Griffith & Farran; Field & Tuer, Ye Leadenhall Press. [Nov.] 1883. No job number. 21.5 cm. 5s. Four parts in 1 vol. Reprinted from the editions of 1807 & 1808. Quarter vellum with drab paper-covered boards, titling in black, paper label on spine. Introduction by Charles Welsh.

1883.22 JOHN HOPPNER AND CHARLES WILKIN; ANDREW W. TUER [annot.]. *Bygone Beauties: "A Select Series of Ten Portraits of Ladies of Rank and Fashion."*

a. First edition: Field & Tuer, the Leadenhall Press; Eyre & Spottiswoode; Simpkin, Marshall; Scribner & Welford. [Nov. 1883]. T.4,567. 19 cm. 21s. Half silk, black flexible card covers, side-stitched, lettering in gilt, red silk ribbon. Engravings on tinted paper from paintings by John Hoppner, R.A., engraved by Charles Wilkin. Annotated by Andrew W. Tuer.

b. Second edition: [Oct.] 1891. 2s. Black flexible card covers, lettering in gilt, side-stitched; gold silk ribbon.

1883.23 [PEDRO CAROLINO]. *English as She Is Spoke: Or, a Jest in Sober Earnest: Her Seconds Part (New Matter)*.

a. First edition: Field & Tuer, ye Leadenhalle Presse; Simpkin, Marshall; Hamilton, Adams. [Nov. 1883]. T.3,202. 14 cm. 1s. Vegetable parchment over flexible boards, lettering in black. Vellum-Parchment Shilling Series of Miscellaneous Literature, no. 1a. With an introduction by James Millington.

b. Special issue: Vellum, gilt lettering, printed on vellum. 6 copies, 1 guinea.

Note: reprinted for Friends of the Gale Research Co., 86th Annual Conference, American Library Association, May 1967.

1883.24 MAX O'RELL [LEON-PAUL BLOUËT]. *John Bull and His Island: Translated from the French, under the Supervision of the Author.*

a. First edition: Field & Tuer, ye Leadenhalle Presse; Simpkin, Marshall.[14] [Dec. 1883]. T.3,258. 296 pp. 18 cm. 3s 6d. Brown cloth, lettering and surrounding rule in black. Translated from the original French of *John Bull et son île*.

b. Yellow wrappers, title page reproduced on cover: [Dec. 1883]. 2s 6d.

c. Cheap edition: C. Scribner's Sons added to imprint. [June 1886]. 242 pp. 16 cm. 1s 6d. Advertisements on endpapers. Olive green cloth, lettering and surrounding rule in black.

d. Cheap edition, wrappers: [June 1886]. 1s.

1883.25 ANDREW WHITE TUER. *London Cries: with Six Charming Children printed direct from stippled plates in the Bartolozzi style, and duplicated in red and brown, and about forty other illustrations including ten of Rowlandson's humorous subjects in facsimile, and tinted; examples by George Cruikshank, Joseph Crawhall, &c. &c.*

a. Regular edition: Field & Tuer, Ye Leadenhall Press; Scribner & Welford. [Dec. 1883]. T.3,236. 30 cm. 21s. Half brown cloth, light gray boards, paper title label. Six copperplate stipple engravings on plates, 48 numbered leaves printed on rectos only, 15 of the large text illustrations hand-colored.

b. Large paper signed proofs: 33 cm. 250 copies, 2 guineas. Signed on preliminary blank "Proof No. __ And. W. Tuer."

---

14. Letters from O'Rell and Field & Tuer in the Scribner's archives at Princeton show that O'Rell demanded that Scribner's negotiate solely with him for rights to the American edition, which appeared in 1884, as well as for later titles. The problem of piracy of his titles may have led O'Rell to relent by the mid-eighties.

c. Large paper copy with signed proofs on satin: 50 copies, 4 guineas. The six stippled plates in duplicate printed in red on satin and window-mounted. Signed on preliminary blank: "Proof No. ___ And. W. Tuer."

Note: A revised, cheaper edition was published in 1885 as *Old London Street Cries and the Cries of To-day* (checklist 1885.29).

1883.26 "Censor" [Oliver Bell Bunce]. *Don't: A Manual of Mistakes & Improprieties More or Less Prevalent in Conduct & Speech*. Field & Tuer, ye Leadenhalle Presse; Simpkin, Marshall; Hamilton, Adams.

a. First edition: [Dec. 1883]. T.2,239. 14 cm. 1s. Vegetable parchment over flexible boards, lettering in black. "Unmutilated with the Additional Matter. The Only Authorised & Complete Edition." Vellum-Parchment Shilling Series of Miscellaneous Literature, no. IX on half-title.[15] "Written by an American for Americans of the better class" (preface).

b. Special issue: Vellum, gilt lettering, printed on vellum. 6 copies, 1 guinea.

c. New edition: [Jan. 1884]. Reissued at 6d without "Vellum-Parchment Shilling Series of Miscellaneous Literature" on half-title or t.p.

Note: reprinted in facsimile by Pryor Publications (Whitstable) in 1982.

1883.27 Capt. R. T. Stevens. *The A B C Mariners' Guide, Containing Complete Information Relative to the Mercantile & Maritime Laws & Customs . . . including a useful set of tables, and the several Merchant Shipping Acts from 1854 to 1880.*

a. First edition: Field & Tuer, ye Leadenhalle Presse, and at all Nautical Warehouses. [1883].[16] T.2,924 (verso of t.p.), B.2,785 (colophon). 297 [1] pp. 22 cm. 7s 6d. Blue cloth, lettering in gilt, rules and anchor-and-rope decorations in black.

b. Second edition: [ca. 1884]. 388 pp. 22 cm. 7s 6d. Red cloth. (Not advertised in publisher's lists until 1891.)

1884.1 James Millington. *Are We to Read ?SDRAWKCAB, or, What Is the Best Print for the Eyes?* Field & Tuer, ye Leadenhalle Presse; Simpkin, Marshall; Hamilton, Adams.

a. First edition: [Jan. 1884]. T.3,215. 14 cm. 1s. Vegetable parchment over flexible boards, lettering in black. The word "?SDRAWKCAB" is printed in backward-facing type. Vellum-Parchment Shilling Series of Miscellaneous Literature, no. V. With an introduction by R. Brudenell Carter.

b. Special issue: Vellum, gilt lettering, printed on vellum. 6 copies, 1 guinea.

---

15. Most series lists show *You Shouldn't* (checklist 1884.8) as no. IX (see Appendix C). Griffith & Farran also published *Don't* with separate rights from Appleton, the original publisher. There was an exchange of letters in *The Academy* in January 1884 concerning compensation: Griffith & Farran paid royalties, while Field & Tuer arranged an exchange of titles, allowing Appleton to publish *English as She Is Spoke* (1883.5), since the Vellum Parchment Series was jointly owned by Field & Tuer and Appleton. However, the mild controversy may have led Tuer to remove *Don't* from the English version of the series and replace it with *You Shouldn't*.

16. Not in *Publishers' Circular* or *English Catalogue of Books*. BL copy has copyright receipt stamp dated 1883.

1884.2   Sir Richard Torkington. *Ye Oldest Diarie of Englysshe Travell: Being the Hitherto Unpublished Narrative of the Pilgrimage of Sir Richard Torkington to Jerusalem in 1517.*

a. First edition: Field & Tuer, ye Leadenhalle Presse; Simpkin, Marshall; Hamilton, Adams. [Jan. 1884]. T.3,216. 14 cm.; 1s. Vegetable parchment over flexible boards, lettering in black. Edited by W. J. Loftie. Vellum-Parchment Shilling Series of Miscellaneous Literature, no. VI.

b. Special issue: Vellum, gilt lettering, printed on vellum. 6 copies, 1 guinea.

1884.3   Thomas, à Kempis. *One Hundred and Forty-Two Selected Texts from The Imitation of Christ.* Field & Tuer, ye Leadenhalle Presse; Simpkin, Marshall; Hamilton, Adams.

a. First edition: [Jan. 1884]. T.3,212. 15 cm. 1s. Vegetable parchment over flexible boards, lettering in black. Vellum-Parchment Shilling Series of Miscellaneous Literature, no. VIII.

b. Special issue: Vellum, gilt lettering, printed on vellum. 6 copies, 1 guinea.

1884.4   [Anna (Bonus) Kingsford and Edward Maitland]. *How the World Came to an End in 1881.* Field & Tuer, ye Leadenhalle Presse; Simpkin, Marshall; Hamilton, Adams. [Jan. 1884]. T.3,250. "Anno Domini 1884. Anno Dominæ 3." 15 cm. 1s. Tan wrappers, lettering in black. Based on *The Perfect Way; or, The Finding of Christ* (checklist 1882.4), published anonymously by Anna (Bonus) Kingsford and Edward Maitland in London, 1882. "The Perfect Way" Shilling Series, no. 1. (No subsequent series publications noted).

1884.5   Joseph Crawhall [illust.]. *Olde ffrendes wyth newe Faces.* Field & Tuer; Simpkin, Marshall; Hamilton, Adams; Scribner & Welford. Imprynted at Ye Leadenhall Presse [at end of each part]. [Apr. 1884]. 1883 on title page, 1883–4 on spine; February 14th, 1883 at end of of last tale (consistent with *Olde Tayles Newlye Relayted*, checklist 1883.4). No job number. 9 parts in 1 vol. 29 cm. 25s. Half cream cloth, light gray boards with lettering in black on upper cover and spine, and hand-colored illustrations and decoration on lower cover. Presumably issued with plain dust jacket lettered on back, similar to companion volume, *Crawhall's Chap-book Chaplets* (1883.15), but no surviving copy in dust jacket located. Reprints of nine ballads and tales, each with hand-colored wrappers and individual pagination. Includes three illustrations by Joseph Crawhall Jr. (i.e., III) for *Ye Loving Ballad of Lorde Bateman, The Long Pack,* and *The Gloamin' Buchte.*

a. I. *Ye Loving Ballad of Lorde Bateman.* 29 cm. Pictorial light gray wrappers.

b. II. *A True Relation of the Apparition of Mrs. Veal to Mrs. Bargrave.* 29 cm. Pictorial light gray wrappers.

c. III. *The Long Pack: a Northumbrian Tale about an Hundred & Sixty Year Old.* By James Hogg. 29 cm. Pictorial beige wrappers.

d. IV. *The Sword-Dancers.* 29 cm. Pictorial light gray wrappers.

e. V. *John Cunningham, the Pastoral Poet.* 29 cm. Pictorial blue-gray wrappers.

f. VI. *Ducks & Green Peas, or, the Newcastle Rider: a Tale in Rhyme.* 29 cm. Pictorial light pink wrappers.

g. VII. *Ducks & Green Peas; a Farce.* 29 cm. Pictorial light green wrappers.

h. VIII. *Andrew Robinson Stoney Bowes Esquire M.P. &c. good deal of &c.* 29 cm. Pictorial light gray wrappers. (Copy located: BL.)

i. IX. *The Gloamin' Buchte.* 29 cm. Pictorial blue-gray wrappers.

1884.6 ARCHIBALD R. COLQUHOUN. *The Truth about Tonquin; Being the Times Special Correspondence.* Field & Tuer, ye Leadenhalle Presse; Simpkin, Marshall; Hamilton, Adams.

a. First edition: [Feb. 1884]. T.3,262. 15 cm. 1s. Vegetable parchment over flexible boards, lettering in black. Vellum-Parchment Shilling Series of Miscellaneous Literature, no. X.

b. Special issue: Vellum, gilt lettering, printed on vellum. 6 copies, 1 guinea.

1884.7 EDWARDA GIBBON [CHARLES JOHN STONE]. *History of the Decline and Fall of the British Empire.* Field & Tuer, the Leadenhall Press; Simpkin, Marshall; Hamilton, Adams. "Aukland 2884" [Feb. 1884]. No job number. 21 cm. 6d. Pamphlet. Ye Leadenhalle Presse Pamphlets no. 1.

1884.8 "BROTHER BOB." *You Shouldn't. Being Hints to Persons of Aristocratic Instincts.* Field & Tuer, ye Leadenhalle Presse; Simpkin, Marshall; Hamilton, Adams.

a. First edition: [Mar. 1884]. T.3,270. 14 cm. 1s. Vegetable parchment over flexible boards, lettering in black. Vellum-Parchment Shilling Series of Miscellaneous Literature, no. IX.

b. Special issue: Vellum, gilt lettering, printed on vellum. 6 copies, 1 guinea.

1884.9 ULICK RALPH BURKE AND ROBERT STAPLES JR. *Business and Pleasure in Brazil.* Field & Tuer, ye Leadenhalle Presse; Hamilton, Adams; Simpkin, Marshall; Scribner & Welford. [Mar. 1884]. T.3,256. 23 cm. 10s 6d. Dark green cloth, lettering in gilt, decoration in black.

1884.10 "W". *Can Parliament Break Faith? A Conversation on the Supply of Water to the Metropolis by Companies Established on the Faith of Private and Public Acts of Parliament.* Field & Tuer, ye Leadenhalle Presse; Simpkin, Marshall; Hamilton, Adams. [Mar., 1884]. T.3,282. 22 cm. 6d. Ye Leadenhalle Presse Pamphlets 2.

1884.11 JOHN OLDCASTLE [WILFRID MEYNELL]. *John Oldcastle's Guide for Literary Beginners.*

a. First edition: Field & Tuer, Ye Leadenhall Press; Simpkin, Marshall; Hamilton, Adams. [Apr.] 1884. T.3,276. Obl. 11 x 14 cm. 1s. Blue spine, pink boards, lettering in black. Ye Leadenhalle Presse Oblong Shilling-Series, no. 1.

Publisher's notice: "The first edition of *Journals and Journalism: with a Guide for Literary Beginners* ... was exhausted in a few days. A second and much larger edition has since been sold ... In order therefore to meet anew the continued demand ... a republication is now made ... of such portions of the original editions as formed most directly 'A Guide for Literary Beginners.'" (See checklist 1880.2.)

b. Special issue: Vellum, gilt lettering, printed on vellum. 6 copies, 1 guinea.

1884.12   FREDERIC CONDÉ WILLIAMS. *Journalistic Jumbles; or, Trippings in Type: Being Notes on Some Newspaper Blunders, Their Origin & Nature, with Numerous Examples.*

a. First edition: Field & Tuer, Ye Leadenhall Press; Simpkin, Marshall; Hamilton, Adams. [Apr. 1884]. T.3,274. Obl. 11 x 14 cm; 1s. Cream spine, tan boards, lettering in black. Ye Leadenhalle Presse Oblong Shilling-Series, no. 2. Printed on pale blue paper.

b. Special issue: Vellum, gilt lettering, printed on vellum. 6 copies, 1 guinea.

1884.13   "A CLERGYMAN." *Decently and in Order: A Few Hints on the Performance of the Orders for Morning and Evening Prayer with a Brief Notice of Mistakes Which Commonly Occur.*

a. First edition: Field & Tuer, Ye Leadenhall Press; Simpkin, Marshall; Hamilton, Adams. [Apr. 1884]. T.3,272. Obl. 11 x 14 cm. 1s. Cream spine, gray boards, titling in black. Ye Leadenhalle Presse Oblong Shilling-Series, no. 3.

b. Special issue: Vellum, gilt lettering, printed on vellum. 6 copies, 1 guinea.

1884.14   ALPHONSE DE FLORIAN. *Holy Blue!*

a. First edition: Field & Tuer, ye Leadenhalle Presse; Simpkin, Marshall; Hamilton, Adams. [Apr. 1884]. T.3,284. 17 cm. 3s 6d. Orange cloth, titling and border rule in black. With an Introduction by J. Millington.

b. Cheap edition: 2s 6d. Wrappers.

1884.15   ROBERT CHAMBERS. *Illustrations of the Author of Waverley: being Notices and Anecdotes of Real Characters, Scenes, and Incidents, supposed to be described in his Works.* Third edition. W. & R. Chambers; Field & Tuer, ye Leadenhalle Presse (verso of t.p.). [June] 1884. T.3,253. 19 cm. 6s. Gray paper spine, blue boards, gray spine label with title in black. With the preface to the second edition of 1825.[17] Originally published in 1822. With a preface by the author's son, typesigned: "R. C. (Secundus)."

1884.16   TREVOR CREIGHTON. *Ethics of Some Modern Novels.* Field & Tuer, ye Leadenhalle Presse; Simpkin, Marshall; Hamilton, Adams.

a. First edition: [June 1884]. T.3,206. 14 cm. 1s. Printed vegetable parchment over cream flexible boards. Vellum-Parchment Shilling Series of Miscellaneous

---

17. Another "second edition" was published in 1884 by William Brown, Edinburgh, printed by Turnbull & Spears.

Literature. A list of the series in this book has *The Truth About Tonquin* as no. IX in the series and *Ethics of Some Modern Novels* as no. X (in conflict with checklist 1883.26, 1884.6 and 1884.8).

b. Special issue: Vellum, gilt lettering, printed on vellum. 6 copies, 1 guinea.

1884.17 BENJAMIN DISRAELI, 1ST EARL OF BEACONSFIELD. *Lord Beaconsfield on the Constitution: 'What Is He?' and 'A Vindication of the English Constitution' / by "Disraeli the Younger."* Field & Tuer, ye Leadenhalle Presse; Simpkin, Marshall; Hamilton, Adams. [June 1884]. T.3,286. Obl. 14 x 17 cm. 2s. 6d. Half cream paper, gray boards, lettering in black. Edited and with an anecdotal preface by Francis Hitchman. Frontis portrait.

1884.18 JULIAN MARSHALL [ed.].[18] *Tennis Cuts and Quips, in Prose and Verse, with Rules and Wrinkles.* Field & Tuer, Ye Leadenhall Presse. [June 1884]. T.3,414. Obl. 14 x 17 cm. 2s 6d. Cream paper spine and tips, gray boards, lettering in black. Dedicated to the All England Lawn-Tennis Club, Wimbledon.

1884.19 JOHN HENRY SALTER. *A Guide to the River Thames, from Its Source to Wandsworth, Together with Particulars of the Rivers Avon, Severn, Wye, Trent, and Ouse, and the Principal Canals in Connection.* Field & Tuer, ye Leadenhalle Presse; John Salter, University Boat-house [Oxford]. [June 1884]. 18 cm. 1s. Originally published by Salter in 1881 as *The River Thames: A Guide to the River and the Principal Places on the Banks, from Its Source to Wandsworth.*

1884.20 DOUGLAS BLACKBURN. *Thought-Reading or Modern Mysteries Explained: Being Chapters on Thought-Reading, Occultism, Mesmerism, &C. Forming a Key to the Psychological Puzzles of the Day.* Field & Tuer, ye Leadenhalle Presse; Simpkin, Marshall; Hamilton, Adams. [July 1884]. T.3,147. 15 cm. 1s. Vegetable parchment over flexible boards, lettering in black.

1884.21 JAMES MILLINGTON. *'Fining Down' on Natural Principles without Banting.* Field & Tuer. [July 1884]. Obl. 6 x 10 cm. 6d. Pamphlet.

1884.22 JAMES GAY. *Canada's Poet.* Field & Tuer, ye Leadenhalle Presse. [July 1884]. T.3,418. Obl. 11 x 14 cm. 1s. Printed cream parchment wrappers over stiff paper covers. With an introduction by J. Millington. (Copies with and without frontis portrait noted.)

1884.23 JOSEPH CRAWHALL. *Old Aunt Elspa's ABC: We'll Soon Learn to Read, Then How Clever We'll Be.*

a. Regular issue: Field & Tuer, ye Leadenhalle Presse. [July] 1884. No job number. Obl. 21 x 24 cm. 2s 6d. Buff wrappers, sewn, hand-lettering and illustration in black. Folded sheets not sewn. With illustrations throughout printed in black. "Imprynted atte ye Signe of Ye Leadenhalle Presse, in ye

---

18. Marshall, who in 1890 revised the rules of tennis, was also a noted collector of prints and bookplates.

Olde London Streete in ye Health Exhibition, South Kensyngton, London Towne, in ye yeare of Grace, 1884" (p. 3 of wrappers).

b. Special edition: illustrations hand-colored, 2s 6d. (Princeton copy inscribed: "Elspeth Crawhall Challoner with Grandfather's love—April 30, 1887.")

Note: reprinted in facsimile by the Scolar Press (London) in 1978 and Pryor Publications (Whitstable) in 2000.

1884.24 *Art Embroidery in the Sewing Machine.* Field & Tuer, the Leadenhall Press. [July 1884]. Pamphlet. (Not located.)[19]

1884.25 ANDREW WHITE TUER. *Quads for Authors, Editors, & Devils.*

a. Midget folio: Field & Tuer, 'ye' Leadenhall Press; Simpkin; Hamilton. [July] 1884. Job number appears in Enlarged edition. 46 pp. 4 cm. 2s 6d. Printed in pearl type on hand-made banknote paper. Full vellum, title in gilt, silk fore-edge ties. Printers' jokes from *The Paper and Printing Trades Journal.*

b. "Enlarged edition" with extra matter: T.3,413. 94 pp. 16 cm. 1s 6d. Japon parchment wrappers, lettering in black.

c. *Quads within Quads*: Enlarged edition in full vellum, lettering in gilt, with a block of extra pages hollowed out to contain the midget folio. Lettered on upper cover: "In unlocking this Forme see that the QUADS do not drop out." 7s 6d. (Lilly copy 3: presentation from Tuer to Thomas Hailing.)

d. *Quads within Quads*, special issue: 12 copies on vellum. "Twelve copies have also been printed on vellum of that bibliographical curiosity, *Quads within Quads*" (from *Recent Books and Something About Them*).

1884.26 RALPH BROWNRIG, BISHOP OF EXETER. *Sermons in Sentences: Being Selected Passages from the Sermons Of... R. Browning.* Field & Tuer, Ye Leadenhall Presse; Simpkin, Marshall; Hamilton, Adams. [Sept. 1884]. T.3,298. 20 cm. 2s 6d. Wrappers, lettering in black. Edited by Rev. A. A. Toms.

1884.27 ALBERT AND GEORGE GRESSWELL. *The Wonderland of Evolution.* Field & Tuer, ye Leadenhalle Presse; Simpkin, Marshall; Hamilton, Adams; Scribner & Welford. [Sept. 1884]. T.3,280. 19 cm. 3s 6d. Cream cloth boards, lettering and pictorial device in gilt. A satire on the theory of evolution.

1884.28 ANDREW W. [WHITE] TUER. *John Bull's Womankind. (Suggestions for an Alteration in the Law of Copyright in the Titles of Books, Called Forth by the Piracy of the Title Originally Proposed for the Translation of Max O'Rell's Work: Les filles de John Bull).*[20] Field & Tuer, the Leadenhall Press. [Sept. 1884]. No job number. 18 cm. 1 farthing. Pamphlet: buff wrappers with "John Bull's Womankind" in

---

19. References: *Catalogue of the International Health Exhibition Library*, 1884, p. 115; *The Health Exhibition Literature*, Vol. XVII, p. 496.
20. Letters in the Scribner's archives at Princeton show that Field & Tuer and O'Rell were concerned about piracy of this work under the title *John Bull and His Daughters* and other translations..

black calligraphic lettering on the cover. At foot of title-page: "The edition of this book consists of one thousand copies." (See checklist 1884.32.)

1884.29 EDWARD TRACY TURNERELLI. *Memories of a Life of Toil: The Autobiography of Tracy Turnerelli "the Old Conservative": A Record of Work, Artistic, Literary, and Political, from 1835 to 1884.*

a. Regular edition: Field & Tuer, the Leadenhall Press; Simpkin, Marshall; Hamilton, Adams. [Oct. 1884]. T.3,423. 20 cm. 6s. Green cloth, lettering in black, decoration in gilt.

b. Supplement: [1884?]. Pamphlet: a note at the back of *Memories of a Life of Toil: The Autobiography of Tracy Turnerelli* indicates that a pamphlet containing reviews and corroborative and explanatory articles will be published and distributed privately and gratuitously. (Not located.)

1884.30 EVELYN FORSYTH. [ed.]. *Ye Gestes of Ye Ladye Anne: A Marvellous Pleasaunt and Comfortable Tayle.* Field & Tuer, ye Leadenhalle Presse; Simpkin, Marshall; Hamilton, Adams; Scribner & Welford. [Nov. 1884]. T.4,182. 21 cm. 2s 6d. Parchment over card covers, lettering and vignette in black. Illustrated by A. Hennen Broadwood.

1884.31 J. M. L. [JAMES MOODY LOWRY]. *The Keys 'at Home': A New Year's-Eve Entertainment.* Field & Tuer, ye Leadenhalle Presse; Simpkin, Marshall; Hamilton, Adams. [Nov. 1884]. T.4,202. 14 cm. 1s. Vegetable parchment over flexible boards, lettering in black. "Vellum-Parchment Shilling Series of Miscellaneous Literature" at head of title, but unnumbered.

1884.32 MAX O'RELL [LEON-PAUL BLOUËT]. *John Bull's Womankind (Les filles de John Bull).*

a. English copyright edition: Field & Tuer, the Leadenhall Press; Simpkin, Marshall; Hamilton, Adams. [Nov. 1884]. T.4,199. 18 cm. 3s 6d. Brown cloth, title in gilt on spine.

b. Cheap edition: [Nov. 1884]. 2s 6d. Yellow wrappers, lettering in black.

1884.33 "PUCK." *This Year, Next Year, Some Time, Never.* Field & Tuer, the Leadenhall Press; Simpkin, Marshall; Hamilton, Adams. [Nov. 1884]. T.4,190. 2 vols. 18 cm. 21s. Tan cloth, titling, floral decoration, and top rule in brown, bottom interwoven fence-like decorative border in red and brown. A novel.

1884.34 ALBERT RHODES. *Monsieur at Home.*

a. First edition: Field & Tuer, the Leadenhall Press; Simpkin, Marshall; Hamilton, Adams. [Nov. 1884]. T.4,188. 19 cm. 3s 6d. Blue-gray cloth, lettering in black.

b. Cheap edition: Merchant advertisements on endpapers. 2s 6d.

1884.35 VISCOUNT E. MELCHIOR DE VOGÜÉ. *The True Story of Mazeppa: The Son of Peter the Great, a Change of Reign.* Field & Tuer, the Leadenhall Press; Simpkin,

Marshall; Hamilton, Adams. [Nov. 1884]. T.3,422. 20 cm. 6s. Olive cloth, lettering in gilt, decorative rules in black. Translation by James Millington from the French of *Le fils de Pierre le Grand*.

1884.36 ARCHIBALD R. COLQUHOUN. *The Opening of China. Six Letters, Reprinted from the Times, on the Present Condition and Future Prospects of China*. Field & Tuer, the Leadenhall Press; Simpkin & Marshall; Hamilton, Adams. [Dec. 1884]. T.4,198. 18 cm. 1s. With an introduction by S. H. Louttit, dated October, 1884. Printed gray wrappers.

1884.37 MRS. ALFRED W. [MARGARET] HUNT. *Our Grandmothers' Gowns*. Field & Tuer, ye Leadenhalle Presse; Simpkin, Marshall; Hamilton, Adams. [Dec. 1884]. T.3,416. 20 cm. 7s 6d. With 24 hand-colored illustrations by George R. Halkett. Leaves printed on rectos only. Printed cloth (pattern varies), printed gray paper labels, four fore-edge ribbon ties.

1884.38 [GEORGE ERIC MACKAY]. *Love Letters by a Violinist*. Field & Tuer, Ye Leadenhall Presse; Scribner & Welford. [Dec.] 1884. T.1,439 on verso of title page; T.3,439 on colophon. 15 cm. 7s 6d. In verse. Vellum, lettering in gilt, gold silk ties. Illustrated with woodcuts. Dedication: "To Marie" (Marie Corelli).

1884.39 W. J. [WILLIAM JAMES] LOFTIE. *An Essay of Scarabs*.
a. First edition: Field & Tuer, the Leadenhall Press; Scribner & Welford. [1884]. T.3,213. 20 cm. 125 copies, 21s. Parchment-covered boards, lettering in gilt. With the catalogue of a private collection of ancient Egyptian amulets, drawings by W. M. Flinders Petrie.
b. Special issue: Six copies on vellum.

1884.40 SIR W. M. [WILLIAM MATTHEW] FLINDERS PETRIE. *The Arts of Ancient Egypt. A Lecture Delivered before the Society for the Encouragement of the Fine Arts*. Field & Tuer, the Leadenhall Press. 1884. No job number. 22 cm. 1s. Brown wrappers, lettering in black. Lecture delivered April 19, 1883.

1884.41 *History of St. Conan*. [Field & Tuer, the Leadenhall Press]. 1884. 14 cm. Price unknown. Printer's device on p. [6]. (Copy located: BL.)

1884.42 [FIELD & TUER]. *Recent Books and Something About Them*. Field & Tuer, the Leadenhall Press. 1884. 19 cm. Pamphlet. "An annotated catalogue of the publications of Messrs. Field & Tuer, a copy of which will be sent to any of our readers who may make application to the publishers. FREE." Categories: Illustrated, Humorous, Theological, Poetry, Fiction, Miscellaneous. (Bound into some books.)

1884.43 JOSEPH CRAWHALL. *Old Aunt Elspa's Spelling Bee, for Chubbies Who Know Well Their A B C. Newly Set Forth by J. Crawhall*.

a. Regular issue: Field & Tuer, Ye Leadenhall Presse. [1884–1885]. No job number. Obl. 21 x 24 cm. 1s. Gray illustrated wrappers, sewn, lettering and illustration in black. With illustrations throughout in black. "Imprynted atte ye Signe of Ye Leadenhalle Presse, London Towne, in ye yeare of Grace, 1884–5." —p. [3] of wrappers.

b. Special edition: illustrations hand-colored, 2s 6d. (Princeton copy inscribed: "Elspeth Crawhall Challoner with Grandfather's love—April 30, 1887.")

1884.44 FIELD & TUER; THE LEADENHALL PRESS. *Extracts from . . . Book List.* Bound into many books, also seen separately. 19–26 cm. depending on trim.

a. *Extracts from Field & Tuer's Book List.* Field & Tuer, the Leadenhall Press. [ca. 1884–1887]. 8 pp.

b. *Extracts from Field & Tuer's List, the Leadenhall Press.* [ca. 1888–1890]. 8 pp. With *Types from the Leadenhall Press* (see Appendix B, EPH.33) as center spread.

c. *Extracts from the Leadenhall Press (Ltd.) Book List.* [1891]. The Leadenhall Press. [ca. 1891–1892]. 16 pp. With *Specimens of Types* . . . as center spread.

d. ———. [ca. 1893–1898]. 16 pp. (Without *Specimens of Types.*)

e. ———. [ca. 1898–1905]. 20 pp. (Without *Specimens of Types.*)

1885.1 [BIBLE]. *The Revelation of Jesus Christ, with Notes for the 144,000, Etc.* Field & Tuer, the Leadenhall Press; Simpkin, Marshall; Hamilton, Adams. [Jan. 1885]. H.2,025. 13 cm. 1s. Black boards, titling in gilt, border rules in blind.

1885.2 ARCHIBALD ROSS COLQUHOUN. *Amongst the Shans.* First edition: Field & Tuer, the Leadenhall Press; Simpkin, Marshall; Hamilton, Adams; Scribner & Welford. [Jan.] 1885. T.3,180. 22 cm. 21s. Green cloth, lettering in gilt. Preceded by an introduction: "The Cradle of the Shan Race" by Terrien de Lacouperie. Folding map, full-page illustrations, and an historical sketch of the Shans by Holt S. Hallett.

1885.3 [ALBERT ETIENNE JEAN BAPTISTE] TERRIEN DE LACOUPERIE. *The Cradle of the Shan Race.* Field & Tuer. [1885]. 22 cm. Pamphlet. Offprint of the introduction to *Amongst the Shans* by Archibald Ross Colquhoun.

1885.4 ATHERTON FURLONG. *Echoes of Memory.* Field & Tuer, the Leadenhall Press; Simpkin, Marshall; Hamilton, Adams; Scribner & Welford. [Jan. 1885]. T.4,205. 20 cm. 21s. Plates dated 1884. Vellum, lettering in gilt. Etchings by Tristram J. Ellis.

1885.5 FRANCIS GEORGE HEATH. *Tree Gossip.* Field & Tuer, the Leadenhall Press; Simpkin, Marshall; Hamilton, Adams. [Jan.] 1885. T.4,196. 19 cm. 3s 6d. Dark olive cloth, title in gilt, author's facsimile signature and geometric design of leaves in concentric rectangular and circular rules in red.

1885.6   ÉMILE [LOUIS VICTOR] DE LAVELEYE. *The Socialism of To-day.* Field & Tuer, the Leadenhall Press; Simpkin, Marshall; Hamilton, Adams. [Jan. 1885]. T.4,183. 19 cm. 6s. Dark olive green cloth, lettering in gilt, rules in black. Translated, and with an account of socialism in England, by Goddard H. Orpen.

1885.7   R. S. DE C. [ROBERT STUART DE COURCY] LAFFAN. *Aspects of Fiction.* Field & Tuer, the Leadenhall Press; Simpkin, Marshall; Hamilton, Adams. [Feb.] 1885. T.4,208. 20 cm. 2s 6d. Peach-orange cloth, lettering in blue, floral device and decorative top and bottom borders in red and blue.

1885.8   SIR MONTAGUE SHEARMAN AND JAMES E. VINCENT. *Foot-Ball: Its History for Five Centuries.* Field & Tuer, the Leadenhall Press; Simpkin, Marshall; Hamilton, Adams. [Feb. 1885]. T.1,492. 18 cm. 1s. Orange or gray wrappers printed in black. Historical Sporting Series, no. 1. (No other titles in series.)

1885.9   ROBERT ROBINSON. *Bewick Memento: Catalogue with Purchasers' Names and Prices Realised of the Scarce and Curious Collection of Books, Silver Plate, Prints, Pictures, Wood Blocks, Copper Plates, and Bewick Relics, Etc., Sold by Auction at Newcastle-Upon-Tyne on February 5th, 6th & 7th, & August 26th, 1884.*

a. Field & Tuer, the Leadenhall Press; Simpkin, Marshall; Hamilton, Adams; Scribner & Welford. [Feb. 1885]. T.4,194. 30 cm. 7s 6d. Half brown cloth, marbled boards, printed gray paper label. In two parts, on different paper. Publishers' note: "Twelve of the cuts . . . embellished the interesting catalogue here reprinted, but the six illustrations at the end . . . are first impressions from blocks hitherto not printed from." Introduction by Robert Robinson.

b. Variant binding: blind-stamped gray cloth, title in gilt on spine.

1885.10   *The Mother: The Woman Clothed with the Sun.*[21]

a. Part the First: Field & Tuer, the Leadenhall Press; Simpkin, Marshall; Hamilton, Adams. [Mar.] 1885. T.4,187. 19 cm. 2s 6d. Blue cloth, titling and sun ray design in gilt, borders in black.

b. Part the Second: 1887. 19cm. 5s.

1885.11   *A Fortnight in a Waggonette: Amusing Experiences by "One of the Party."* Field & Tuer, the Leadenhall Press. [Mar. 1885]. T.4,207. 15 cm. 1s. Vegetable parchment wrappers, one shilling.

1885.12   "A CIVIL SERVANT." *Eighteen-Eighty-Five. The Story of a Black Bag, a Big Bribe, & a Crushing Crime. By a Civil Servant.* Field & Tuer, the Leadenhall Press;

---

21. Authorship is sometimes attributed to Anna B. Kingsford, because of the similarity of the title to Kingsford's *Clothed with the Sun* (London: Watkins, 1889), but the anonymous narrator is male, and his identity remains unknown. The "Mother" is shown by William Oxley in *Modern Messiahs and Wonder Workers* (London: Trübner, 1889) to be a mysterious woman who surfaced in 1877 as a rival to Mary Ann Girling (founder of an English Shaker Community) for the claim of the Second Coming in female form. See also Philip Hoare, *England's Lost Eden: Adventures in a Victorian Utopia* (London: Harper Collins/Fourth Estate, 2005).

Simpkin, Marshall; Hamilton, Adams. [Mar. 1885]. T.4,233. 18 cm. 1s. Cover title: "1885." Advertisements pasted on endpapers.

1885.13 JOHN F. DEXTER; FRANCIS PHILLIMORE [ALICE MEYNELL]. *Dickens Memento: Catalogue with Purchasers' Names & Prices Realised of the Pictures, Drawings and Objects of Art of the Late Charles Dickens Sold by Auction in London by Messrs. Christie, Manson & Woods on July 9th 1870.*

a. First edition: Field & Tuer, the Leadenhall Press; Simpkin, Marshall; Hamilton, Adams; Scribner & Welford. [Mar. 1885]. T.4,193. 2 parts in 1 vol. 29 cm. 7s 6d. Half blue cloth and marbled boards, printed gray paper label. Introduction by Francis Phillimore (Alice Meynell) and "Hints to Dickens Collectors" by John F. Dexter. (BL copy: J. F. Dexter's presentation copy with letters and two reproductions of paintings inserted.)

b. Variant binding: blind-stamped brown cloth, title in gilt on spine.

1885.14 "HERCULES." *British Railways and Canals in Relation to British Trade and Government Control.* Field & Tuer, the Leadenhall Press; Simpkin, Marshall; Hamilton, Adams. [Mar. 1885]. T.4,235. 18 cm.; 3s 6d. Cream cloth boards, lettering in black on upper cover, white label on spine.

1885.15 COLONEL TCHENG-KI-TONG. *The Chinese Painted by Themselves.* Field & Tuer, the Leadenhall Press; Simpkin, Marshall; Hamilton, Adams. [Mar. 1885]. T.4,203. 20 cm. 6s. Olive cloth, lettering in gilt, decorations in red. Translated by James Millington. Tcheng-Ki-Tong was China's Military Attaché at Paris.

1885.16 *Slip-shod English in Polite Society. A Manual for the Educated but Careless.* Field & Tuer. [Apr. 1885]. T.4,240. 14 cm. 6d. Yellow wrappers printed in black.

1885.17 SAMUEL BAGSHAW [WALTER MARISTOW WATKINS-PITCHFORD]. *Amateur Tommy Atkins. Being a Volunteer's Experiences Related in the Letters of Private S. Bagshaw to His Mother.* Field & Tuer, the Leadenhall Press; Simpkin, Marshall; Hamilton, Adams. [Apr. 1885]. T.4,175. 18 cm. 1s. Gray wrappers, lettering, silhouette and decorative rules in black. Illustrated throughout with silhouettes.

1885.18 SIR JAMES CANTLIE. *Degeneration Amongst Londoners.* Field & Tuer, the Leadenhall Press; Simpkin, Marshall; Hamilton, Adams. [Apr. 1885]. T.4,236. 17 cm. 1s. Wrappers. "A lecture delivered at the Parkes museum of hygiene, January 27, 1885."

1885.19 RIGHT HON. SIR FAIRFAX LEIGHTON CARTWRIGHT, G.C.V.O. *The Emperor's Wish. A Play in Five Acts.* Field & Tuer, the Leadenhall Press. [Apr. 1885]. T.4,209. 19 cm. 3s 6d. Brown cloth, black design, lettering in black and gilt.

1885.20 ARCHIBALD ROSS COLQUHOUN. *Burma and the Burmans; or, "the Best Unopened Market in the World."* Field & Tuer, the Leadenhall Press; Simpkin, Marshall;

Hamilton, Adams. [Apr. 1885]. T.4,209. 17 cm. 1s. Pamphlet: wrappers, lettering in black. With folding map of the country.

1885.21 JEROME K. [KLAPKA] JEROME. *On the Stage–and Off: The Brief Career of a Would-Be-Actor.*

a. First edition: Field & Tuer, the Leadenhall Press; Simpkin, Marshall, Hamilton, Kent. [Apr. 1885]. T.4,211. 17 cm. 1s. Light pink wrappers, lettering in black.

b. New edition: Field & Tuer, the Leadenhall Press; Simpkin, Marshall, Hamilton, Kent; Scribner & Welford. [Mar. 1890]. 1s.

Illustrated edition: (see checklist 1891.21).

1885.22 RIGHT HON. SIR FAIRFAX LEIGHTON CARTWRIGHT, G.C.V.O. *Lorello. A Play in Five Acts.* Field & Tuer, the Leadenhall Press; Simpkin, Marshall; Hamilton, Adams. [May 1885]. T.4,209.[22] 19 cm. 3s 6d. Venetian red cloth, title in gilt, author's name, decorative frame, and border rule in black.

1885.23 VINCENT M. HOLT. *Why Not Eat Insects?* Field & Tuer, the Leadenhall Press; Simpkin, Marshall; Hamilton, Adams. [May 1885]. T.4,239. 17 cm. 1s. Light blue-gray paper wrappers, lettering and illustration in darker blue-gray. With two menus including various insects.

Note: reprinted in facsimile by Pryor Publications (Whitstable) in 1992.

1885.24 A. E. N. [ALICIA E. NEVA] BEWICKE. *Mother Darling!* Field & Tuer, the Leadenhall Press; Simpkin, Marshall; Hamilton, Adams. [June 1885]. T.4,243. 15 cm. 1s. Vegetable parchment over flexible boards, lettering in black. A novel about the rights of married women.

1885.25 JAMES COTTER MORISON. *Madame de Maintenon; an Etude.* Field & Tuer, the Leadenhall Press; Simpkin, Marshall; Scribner & Welford. [June 1885]. T.4,241. 15 cm. 1s. Vegetable parchment wrappers, lettering in black. Concernin Françoise d'Aubigné, Marchioness de Maintenon.

1885.26 A. C. [ANNE CAMPBELL] MACLEOD AND SIR HAROLD EDWIN BOULTON [eds.]; MALCOLM LEONARD LAWSON [arr.]. *Songs of the North, Gathered Together from the Highlands and Lowlands of Scotland.*

a. First edition: Field & Tuer, the Leadenhall Press; Simpkin, Marshall, Hamilton, Kent; J. B. Cramer; Scribner & Welford. [June 1885]. T.4,230. 32 cm. 21s. Half gray-blue cloth, cream boards, titling and ornament in gilt. Also seen bound by Maclehose (Glasgow) in half olive morocco, pale green boards, lettering in green, maroon leather spine label. Date given in Roman numerals on cover. With frontispiece "A Jacobite lament" by E. Burne-Jones and illustrations by James Archer, Mrs. Hugh Blackburn, Colin Hunter,

---

22. Duplicate job number (see checklist 1885.19). Apparently these two Cartwright plays were grouped as one job.

C. Keene, Cecil Lawson, R. Little, W. E. Lockhart, J. H. Lorimer, R. W. Macbeth, W. D. Mackay, J. MacWhirter, Albert Moore, Sir Noel Paton, John Pettie, George Reid, Frederick Sandys, J. M. Whistler, others. Edited by A. C. Macleod and H. Boulton, music arranged by M. Lawson.

b. Second edition:[23] [1887]. 32 cm. 12s 6d. Light brown cloth, lettering in gilt, border and vignette in black. Omits all plates except "Proud Maisie" by Frederick Sandys, which appears as the frontispiece.

c. Later editions: maroon cloth, lettering in gilt.

1885.27 "POOF." *The Fowl Deceiver. A Lay of the Inventions Exhibition.* Field & Tuer, the Leadenhall Press; Simpkin, Marshall; Hamilton, Adams. [June 1885]. T.1,245. Sq. 15 cm. 6d. Gray wrappers, lettering in black. Illustrated by "Gil."

1885.28 CHARLES SEARLE. *Look Here!: A Book for the Rail . . . to Be Digested Bit by Bit by Those Who Object to Continuous Reading in a Train.* Field & Tuer, the Leadenhall Press; Simpkin, Marshall; Hamilton, Adams. [July 1885]. T.4,244. Sq. 15 cm. 1s. Green cloth, spine lettered in gilt, edges sprinkled brown. At head of title: "Laugh, laugh, laugh, and shed sweet tears."

1885.29 ANDREW WHITE TUER. *Old London Street Cries and the Cries of To-day, with Heaps of Quaint Cuts.* Field & Tuer, the Leadenhall Press; Scribner & Welford. [July] 1885. T.4,237. 13 cm. 1s. Marbled boards, paper title labels, fore-edge ties. Hand-colored frontispiece. "The 'Cries' have been sufficiently well received in bolder form at a guinea, to induce the publication of this additionally illustrated extension at the . . . price of a shilling." – Introd. (See checklist 1883.25.) (Variant copy at Lilly without this statement, note on p. 125, or index.) Illustrations by Rowlandson, Cruikshank, Crawhall, others.

Note: reprinted for the Old London Street Company (New York) in 1887; reprinted in facsimile by the Scolar Press (London) in 1978.

1885.30 J. [JAMES] REDDING WARE AND R. K. MANN. *The Life and Times of Colonel Fred Burnaby.* Field & Tuer, the Leadenhall Press; Simpkin, Marshall; Hamilton, Adams; Scribner and Welford. [July 1885]. T.4,243. 20 cm. 7s 6d. Green cloth lettered in gilt. Frontis portrait.

1885.31 [GLADWELL'S GALLERY]. *Summer Exhibition, 1885: Catalogue of the Collection of Water Colour Drawings, Paintings, Choice Modern Etchings and Bartolozzi Prints, &c., &c.* The Leadenhall Press. [1885]. 23 cm. Catalogue, published to accompany an exhibition held at Gladwell's Gallery, London.

1885.32 ARCHIBALD R. [ROSS] COLQUHOUN, F.R.G.S. *English Policy in the Far East. Being the Times Special Correspondence.* Field & Tuer, the Leadenhall Press; Simpkin, Marshall; Hamilton, Adams. [Sept.] 1885. T.4,252. 22 cm. 6d. Brown wrappers with title page reproduced on upper cover in black.

---

23. Later editions were labeled "Volume I"; Volumes II (1895) and III (1925) were published by J. B. Cramer.

1885.33   H. [HOVELL] CRICKMORE. *Ye Foure Etchynges By Maister H. Crickmore After ye Originales in ye Nationale Gallerie, Painted by Sir Augustus Calcott, R.A.* Raphael Tuck; [printed by] ye Leadenhalle Press. September, 1885. H.1,545. Obl. 20 x 25 cm. Price unknown. Buff paper covers, "Edition de Luxe" in red, "With ye Season's Greetynges" and lettering in black, white silk ribbon tie at left edge. Subjects: I. The Wooden Bridge; II. A Dutch Ferry; III. Old Pier, Littlehampton; IV. The Return from Market. "Published Sept. 1st. 1885 by Raphael Tuck & Sons" in each plate. "Ye Leadenhalle Press, E.C." at foot of back cover.

1885.34   S. MYERS. *Ye Foure Etchynges By Maister S. Myers After ye Originales in ye South Kensington Museum, Painted by David Cox.* Raphael Tuck; [printed by] ye Leadenhalle Press. September, 1885. H.1,752. Obl. 20 x 25 cm. Price unknown. Buff paper covers, "Edition de Luxe" in red, "With ye Season's Greetynges" and lettering in black, white silk ribbon tie at left edge. Subjects: I. Windsor Castle, from Sandgate Pit; II. Conway Castle; III. Harlech Castle; IV. Penrhyn Castle. At head of title: "Edition de Luxe. With ye Season's Greetynges." "Published Sept. 1st. 1885 by Raphael Tuck & Sons" in each plate. "Ye Leadenhalle Press, E.C." at foot of back cover.

1885.35   ANDREW WHITE TUER. *Bartolozzi and His Works. A Biographical & Descriptive Account of the Life & Career of Francesco Bartolozzi, R.A. Second edition, corrected and revised with additional matter.* [Sept.] 1885. No job number. 1 vol. 20 cm. 500 copies, 12s 6d. Full vellum, black and red lettering, with wide dark green silk bands lettered in gilt mounted around covers through slits; in gray cloth case with printed paper labels. Engraved title, 2 plates and 2 folding lottery tickets. (Lilly: presentation copy from Tuer to Charles E. Fagan.)

First edition: (see checklist 1882.1).

1885.36   IZAAK WALTON; JOSEPH CRAWHALL [illust.]. *Izaak Walton: His Wallet Booke.*

a. Small paper edition: Field & Tuer, the Leadenhall Press; Sampson Low, Marston, Searle and Rivington. [Sept.] 1885. T.4,232. 20 cm. 500 copies, 21s. Cream spine, green-blue boards, hand-lettering in gilt. Hand-colored woodcut illustrations by Joseph Crawhall. Issued without the sewn pockets and blank pages included in the Large Paper edition.

b. Large paper edition: 24 cm. 100 copies, 42s. Half white parchment, natural vellum boards, hand-lettering and ornament in gilt on upper cover, vignette in gilt on lower cover, linen ties, yellow silk page marker. Linen pockets mounted to pastedowns labeled in black: "Baccy," "Fysshe stories I Believe," "Fysshe Stories I Don't Believe," etc. Blank pages at end for "Fysshe stories." Publisher's listing in *1,000 Quaint Cuts from Books of Other Days* states: "One of Mr. Crawhall's engraved blocks—that is, the boxwood block itself—is attached as a pendant to a silk book marker to *each copy of the large paper edition only.*" (No copy located with the block still attached.)

1885.37   EMILY JANE PFEIFFER. *Flying Leaves from East and West.* Field & Tuer, the Leadenhall Press; Simpkin, Marshall; Hamilton, Adams; Scribner & Welford. [Oct.] 1885. T.4,246. 20 cm. 6s. Blue cloth, lettering and corner decorations in gilt.

1885.38   MAX O'RELL [LEON-PAUL BLOUËT]. *The Dear Neighbours!*
a. First edition: Field & Tuer, the Leadenhall Press; Simpkin, Marshall; Hamilton, Adams. [Oct. 1885]. T.4,250. 19 cm. 3s 6d. Light blue cloth, lettering in black. Translated from the French *Chers Voisins,* by Madame Blouët.
b. Cheap edition: [Oct. 1885]. 2s 6d. Wrappers.
Note: The *Publishers' Circular* of September 1, 1885, ran a notice: "Messrs. Field & Tuer have issued an advertisement of M. Max O'Rell's *Les Chers Voisins—The Dear Neighbours.* The advertisement is issued in a booklet form in order to secure the copyright of the title." (Not seen.)

1885.39   ALICE CORKRAN [ed.]. *The Bairns' Annual.* Field & Tuer, the Leadenhall Press; Simpkin, Marshall; Hamilton, Adams; Scribner & Welford (beginning with second year). 1885–1889. Illustrated by Lizzie Lawson. First issue with original material; later issues reprint old fairy tales, adding subhead: . . . *of Old Fashioned Fairy Tales, &c.*
a. 1885-6. [Nov. 1885]. T.4,249. 15 cm. 1s. Blue paper boards with diamond-shaped labels on front cover and spine. Frontis aquatint, "In Disgrace" by William Luker: "A limited number of India Proofs on large paper may be had at one shilling each through the Bookseller or Publishers." —inserted slip. Includes a story, "The Child's Dream," by Lady Jane Wilde.
b. 1886-7: [Nov. 1886]. T.4,292. 21 cm. 1s. Chromolithographed wrappers.
c. 1887-8: [Nov. 1887]. T.4,325. 21 cm. 1s. Chromolithographed wrappers.
d. 1888-9: [Oct. 1888]. T.4,356. 21 cm. 1s. Chromolithographed wrappers.
e. 1889-90: [Nov. 1889]. T.4,380. 21 cm. 1s. Chromolithographed wrappers.

1885.40   A. Y. D. *The Owls of Olynn Belfry. A Tale for Children.* Field & Tuer, the Leadenhall Press; Simpkin, Marshall; Hamilton, Adams. [Nov. 1885]. T.4,253. 15 cm. 1s. Vegetable parchment with illustration and lettering in black. Illustrated throughout by Randolph Caldecott.

1885.41   E. M. [ELEANOR MARY] MARSH. *Marah. A Prose Idyll.* Field & Tuer, the Leadenhall Press; Simpkin, Marshall; Hamilton, Adams. [Nov. 1885]. T.4,257. 19 cm. 1s. Pale blue wrappers, lettering in darker blue as part of decorative artwork.

1885.42   AN EX-M.P. *A Radical Nightmare, or, England Forty Years Hence. By an Ex-M.P.* Field & Tuer. [Nov. 1885]. T.4,265. 16 cm. 6d. Orange wrappers. lettering in black.

1885.43 TEUFELSDRÖCKH JUNIOR [SIR EDWARD ABBOTT PARRY]. *Gladstone Government: a Chapter of Contemporary History.* Field & Tuer, the Leadenhall Press; Simpkin, Marshall; Hamilton, Adams; Scribner & Welford. [Nov. 1885]. T.4,251. 21 cm. 6d. Pamphlet.

1885.44 W. A. WATLOCK. *The Next Ninety-Three, or Crown, Commune and Colony, Told in a Citizen's Diary.* Field & Tuer, the Leadenhall Press; Simpkin, Marshall; Hamilton, Adams. [Nov. 1885]. T.4,264. 21 cm. 6d. Wrappers.

1885.45 FORTNIGHTLY CLUB [GLASGOW, SCOTLAND]. *The Proceedings of the Fortnightly Club.* Field & Tuer, the Leadenhall Press. Printers in Ordinary to the Fortnightly Club (imprint follows text but precedes member profiles). 3 vol.: 1885–86, 86–89, 89–94. 30 cm. Half maroon leather and maroon boards, gilt tooling on covers, titling in gilt on spine. Each issue a limited edition of 18 to 20 copies. (Later volumes printed by Robert MacLehose and Co., Glasgow.)
a. 1885–86: K.1,593
b. 1886–89: W.1,600
c. 1889–94: W.1,503

1886.1 W. [WALTER] ELDRED WARDE. *Lines Grave and Gay.* Field & Tuer, the Leadenhall Press; Simpkin, Marshall; Hamilton, Adams; Scribner & Welford. [Feb. 1886]. T.4,263. 21 cm. 3s 6d. Parchment spine, brown floral-patterned cloth, lettering in gilt on spine, printed label upside down on lower cover.

1886.2 "LOCHNELL." *Saxon Lyrics and Legends after Aldhelm.* Field & Tuer, the Leadenhall Press; Simpkin, Marshall; Hamilton, Adams; Scribner & Welford. [Feb. 1886]. T.4,259. 14 cm. 1s. Cream printed wrappers.

1886.3 LEWIS LORRAINE. *The Corpse in the Copse or the Perils of Love. A Sensational Story.* Field & Tuer, the Leadenhall Press; Simpkin, Marshall; Hamilton, Adams. [Feb. 1886]. T.4,261. 17 cm. 1s. Yellow wrappers, ornamental lettering in black.

1886.4 HUGH CONWAY [FREDERICK JOHN FARGUS]. *"Somebody's" Story.* Field & Tuer, the Leadenhall Press. [Mar. 1886]. T.4,268. Obl. 14 x 22 cm. 1s. Stiff wrappers, with handwritten title printed in green. Edited by J. S. Wood. "An Exact Lithographed reproduction of *'Hugh Conway's' Original Manuscript of 'Somebody's' Story. A True Story of 'Somebody.'*" Lithographed manuscript, followed by the story in type. A fund-raising vehicle, with detachable Bank Order payable to the Chelsea Hospital for Women at the rear.

1886.5 HENRY WILLIAM AND GEORGE GRESSWELL. *How to Play the Fiddle, or, Hints to Beginners on the Violin.* Field & Tuer, the Leadenhall Press. [Mar. 1886]. 19 cm. 1s. Also published by William Reeves, London.

1886.6   FRED C. MILFORD. *Lost! A Day.* Field & Tuer, the Leadenhall Press; Simpkin, Marshall; Hamilton, Adams. [Mar. 1886]. T.4,277. 16 cm. 1s. Wrappers in light blue, dark blue, and red; title and subtitle in red and dark blue cursive script, author in white cursive script on blue ground, all set diagonally across cover from bottom left to top right. "The thrilling story of an extraordinary Mesmeric Theft" (publisher's ads).

1886.7   MAURICE NOEL. *"Evidence."* Field & Tuer, the Leadenhall Press; Simpkin, Marshall; Hamilton, Adams. [Mar. 1886]. T.4,262. 18 cm. 1s. Brown wrappers, title and author in black cursive script set vertically. A novel.

1886.8   MRS. [MARY ELIZA JOY] HAWEIS. *Rus in Urbe: Or, Flowers That Thrive in London Gardens and Smoky Towns.* Field & Tuer, the Leadenhall Press; Scribner & Welford. [May 1886]. T.4,271. 14 cm. 1s. Colored floral-patterned cloth, printed paper labels on upper cover and spine. Frontis copperplate engraving after Corbold in sepia.

1886.9   JEROME K. [KLAPKA] JEROME. *The Idle Thoughts of an Idle Fellow: A Book for an Idle Holiday.* Field & Tuer, the Leadenhall Press; Simpkin, Marshall, Hamilton, Kent; Scribner & Welford. [June 1886]. T.4,283. 20 cm. 2s 6d. Yellow cloth, lettering in black, floral design in blue.

Note: This book went through many printings, each thousand representing an "edition," stamped on the front cover. Beginning in 1890, the imprint changed to "The Leadenhall Press" and the date appeared on the title page. (Henry Holt also published an edition in New York in 1890.) Around 1899 the cloth color changed from light yellow to orange-yellow, with a different floral decoration. Throughout, there was no significant change in content except for the ads for Jerome's books at the back.

1886.10   RIGHT HON. SIR FAIRFAX LEIGHTON CARTWRIGHT, G.C.V.O. *Bianca Capello. A Tragedy.* Field & Tuer, the Leadenhall Press. [Aug.] 1886. T.4,282. 19 cm. 3s 6d. Japanese vellum, lettering in gilt.

1886.11   SAMUEL RICHARDSON. *Sir Charles Grandison.* Field & Tuer, the Leadenhall Press; Simpkin, Marshall; Hamilton, Adams; Scribner & Welford. [Sept. 1886]. T.4,284. 21 cm. 1s 4d. Brown wrappers over thin card, lettering in gilt and black. "With six illustrations from the original copper-plates engraved in 1778 by Isaac Taylor." The Leadenhall Press Sixteenpenny Series: Illustrated Gleanings from the Classics, no. 1. Preface by John Oldcastle (Wilfrid Meynell).

1886.12   SOLOMON GESSNER. *Solomon Gessner: "The Swiss Theocritus."* Field & Tuer, the Leadenhall Press; Simpkin, Marshall; Hamilton, Adams; Scribner & Welford. [Sept. 1886]. T.4,285. 22 cm. 1s 4d. Brown wrappers over thin card, titling in gilt and black. "With six illustrations and extra portrait from the original copper-plates engraved in 1802 by Robert Cromek, from drawings by Thomas Stothard." The Leadenhall Press Sixteenpenny Series: Illustrated Gleanings from the Classics, no. 2. Selections from "Idyllen" in English translation. Preface by John Oldcastle (Wilfrid Meynell).

1886.13 "MABEL." *Views of English Society: by a Little Girl of Eleven.*

a. Field & Tuer, the Leadenhall Press; Simpkin, Marshall; Hamilton, Adams; Scribner & Welford. [Aug. 1886]. T.4,278. 22 cm. 2s 8d. Signed in facsimile following t.p.: "From your little friend Mabel," and "Mabel" at end of text and addendum. Floral-patterned cotton laced over boards, printed title label on lower right front cover. Design proposed by the author "after a fashion my mamma had taught me" (addendum). Illustrations by the author.

b. Variant binding: Brown cloth spine, tan boards, printed title label.

1886.14 R. I. [REGINALD ILLINGWORTH] WOODHOUSE. *What Is the Church? Or Plain Instruction About the Church, Especially in England: Her Doctrine, Her Discipline, Her Offices.* Field & Tuer, Leadenhall Press. [Aug. 1886]. 15 cm. 1s.

1886.15 FRED. C. MILFORD. *55 Guineas Reward.* Field & Tuer, the Leadenhall Press; Simpkin, Marshall; Scribner & Welford. [Sept. 1886]. T.4,296. 20 cm. 2s 6d. Blue cloth spine, cover printed in black with large reverse type: 55 GUINEAS REWARD (TWO AND EIGHT-PENCE) revealing newspaper "notices" about a reward for information leading to the apprehension of a culprit.

1886.16 CHARLES JAMES SCOTTER. *Who Is His Father? A Story of Poverty and Fortune.* Field & Tuer, the Leadenhall Press; Simpkin, Marshall; Hamilton, Adams. [Sept.] 1886. T.4,283. 19 cm. 1s. Gray card, lettering and ornaments in black.

1886.17 ANDREW W. [WHITE] TUER. *The Follies & Fashions of Our Grandfathers (1807).*

a. "Demy octavo": Field & Tuer, the Leadenhall Press; Scribner & Welford. 1886–1887. [Sept. 1886]. T.4,258. 23 cm. 25s. Half natural suede, rough brown boards, embroidered labels, floral-patterned chintz endpapers, embroidered linen page marker with title on both sides. "Embellished with Thirty-seven whole-page Plates including Ladies' and Gentlemen's Dress (hand-coloured and heightened with gold and silver), Sporting and Coaching scenes (hand-coloured), Fanciful Prints, Portraits of Celebrities, &c. (many from original copper-plates)." List of magazines on leaf 3 of prelims, statement of editions on verso. "Dedicated by Gracious Permission to Her Majesty the Queen."

b. "Large Paper crown quarto": 27 cm. The earliest impressions of the plates, extra-carefully tinted and heightened. 250 copies only, 63s. Numbered and signed "Field & Tuer."

c. "Special Large Paper": printed on brown paper. Three copies only, 10 guineas. Inked and initialed by Andrew W. Tuer. Statement of editions on recto of leaf 3 of prelims, list of magazines on verso. (Copies located: BL, Lilly.)

1886.18   THOMAS GRAY. *Gray's Elegy in a Country Churchyard.* Field & Tuer, the Leadenhall Press; Simpkin, Marshall; Hamilton, Adams; Scribner & Welford. [Oct. 1886]. T.4,254. 29 cm. 21s. Fell vellum, lettering in gilt, two gold silk ribbons around covers and spine, stitched into covers. Printed on one side of the leaf only. Illustrated by Norman Prescott Davies. Introduction by Professor John W. Hales.

1886.19   A. W. T. [ANDREW WHITE TUER]. *1,000 Quaint Cuts from Books of Other Days, Including Amusing Illustrations from Children's Story Books, Fables, Chap-Books, &c., &c., a Selection of Pictorial Initial Letters & Curious Designs & Ornaments from Original Wooden Blocks Belonging to the Leadenhall Press.*

a. Regular issue: Field & Tuer, the Leadenhall Press; Simpkin, Marshall; Hamilton, Adams; Scribner & Welford. [Nov. 1886]. T.4,291. 25 cm. 1s 4d. Light gray-blue card covers, ornamental lettering in gilt and black within frame artwork in black.

b. Special issue: 2s 8d. A limited number printed on one side of the paper only. Light gray-blue or pink covers.

Note: reprinted by the Singing Tree Press (Detroit) in 1968 and Art Direction Book Co. (New York) in 1973.

1886.20   MAX O'RELL [LEON-PAUL BLOUËT]. *Drat the Boys!: or, Recollections of an Ex-Frenchmaster in England.* Field & Tuer, the Leadenhall Press; Simpkin, Marshall; Hamilton, Adams; Scribner & Welford. [Nov. 1886]. T.4,299. 19 cm. 2s. Dark blue cloth, decoration in black, lettering in gilt, Velveteen ad on lower cover.

1886.21   ELIZABETH STILL, DOWAGER COUNTESS OF HARRINGTON. *The Foster-Brother and The Creoles. Plays for Young People.* Field & Tuer, the Leadenhall Press; Simpkin, Marshall; Hamilton, Adams; Scribner & Welford. [Nov. 1886]. T.4,300. 14 cm. 1s. Brown wrappers over card covers, title and author in black, "Plays for Young People" in gilt. Each play in three acts and in prose.

1886.22   JOHN BICKERDYKE [CHARLES HENRY COOK]. *The Curiosities of Ale & Beer: An Entertaining History.* Field & Tuer, the Leadenhall Press; Scribner & Welford. [Dec. 1886]. T.4,275. 27 cm. 21s. Cream boards, ornamental lettering in gilt. "In Part collected by the late J. G. Fennell; now largely augmented with manifold matters of singular note and worthy memory by the author and his friend J. M. D___." (J. M. Dixon). Illustrated.

1886.23   EMILY JANE PFEIFFER. *Sonnets. Revised and Enlarged Edition.* Field & Tuer, the Leadenhall Press; Scribner & Welford. [Dec. 1886]. T.4,293. 16 cm. 6s. Blue cloth, lettering and corner decorations in gilt. Edited by J. E. Pfeiffer.

1886.24   [JESSIE A. H. MUIR]. *Diary J. A. H. M.* "Imprinted at The Leadenhall Press by Field & Tuer In the month of June, 1886 . . . Privately Printed." No job number. 24 cm. Japanese-style floral velvet without titling, printed silk endpapers. Printed on hand-made paper, with woodcut title page and other woodcuts, and with an etched folding map by Tristram Ellis. Preface, signed in facsimile: "Jessie A. Muir," states that only a few copies were printed.

1887.1   HEINRICH OSCAR VON KARLSTEIN [PSEUD.]. *Gotham and the Gothamites (New York and the New Yorkers)*. Field & Tuer, the Leadenhall Press; Simpkin, Marshall; Hamilton, Adams. [Jan.] 1887. 19 cm. 2s 6d. Observations on New York social life. Translated by F. C. Valentine. Published as *Gotham and the Gothamites, or Gay Girls of New York* by Laird & Lee, Chicago, 1886.

1887.2   ISLAY HAMILTON. *A Splendid Rally: A Story of a Love Set*. Field & Tuer, the Leadenhall Press; Simpkin, Marshall; Hamilton, Adams. [Mar. 1887]. T.4,307. 16 cm. 1s. Wrappers.

1887.3   L. FLORENCE FFOULKES. *Short Poems in Sunlight and Shade*. Field & Tuer, the Leadenhall Press; Simpkin, Marshall; Hamilton, Adams; Scribner & Welford. [Apr. 1887]. T.4,311. 20 cm. 6s. Vellum parchment, lettering in gilt, yellow silk page marker.

1887.4   W. B. GILPIN. *A Set of Four Hunting and Racing Stories*. Field & Tuer, the Leadenhall Press. [Apr. 1887]. T.4,302. 19 cm. 2s. Red boards, lettering and vignettes in black on upper cover, ad for Cooper Cooper & Co. Tea on lower cover. Stories: "Played Out," "A Ride in a Snowstorm," "My Good Lady," and "Don't Always Judge from Appearances."

1887.5   WILHELM FERDINAND BRAND. *London Life Seen with German Eyes. (Londoner Streifzüge)*. Field & Tuer, the Leadenhall Press; Simpkin, Marshall; Hamilton, Adams. [June 1887]. T.4,302. 19 cm. 2s. Dark green paper-coverd boards, lettering (title, author, contents, and price) in yellow.

1887.6   ANDREW W. TUER AND CHARLES EDWARD FAGAN. *The First Year of a Silken Reign (1837-8)*. Field & Tuer, the Leadenhall Press; Simpkin, Marshall; Hamilton, Adams; Scribner & Welford. [June] 1887. T.4,308. 24 cm. 6s. Dark blue cloth, lettering in gilt. With ten illustrations from contemporary original plates. Intended as a memorial of the Jubilee of the 50-year reign of Queen Victoria. (Presentation copy in full vellum with gilt dentelles reported.)

1887.7   G. H. [GEORGE HENRY] ADDY. *A Song of Love and Liberty or Fifty Golden Years*. Field & Tuer, the Leadenhall Press. [July] 1887. 14 cm. 1s. Parchment. Dismissed, with other Jubilee poets, by G. B. Shaw as "knowing nothing, or thereabouts, of the history of the reign, the geography of the Empire, or the personal characteristics of the Royal family, yet loyally ready."[24] (Not located.)

Note: The *Publishers' Circular* for March 1, 1887, listed a new work, *"Shelley Primer*, By H. Salt . . . Field & T." The listing was an error; a review in the same issue correctly gave the publisher as Reeves & Turner. The mistake was repeated by William Swan Sonnenschein in *A Bibliography of Literature* (London: Swan Sonnenschein, 1897).

24. G. B. Shaw, "Some Small Poetry of 1877," *The Pall Mall Gazette*, Dec. 27, 1877.

1887.8 ELIZABETH STILL, DOWAGER COUNTESS OF HARRINGTON. *The Prime Minister and Tom. Plays for Young People.* Field & Tuer, the Leadenhall Press; Scribner and Welford. [July 1887]. T.4,317. 16 cm. 1s. Brown wrappers over card covers, title and author in black, "Plays for Young People" in gilt.

1887.9 E. W. L. [EDWARD WILLIAM LEWIS] DAVIES. *Our Sea-Fish and Sea-Food.* Field & Tuer, the Leadenhall Press; Simpkin, Marshall; Hamilton, Adams. [Oct.] 1887. T.4,320. 19 cm. 1s. Yellow card wrappers with title and illustration in black on upper cover, advertisement for Cooper, Cooper & Co. Tea on lower cover.

1887.10 CHARLES LAMB. *Beauty and the Beast.*

a. Regular edition: Field & Tuer, the Leadenhall Press; Simpkin, Marshall; Hamilton, Adams; Scribner & Welford. [Oct. 1887]. T.4,318. 18 cm. 3s 6d. Black boards, titling in gilt. Frontis and 7 steel plate engravings from the original edition. Authorship attributed to Lamb. With an Introduction by Andrew Lang. Facsimile of original edition printed for M. J. Godwin (1811).

b. Special edition: Brown boards, gilt lettering, yellow silk page marker. 100 signed copies, 10s 6d (raised to 2 guineas). With a set of earliest open-letter proofs of the illustrations in red, and a duplicate set in brown.

1887.11 "A MODERN MAID" [CHARLOTTE O'CONNOR ECCLES].[25] *Modern Men. By a Modern Maid.* Field & Tuer, the Leadenhall Press; Simpkin, Marshall; Hamilton, Adams. [Oct.] 1887. T.4,339. 19 cm. 2s. Tan cloth spine over gray paper boards with black lettering and decoration.

1887.12 F. S. JANET BURNE. *Sybil's Dutch Dolls.* Field & Tuer, the Leadenhall Press; Simpkin, Marshall; Hamilton, Adams; Scribner and Welford. [Nov.] 1887. T.4,314. 21 cm. 2s 6d. Illustrated. Quarter green or brown cloth and gray boards, title and vignettes in black.

1887.13 INCORPORATED SOCIETY OF AUTHORS. *The Grievances between Authors & Publishers; Being the Report of the Conferences of the Incorporated Society of Authors, Held at Willis's Rooms, in March, 1887; with Additional Matter and Summary.* Field & Tuer, the Leadenhall Press; Simpkin, Marshall; Hamilton, Adams. [Nov.] 1887. T.4,328. 20 cm. 2s. Brown wrappers, blue wrap-around label with title in black. Contributions by Sir Francis O. Adams, Walter Besant, Edmund Gosse, John Hollingshead, Lord Lytton, Frederick Pollock; appendices by Geo. Haven Putnam, Geo. M. Smith, Andrew W. Tuer.

1887.14 LOUISE BLENNERHASSETT POIREZ. *Eight Tales of Fairyland.* Field & Tuer, the Leadenhall Press; Simpkin, Marshall; Hamilton, Adams; Scribner & Welford. [Dec.] 1887. T.4,342. 19 cm. 2s 6d. Twenty-four illustrations by V. Gertrude Muntz. Illustrated. Brown cloth spine, marbled boards, printed paper label.

---

25. The author identified herself in an unsigned article: "The Experiences of a Woman Journalist," *Blackwood's Edinburgh Magazine* 153, June 1893.

1887.15   F. G. [FREDERICK GEORGE] HILTON PRICE, F.S.A; JAMES WEST [illust.]. *The Signs of Old Lombard Street.*

a. First edition: Field & Tuer, the Leadenhall Press; Simpkin, Marshall; Hamilton, Adams; Scribner & Welford. [Dec. 1887]. T.4,298. 112 leaves, 60 illustrations on plates by James West, 1 folding map. 26 cm. 1 guinea. Cream paper spine, gray boards, sign artwork in black containing red label with lettering in black. 109 signs of tradesmen of old Lombard Street described and pictured. (Tuer's copy, with original drawings mounted, at Lilly.)

b. Second edition: 1887–1902 [Dec. 1902]. T.4,754. 208 pp. 23 cm. 6s. Gray-brown boards, art and lettering in black and white. 168 signs described, with additional illustrations.

1887.16   WILLIAM LAMBERT RICHARDSON. *The Duties and Conduct of Nurses in Private Nursing: An Address Delivered at the Boston Training School for Nurses, June 18, 1886 . . . with Some Notes on Preventing the Spread of Infectious Disease.* Field & Tuer, the Leadenhall Press; Simpkin, Marshall; Hamilton, Adams. [Oct.] 1887. T.4,327. 15 cm. 1s. Cream spine, marbled boards, printed paper label.

1887.17   [RICHARD SCRAFTON SHARPE; MRS. PEARSON]. *Dame Wiggins of Lee and her Seven Wonderful Cats: A Humorous Tale. Written Principally by a Lady of Ninety.* Republished by Field & Tuer, the Leadenhall Press. [Oct.] 1887. No job number. 19 cm. 1s. Gray-green wrappers, lettering in black with hand-colored illustration. "Embellished with Sixteen Coloured Engravings." Printed on one side of leaf only. The Leadenhall Press Series of Forgotten Picture Books for Children, no. 1. Introduction by Andrew Tuer attributes authorship to Richard Scrafton Sharpe and Mrs. Pearson, illustrations to R. Stennet. Original imprint: London, 1823. Dean & Munday; A. K. Newman, The Minerva Press.

1887.18   *The Gaping, Wide-mouthed, Waddling Frog: A New and Entertaining Game of Questions and Commands with Proper Directions for Playing the Game and Crying Forfeits.* Republished by Field & Tuer, the Leadenhall Press. [Nov.] 1887. T.4,329. 19 cm. 1s. Gray-green wrappers, lettering in black with hand-colored illustration. "Embellished with Thirteen Coloured Engravings." Printed on one side of leaf only. The Leadenhall Press Series of Forgotten Picture Books for Children, no. 2. Introduction by Andrew W. Tuer. Original imprint: London, 1823. Dean & Munday; A. K. Newman, The Minerva Press.

1887.19   *Deborah Dent and Her Donkey: a Humorous Tale.* Republished by Field & Tuer, the Leadenhall Press. [Nov.] 1887. No job number. 19 cm. 1s. Gray-green wrappers, lettering in black with hand-colored illustration. "Embellished with Ten Beautifully-Coloured Engravings." Printed on one side of leaf only. The Leadenhall Press Series of Forgotten Picture Books for Children no. 3. Introduction by Andrew W. Tuer. Original imprint: London, 1823. Dean & Munday; A. K. Newman, The Minerva Press.

1887.20 *Silver-Voice: A Fairy Tale; Being the Adventures of Harry's Mother, Harry's Sweetheart, and Harry Himself.* Field & Tuer, the Leadenhall Press; Simpkin, Marshall; Hamilton, Adams; Scribner & Welford. [Nov. 1887]. T.4,340. 18 cm. 1s 6d. Pale green stiff wrappers, lettering in black, hand-colored illustration. With hand-colored wood-engravings, including frontispiece.

1887.21 JAMES TENNANT CAIRD; J. C. P. [ed.]. *A Celebrity at Home. Mr. James Tennant Caird on Board the Yacht 'Morves' in Southampton Water.* Field & Tuer, the Leadenhall Press. "For private circulation" on upper wrapper. [1887]. T.3,576. 18 cm. Vegetable tissue wrappers over buff paper cover. Reprinted from *The World And The P. & O. Steamer Victoria* and *The Times*.

1888.1 J. M. L. [JAMES MOODY LOWRY] [ed.]. *A Book of Jousts.* Field & Tuer, the Leadenhall Press. [Jan. 1888]. T.4,343 18 cm. 1s. Includes the poem "A Night Vision" by Oscar Wilde, as well as poems by J. (John) Todhunter, W. (William) C. K. Wilde, and others, all of which originally appeared in *Kottabos,* a Trinity College Dublin magazine.

1888.2 JAMES THOMSON. *The Seasons.* Field & Tuer, the Leadenhall Press; Simpkin, Marshall; Hamilton, Adams; Scribner & Welford. [Feb. 1888]. T.4,331. 23 cm. 1s 4d. Brown wrappers over thin card, lettering in gilt and black. The Leadenhall Press Sixteenpenny Series: Illustrated Gleanings from the Classics, no. 3. "Four illustrations and extra portrait, printed from original copper-plates engraved in 1792." Preface by John Oldcastle (Wilfrid Meynell).

1888.3 LAURENCE STERNE. *Tristram Shandy.* Field & Tuer, the Leadenhall Press; Simpkin, Marshall; Hamilton, Adams; Scribner & Welford. [Feb. 1888]. T.4,332. 21 cm. 1s 4d. Brown wrappers over thin card, lettering in gilt and black. "Six unpublished illustrations in aquatint from the original copper-plates engraved in 1820 for John Bumpus." The Leadenhall Press Sixteenpenny Series: Illustrated Gleanings from the Classics, no. 4. With an ntroductory note by John Oldcastle (Wilfrid Meynell) and the statement: "The Publishers regretfully announce that No. 4, Tristram Shandy, finishes this series, which, for lack of further material in the way of original copper-plates, they are unable to continue."

1888.4 *The Dawn of the Twentieth Century. 1st January 1901.* Field & Tuer, the Leadenhall Press; Simpkin, Marshall; Hamilton, Adams. [Mar.] 1888. T.4350. 19 cm. 1s. Gray wrappers, decorative title in black & gilt. Fictional government reports about the state of world affairs in 1901.

1888.5 [GEORGE] ERIC MACKAY. *A Lover's Litanies.* Field & Tuer, the Leadenhall Press; Simpkin, Marshall; Hamilton, Adams; Scribner & Welford. [Apr.] 1888. T.4,258. 17 cm. 10s 6d. 250 copies. In verse. Vellum with two white silk ribbons, woven through slits, around covers.

1888.6   THOMAS HOOD, THE ELDER; F. DRUMMOND NIBLETT [illust.]. *The Henry Irving Dream of Eugene Aram.* The Leadenhall Press;[26] Simpkin & Marshall; Scribner & Welford. [Apr. 1888]. No job number. 24 cm. 1s. Wrappers, hand-lettering and illustrations by F. Drummond Niblett in red on black ground throughout. Lettering of dedication to J. L. (John Lawrence) Toole on front cover deliberately out of register. "Forwards" *(sic)* dated 1887, but with insert slip: "Publication delayed until Mr. Irving's return from America."

1888.7   SIR W. M. [WILLIAM MATTHEW] FLINDERS PETRIE. *A Season in Egypt 1887.* Field & Tuer, the Leadenhall Press; Trübner. [Apr.] 1888. T.4,347. 32 cm. 12s. Red cloth-backed boards. With illustrations on plates, by W. M. Flinders Petrie and F. L. L. Griffith, of inscriptions, names, balances, funereal cones, pyramids, columns and capitals, the Fayum road, weights of Memphis, and index of names in hieroglyph.

1888.8   ANNA BONUS KINGSFORD. *Chapters from "the Perfect Way." The Nature and Constitution of the Ego: With an Appendix: "Concerning the Mysteries," and a "Hymn to the Planet-God."* Field & Tuer, the Leadenhall Press; Simpkin, Marshall; Hamilton, Adams; George Redway. [July] 1888. T.4,357. 21 cm. 1s. Pale blue wrappers, lettering in black. A Selection from *The Perfect Way; or The Finding of Christ* (checklist 1882.4).

1888.9   *The Dame and Her Donkeys Five.* Republished by Field & Tuer, the Leadenhall Press. [Oct.] 1888. No job number. 19 cm. 1s. Gray-green wrappers, black lettering, hand-colored illustration. The Leadenhall Press Series of Forgotten Picture Books for Children, no. 4. With 31 hand-colored engravings. Original imprint: 1823. London: Dean & Munday; A. K. Newman, The Minerva Press.

1888.10 "CYLINDER." *Prince Bismarck's Map of Europe.* Field & Tuer, the Leadenhall Press; Simpkin, Marshall; Hamilton, Adams; Scribner & Welford. [Oct. 1889]. T.4,389. 16 cm. 6d. Pale gray wrappers, title and map of Europe in black.

1888.11 CHARLES SELLERS. *Tales from the Lands of Nuts and Grapes: (Spanish and Portuguese Folklore).* Field & Tuer, the Leadenhall Press; Simpkin, Marshall; Hamilton, Adams. [Oct.] 1888. T.4,355. 20 cm. 2s 6d. Green cloth, lettering in gilt, red decorations and rules, spine lettering in blind.

1888.12 *Delamar's Fetich. A Story of the Riviera.* Field & Tuer, the Leadenhall Press; Simpkin, Marshall; Hamilton, Adams; Scribner & Welford. [Nov.] 1888. T.4,326. 19 cm. 1s. Wrappers.

1888.13 *Hieroglyphic Bible: Being a Careful Selection of the Most Interesting and Important Passages in the Old and New Testaments: Regularly Arranged from Genesis to*

---

26. The first book noted without "Field & Tuer" as part of the imprint.

Revelations: Embellished and Illustrated with Hundreds of Engravings on Wood. Field & Tuer, the Leadenhall Press; Simpkin, Marshall; Hamilton, Adams; Scribner & Welford. [Nov.] 1888. T.4,366. 17 cm. 1s. Gray card wrappers, lettering in black on both covers. Printed on light gray-blue paper. Illustrations from original blocks (some or all possibly by Bewick).

1888.14 JOHN ASHTON. *Men, Maidens and Manners a Hundred Years Ago.* Field & Tuer, the Leadenhall Press; Simpkin, Marshall; Scribner & Welford. [Nov.] 1888. T.4,367. Obl. 14 x 17 cm. 1s. Brown stiff wrappers with illustrated paper labels. "With thirty-four contemporary illustrations." Errata slip facing page 91.

1888.15 FAIRFAX L. CARTWRIGHT, B.A. *The Baglioni. A Tragedy [in Verse].* Field & Tuer, the Leadenhall Press; Simpkin, Marshall; Hamilton, Adams. [Nov. 1888]. T.4,360. 21 cm. 3s 6d. Blue-gray cloth, lettering in gilt and red.

1888.16 CHARLES F. RIDEAL. *People We Meet.*

a. First edition: Field & Tuer, the Leadenhall Press; Simpkin, Marshall; Hamilton, Adams; Scribner & Welford. [Nov. 1888]. L.1,299. 21 cm. 1s. Brown card covers, printed gray paper label. Illustrated by Harry Parkes. Printed on one side of the page.

b. Special edition: Proof copies, signed and numbered. 250 copies, 5s.

1888.17 CHARLES F. STEEL. *Is There Any Resemblance between Shakespeare & Bacon?* Field & Tuer, the Leadenhall Press; Simpkin, Marshall; Hamilton, Adams. [Nov.] 1888. T.4,354. 20 cm. 3s 6d. Dark blue cloth, lettering in gilt and red. "Copyrighted at Washington, U.S.A. by Charles F. Steel" on verso of t.p.

1888.18 [TIT-BITS]. *Prize Specimens of Handwriting, Ladies' and Gentlemen's.* Field & Tuer, the Leadenhall Press; *Tit-Bits.* [Nov. 1889]. T.4,393. Obl. 10 x 17 cm. 6d. Green wrappers, lettering in black. "The specimens . . . are the outcome of prizes offered in *Tit-Bits* for the best handwriting executed by members of either sex." Newberry copy has original mss. mounted and inserted: ms. letter from Tit-bits to Tuer authorizing the retention of the originals, dated 1900.

1888.19 *The Christmas Box, or New Year's Gift.* Field & Tuer, the Leadenhall Press; Simpkin, Marshall; Hamilton, Adams; Scribner & Welford. 1889-90 [Dec. 1889]. T.4,397. 20 cm. 1s. Blue cloth spine, gray card covers, titling and woodcut in black. With introduction signed: S. G. (Samuel Gosnell) Green, 1889. Originally published by the Religious Tract Society, 1825.

1888.20 CELIA FIENNES. *Through England on a Side Saddle: In the Time of William and Mary.* Field & Tuer, the Leadenhall Press; Simpkin, Marshall; Hamilton, Adams; Scribner & Welford. [Dec.] 1888. T.4,346. 23 cm. 12s 6d. Dark red-brown cloth, spine lettered in gilt. "Being the Diary of Celia Fiennes; with an Introduction by the Hon. Mrs. Griffiths" (Emily W. Griffiths).

1888.21 W. J. [WILLIAM JOHN] LOFTIE. *Kensington Picturesque & Historical.*

a. Regular issue: Field & Tuer, the Leadenhall Press; Scribner & Welford. [Dec.] 1888. T.4,323. 26 cm. 45s. Dark blue cloth, lettering in gilt. Illustrations (some in color) by William Luker Jr., engraved by Ch. Guillaume et Cie., Paris. "By command dedicated to Her Majesty the Queen."

b. Proof issue: 50 copies, numbered and signed, 5 guineas. Full brown morocco gilt, fore-edge painting of two scenes concealed under gilt edges.

c. Special issue: "25 special copies on thick super-calendered paper." Signed and numbered. 63s. Dark blue cloth, titling in gilt.

1888.22 "E. M., A FARMER." *The Art of Making and Selling Butter: By a Farmer (Subscribing Himself, E. M.).* Field & Tuer, the Leadenhall Press; Simpkin, Marshall; Hamilton, Adams. [1888]. No job number. 16 cm. 6d. Pamphlet: light yellow wrappers, lettering and decoration in black.

1888.23 WILLIAM SHAKESPEARE. *The Winter's Tale, a Comedy in Five Acts.* Field & Tuer, the Leadenhall Press; Scribner & Welford. [1888]. T.4,348. Obl. 17 x 25 cm. White card covers, illustrations and hand-lettering in brown. Arranged by Miss Mary Anderson, illustrations by Edwin John Ellis and Joseph Anderson, selections from incidental music by Andrew Levey.

1889.1 THOMAS CARLYLE. *A Pearl of English Rhetoric. Thomas Carlyle on the Repeal of the Union.* Field & Tuer, the Leadenhall Press; Simpkin, Marshall; Hamilton, Adams. [Mar.] 1889. T.4,374. 16 cm. 6d. Light blue-gray wrappers, Title in red and black. Prefatory note by P. E. N. (Percy E. Newberry).

1889.2 "B." *A Political Catechism.* Field & Tuer, the Leadenhall Press; Simpkin, Marshall; Hamilton, Adams. [Mar. 1889]. T.4,373. 19 cm. 1s. Yellow card covers, decorative title in blue, red, and green.

1889.3 GWENDOLINE DAVIDSON. *Kitten's Goblins.* Field & Tuer, the Leadenhall Press; Scribner & Welford. [Apr. 1889]. T.4,372. 23 cm. 5s. Light gray-blue cloth, illustration in blue, lettering in blue and gilt. "Illustrations by the authoress."

1889.4 [THE LEADENHALL PRESS]. *A New Shilling Book of Alphabets Plain and Ornamental.*

a. Thick paper edition: Field & Tuer, the Leadenhall Press; Simpkin, Marshall, Hamilton, Kent; Scribner & Welford. [May 1889]. T.4,368. Obl. 15 x 25 cm. Gray card covers printed in black. Printed on rectos only. "The alphabets shewn herein are selected from those in everyday use at The Leadenhall Press."

b. Thin paper edition: T.4,368/400. 1s. Brown card covers, printed in black. (Later issue with number: J.6,175/2000 noted.)[27]

1889.5 SIR W. M. [WILLIAM MATTHEW] FLINDERS PETRIE. *Hawara, Biahmu, and*

---

27. One later issue seen with two tipped-in Stickphast ads. See Appendix B, EPH-43 and EPH-44.

Arsinoe, with Thirty Plates. Field & Tuer, the Leadenhall Press; Trübner. [May] 1889. No job number. 32 cm. 16s. Green cloth, lettering in gilt on spine. With sections on "Inscriptions" by F. L. Griffith, "Papyri" by Prof. Sayce, "Pictures" by C. Smith, and "Ancient Botany" by P. E. Newberry.

1889.6 *Blots & Blemishes: From Liars Let Loose, and Tale-Bearers on the Trot, Save Us!* The Leadenhall Press; Simpkin, Marshall; Scribner & Welford. [June] 1889. T.4,386. 17 cm. 1s. Red wrappers, lettering in black.

1889.7 T. WILLIAMS, MISCELLANEOUS WRITER. *Political Wit and Humour in Our Own Times. Collected and Edited by T. W.* Field & Tuer, the Leadenhall Press; Simpkin, Marshall; Hamilton, Adams. [July] 1889. T.4,381. 18 cm. 1s. Red wrappers, title and names of politicians (in two columns) in black. Excerpts of speeches by Randolph Churchill, Disraeli, Gladstone, Robert Peel, Lord Roseberry, Lord Salisbury, and others.

1889.8 "R. I. W." [REGINALD ILLINGWORTH WOODHOUSE]. *Baby's Record: (Mother's Notes About Her Baby).*

a. First edition: Field & Tuer, the Leadenhall Press; Simpkin & Marshall, Hamilton, Adams; Scribner & Welford. [July 1889]. G.2,332. 18 cm. 1s.

b. Edition de Luxe: White vellum and green morocco, silk ties, 21s. With two Bartolozzi engravings from the original copperplates, one hand-colored.

c. Revised and improved edition: [Mar.] 1895. 1s. "... as used by the Royal Mother of the future King of England." Preface dated July 2nd, 1894. Sponsored by Mellin's Food. Green paper boards, lettering in gilt.

d. Third edition: 1905. Red textured paper, lettering in gilt.

1889.9 CHARLES TEMPEST CLARKSON AND JOSEPH HALL RICHARDSON. *Police!* Field & Tuer, the Leadenhall Press; Simpkin, Marshall; Hamilton, Adams; Scribner and Welford. [Oct.] 1889. T.4,376. 23 cm. 6s. Blue cloth, lettering and decoration in gilt and red. A general account of the work of the police in England and Wales. Includes a brief discussion of the Jack the Ripper murders.

1889.10 CHARLES LAMB. *Prince Dorus.*

a. "Proof copy" issue: Field & Tuer, the Leadenhall Press; Simpkin, Marshall; Hamilton, Adams; Scribner & Welford. [Oct.] 1889. T.4,379. 20 cm. 5s. Half vellum over gray-blue boards, lettering in gilt. 500 copies, each numbered and signed by the publishers. With facsimile of 1811 title page and nine hand-colored illustrations in facsimile. Introduction by Andrew W. Tuer.

b. New edition: 1890–1. [Sept. 1890]. T.4,442. 15 cm. 1s. Imitation pigskin brown stiff wrappers, lettering in black. Nine hand-colored illustrations.

1889.11 MAX O'RELL [LEON-PAUL BLOUËT]. *John Bull Junior or French as She Is Traduced: Enlarged from "Drat the Boys."* Field & Tuer, the Leadenhall Press.

[Oct. 1889]. T.4,387. 15 cm. 1s. Dark blue cloth, printed paper label on spine. Published separately in New York by Cassell & Co.

1889.12 CHARLES NEWTON SCOTT. *The Age of Marie Antoinette, a Sketch of the Period of European Revival, Which Claims among Its Representatives Goethe, Prudhon, Gainsborough, and Mozart.*

a. First edition: Field & Tuer, the Leadenhall Press; Simpkin, Marshall, Hamilton, Kent; Scribner & Welford. [Nov. 1889]. B.3,330. 17 cm. 2s.

b. Revised edition: [Apr.] 1905. 19 cm. 3s 6d. Blue cloth, decoration in gilt at top of upper cover, title in gilt on spine.

c. Third revised edition: 1912. 2s.

1889.13 WILFRID ALLAN. *Weather Wisdom from January to December, Wherein Will Be Found Much That Is Curious, Entertaining, and Instructive.* Field & Tuer, the Leadenhall Press; Simpkin, Marshall; Hamilton, Adams; Scribner & Welford. [Dec. 1889]. T.4,392. 17 cm. 6d. Printed red wrappers.

1889.14 JOHN MAX. *In Chains of Fate.* Field & Tuer, the Leadenhall Press; Simpkin, Marshall; Hamilton, Adams. [Dec. 1889]. T.4,398. 18 cm. 1s. Red wrappers, title and detail from frontispiece illustration in black. A novel.

1889.15 RICHARD WAKE. *A Selection of Sketches and Letters on Sport and Life in Morocco.* Field & Tuer, the Leadenhall Press; Simpkin, Marshall; Hamilton, Adams; Scribner & Welford. [Dec. 1889]. T.4,391. Obl. 29 x 39 cm. Quarter green cloth, tan boards, lettering in black. Drawings printed in sepia on rectos only; 20 are mounted. The author died on Dec. 6, 1888, from Arab fire at the Gemaizeh fort (from the "Memoir" preceding the drawings).

1889.16 SIR RICKMAN JOHN GODLEE. *Introductory Address in the Faculty of Medicine at University College, London. October 1889.* Field & Tuer, the Leadenhall Press. 1889. T.4,399. 24 cm. Price unknown. Half cream paper, gray boards. Title & block of UCL on front board (same as t.p.) in black.

1889.17 H. DE W. [HARRY DE WINDT]. *Ennui de Voyage.* Field & Tuer, the Leadenhall Press. [1889]. L.1,622. 17 cm. 2s. White wrappers, lettering blind-stamped in Gothic script, white dust jacket with lettering in gilt.

1890.1 C. J. [CHARLES JAMES] SCOTTER. *Lost in a Bucket-Shop. A Story of Stock Exchange Speculation.* Field & Tuer, the Leadenhall Press; Simpkin, Marshall; Hamilton, Adams. [Jan. 1890]. T.4,401. 17 cm. 1s. Pale blue wrappers, title and illustration in black.

1890.2 "AN ENVOY EXTRAORDINARY." *King Squash of Toadyland. By an Envoy Extraordinary.* Field & Tuer, the Leadenhall Press; Simpkin, Marshall; Hamilton, Adams; Scribner & Welford. [Feb. 1890]. T.4,402. 20 cm. 2s 6d.

Light blue cloth, lettering and illustration in black and blue.

1890.3 PERCY FITZGERALD. *The Story of "Bradshaw's Guide."* Field & Tuer, the Leadenhall Press; Simpkin, Marshall; Hamilton, Adams; Scribner & Welford. [Mar. 1890]. T.4,396. 15 cm. Printed blue-gray wrappers over cream card covers, reduced facsimile of *Bradshaw's Guide for Great Britain and Ireland* mounted on upper cover.

1890.4 ANDREW LANG. *How to Fail in Literature: A Lecture.* Field & Tuer, the Leadenhall Press; Simpkin, Marshall, Hamilton, Kent. [Mar.] 1890. T.4,439. 16 cm. 1s. Imitation pigskin brown stiff wrappers, lettering in black. Publisher's catalogue bound at end of volume.

1890.5 MARY BOYLE. *Æsop Redivivus.* Field & Tuer, the Leadenhall Press; Simpkin, Marshall, Hamilton, Kent; Scribner & Welford. [Apr.] 1890. T.4,359. 20 cm. 1s. Illustrated gray wrappers printed in black. "Old cuts are here wedded to Fables new. But I'd skip the Morals if I were you."

1890.6 CHARLES TEMPEST CLARKSON AND JOSEPH HALL RICHARDSON. *The Rogues' Gallery. Portraits from Life of Burglars, Receivers, Forgers, Cracksmen, Smashers, Bank Sneaks, House Thieves, Swell Mobsmen, Pickpockets, Swindlers, & Tricksters.* Field & Tuer, the Leadenhall Press. [Apr.] 1890. T.4,438. 18 cm. 1s. Red wrappers, lettering and illustration in black. Illustrated by Harry Parkes.

1890.7 ROBERT ST. JOHN CORBET. *The Handsome Examiner: His Adventures in Learning and Love. An Incident in the Life of an Original Thinker Told in One Volume.* The Leadenhall Press; Simpkin, Marshall, Hamilton, Kent. [June] 1890. T.4,456. 18 cm. 1s. Brown wrappers, title and "A New Story" in black.

1890.8 [ANDREW WHITE TUER]. *"Thenks Awf'lly!" Sketched in Cockney and Hung on Twelve Pegs.* Field & Tuer, the Leadenhall Press; Simpkin, Marshall, Hamilton, Kent; Scribner & Welford. [June] 1890. T.4,453. 16 cm. 1s. Red wrappers with diagonal white printed label. Each line of text "translated" into regular English in smaller type.

1890.9 "B." *Palaver; or, the Fairy Genius of Atlantis.* The Leadenhall Press; Simpkin, Marshall, Hamilton, Kent; Scribner & Welford. [Aug. 1890]. T.4,458. 19 cm. 1s. Brown wrappers, title in black.

1890.10 [ANDREW WHITE TUER]. *London City* [copyright pamphlet]. The Leadenhall Press. [Aug. 1890].[28] No job number. 12.5 cm. 1 farthing. Registered and issued in an edition of 500 copies to secure the title of W. J. Loftie's *London City* (in preparation) and attacking "the Unrepentant Publisher." On slip tipped onto cover: "For bibliographical trifles such as this—issued to serve

---

28. Review in *Punch,* Aug. 9, 1890.

a special purpose—fancy prices are often paid by the collector. An example that appeared some time ago from The Leadenhall Press recently changed hands at about a thousand times its published price."

1890.11 C. E. W. [CHARLOTTE ELIZABETH WOODS]. *Gatherings.* The Leadenhall Press; Simpkin, Marshall, Hamilton, Kent; Scribner & Welford. [Aug. 1890].[29] T.4,459. 19 cm. 5s. Light brown cloth, lettering and decorations in black.

1890.12 W. B. GILPIN. *Ranch-Land, a Romance of Adventure and Adventurers.* The Leadenhall Press; Scribner & Welford. [Sept.] 1890. T.4,451. 19 cm. 6s. Gray cloth, lettering in gilt and black.

1890.13 ANDREW LANSDOWNE. *A Life's Reminiscences of Scotland Yard: In One-and-Twenty Dockets.*

a. First edition: The Leadenhall Press; Simpkin, Marshall, Hamilton, Kent; Scribner & Welford. [Sept. 1890]. T.4,465. 188 pp. 19 cm. 2s 6d. Blue cloth, title and rule in dark blue.

b. Illustrated edition: [Oct. 1893]. 202 pp. 19 cm. 1s. "... with one hundred and twenty-one suggestive illustrations by Ambrose Dudley." Bind Me As You Please Series, no. 1. (No other titles noted in this series.)

1890.14 MILLWOOD MANNERS. *Three Beauties; or, the Idols of the Village.* The Leadenhall Press; Simpkin, Marshall, Hamilton, Kent. [Sept. 1890]. T.4,455. 19 cm. 1s. Red wrappers, title in black.

1890.15 F. G. [FREDERICK GEORGE] HILTON PRICE, F.S.A. *A Handbook of London Bankers; with Some Account of Their Predecessors the Early Goldsmiths. Together with Lists of Bankers, from the Earliest One Printed in 1677 to That of the London Post-Office Directory of 1876.* The Leadenhall Press; Simpkin, Marshall, Hamilton, Kent; Scribner & Welford. 1890, 1891 [Sept. 1890]. T.4,462. 27 cm. 15s. Brown cloth, title in gilt. New and Enlarged edition.

1890.16 *Diary of Eve in Eden, A.M., I. Edited by a Daughter of Eve, A.D., 1890.* [The Leadenhall Press]. [Sept. 1890]. T.4,470. 14 cm. 1s. Blue-gray wrappers, lettering in dark blue.

1890.17 E. H. [EDMUND HENRY] LACON WATSON. *Ephemera: Essays on Various Subjects.* The Leadenhall Press; Simpkin, Marshall, Hamilton, Kent; Scribner & Welford. [Sept. 1890]. T. 457 (T.4,457?). 18 cm. 1s. Rust red wrappers, title in black.

1890.18 A. DEWAR WILLOCK, M.J.I. *"Never Hit a Man Named Sullivan!"* The Leadenhall Press; Simpkin, Marshall, Hamilton, Kent; Scribner & Welford. [Sept.] 1890. T.4,461. 20 cm. 2s 6d. Orange cloth, lettering in black and gilt. The "Preface" appears on the upper cover in gilt.

29. Review in the *Literary World,* Aug. 29, 1890.

1890.19 [ANDREW WHITE TUER]. *Told after Supper.* The Leadenhall Press. [Sept. 1890].[30] No job number. 12.5 cm. 1 farthing. Registered and issued in an edition of 500 copies to secure the title of Jerome K. Jerome's *Told After Supper.*

1890.20 MRS. [GWENDOLINE] DAVIDSON. *A Story of Stops.* The Leadenhall Press; Simpkin, Marshall, Hamilton, Kent; Scribner & Welford. [Oct. 1890]. T.4,400. 22 cm. 5s. "With Fourteen whole-page Illustrations by the Authoress." Red cloth, lettering and vignette in gilt and dark blue.

1890.21 WILLIAM SHAKESPEARE; ARTHUR SYMONS. *Shakespeare's Play of Antony & Cleopatra, as Performed for the First Time under Mrs. Langtry's Management, at the Royal Princess's Theatre, London, on Tuesday, 18th November, 1890.* The Leadenhall Press. 1890. T.3,704. Obl. 15 x 25 cm. Half blue cloth, light blue boards, hand-lettering and illustration in brown and red-brown. "Antony, Mr. Coghlan. Cleopatra, Mrs. Langtry... Pictorial illus. of the principal scenes by Edwin J. Ellis. The historical introd. by Arthur Symons." Produced under the direction of the Hon. Lewis Wingfield.

1890.22 ALBERT E. HOOPER. *Up the Moonstair, a Story for Children.* The Leadenhall Press; Simpkin, Marshall, Hamilton, Kent; Scribner & Welford. [Dec.] 1890. T.4,440. 19 cm. 3s 6d. Blue cloth, ornamental lettering in dark blue, vignette in gilt. With 12 illustrations by Harry Parkes.

1890.23 "BLUE PETER." *A Week in a Wherry on the Norfolk Broads.* The Leadenhall Press; Simpkin, Marshall, Hamilton, Kent; Scribner & Welford. [Dec. 1890]. T.4,467. 20 cm. 5s. Tan cloth, lettering in black and gilt. Illustrated by "The Purser."

1890.24 "A NORTH-COUNTRYWOMAN." *Geordie: The Adventures of a North-Country Waif and Stray.* The Leadenhall Press; Simpkin, Marshall, Hamilton, Kent; Scribner & Welford. [Dec. 1890]. T.4,468. 13 cm. 1s. Pale pink wrappers, title in black.

1890.25 JEROME K. [KLAPKA] JEROME. *Told after Supper.*

a. First edition:[31] The Leadenhall Press; Simpkin, Marshall, Hamilton, Kent; Scribner & Welford. 1891 [Dec. 1890]. T.4,471. 19 cm. 3s 6d. "With 96 or 97 illustrations by Kenneth M. Skeaping." Red cloth, lettering, vignette and price 3/6 in black. Printed in dark blue ink on light blue paper.

b. Authorized American edition: Identical to English edition except for "Authorised American Edition" on title page.

1890.26 Rev. JOSEPH LL. [LLEWELYN] THOMSON, M.A. *Oxford to Palestine, Being Notes of a Tour in 1889.* The Leadenhall Press; Simpkin, Marshall, Hamilton, Kent.

---

30. Notice in the *Publishers' Circular*, September 15, 1890.
31. A second printing was halted while in the press. A notice in *The Academy*, Feb. 21, 1891, read: "At the request of the author, who is dissatisfied with its price and 'dress,' the second edition of Mr. Jerome K. Jerome's book *Told After Supper* has been withdrawn." Remaining copies were sold with "3/6" cancelled on the cover, and American rights were apparently transferred to Henry Holt and Altemus, who issued editions in 1891.

[Dec.] 1890. T.4,473. 20 cm. 2s 6d. Light blue cloth, title in gilt, author's name in blue. Reprinted from the *Oxford Times*.

1890.27 JOHN WATSON, F.L.S. [ed.]. *The Confessions of a Poacher*.

a. First edition: The Leadenhall Press; Simpkin, Marshall, Hamilton, Kent; Scribner & Welford. [Dec.] 1890. T.4,463. 20 cm. 2s 6d. Illustrated by James West. Green cloth, lettering and vignette in gilt.

b. First edition (variant binding): Gray-blue cloth, title in gilt, rule and lettering in black.

c. Second edition: The Leadenhall Press; Simpkin, Marshall, Hamilton, Kent; C. Scribner's Sons. [Oct.] 1893. 20 cm. 1s. Gray illustrated wrappers printed in black and red.

1891.1 "B." *The Truth About Democracy*. The Leadenhall Press; Simpkin, Marshall, Hamilton, Kent; Scribner & Welford. [Mar. 1891]. T.4,541. 19 cm. 2s 6d. Green cloth, beveled edges, title in gilt.

1891.2 W. J. [WILLIAM JOHN] LOFTIE. *London City: Its History—Streets—Traffic—Buildings—People*.

a. Regular edition: The Leadenhall Press; Scribner & Welford. [May] 1891. T.4,443. 29 cm. 42s (21s to subscribers). Blue morocco grain cloth, titling in gilt. Photo-zincotypes from drawings by W. Luker Jr., engraved by Ch. Guillaume et Cie., Paris. "By Command Dedicated to Her Majesty the Queen."

b. Large paper edition: 33 cm. 45s.

Note: Republished as *Victoria's London, Vol. 1: The City* (Alderman Press, 1984).

1891.3 *The Devil's Acres*. The Leadenhall Press; Simpkin, Marshall, Hamilton, Kent; Scribner & Welford. [June 1891]. T.4,544. 20 cm. 2s 6d. Illustrations by Kenneth M. Skeaping. Light blue cloth, lettering in gilt and blue.

1891.4 REV. SYDNEY [GWENFFRWD] MOSTYN.[32] *My First Curacy*. The Leadenhall Press; Simpkin, Marshall, Hamilton, Kent. [June] 1891. T.2,452. 19 cm. 2s 6d. Curatica, or Leaves from a Curate's Note-book, I. (No other titles noted in this series.)

1891.5 NORMAN PORRITT. *"Cornered."* The Leadenhall Press; Simpkin, Marshall, Hamilton, Kent; Scribner & Welford. [June 1891]. T.4,546. 20 cm. 2s 6d. Gray-green cloth, lettering in black. A novel of villainy and the Stock Exchange.

1891.6 AL-SO [ALEXANDER SOMERS]. *Lays of a Lazy Lawyer*. The Leadenhall Press;

---

32. Adrian Poole, in an explanatory note in the Oxford University Press "World's Classics" edition of Henry James' *What Maisie Knew* (1996), mistakenly attributes authorship of *My First Curacy* to William Clark Russell, who wrote nautical novels as "Sydney Mostyn" in the 1870s. Rev. Sydney Gwenffrwd Mostyn graduated from Oxford and was a lecturer and teacher.

Simpkin, Marshall, Hamilton, Kent; C. Scribner's Sons.[33] [June] 1891. T. ,551. (T.4,551?). 19 cm. 1s. Blue wrappers, title in black, heavy sans serif. Poetry.

1891.7 EDWARD MOXON. *Contemporary Notices of Charles Lamb.* The Leadenhall Press. 100 copies privately re-printed for L. W. Bangs, September, 1891. R.1,355. 23 cm. Gray wrappers, lettering in black. Containing "Charles Lamb" by Edward Moxon, dated January 27th, 1835, and an article from *The Mirror,* no. 703, January 24th, 1835.

1891.8 *Curious Old Cookery Receipts: Including Simples for Simple Ailments.* The Leadenhall Press; C. Scribner's Sons. [Oct. 1891]. T.4,568. 19 cm. 1s. Gray wrappers. lettering and illustration of knife and fork in black. "Printed from a Manuscript now dropping to pieces through much thumbing." The MS. dated at end Sept. 24, 1709.

1891.9 GUY BALGUY. *The Bantams of Sheffield.* The Leadenhall Press; Simpkin, Marshall, Hamilton, Kent; Scribner & Welford. [Oct.] 1891. T.4,563. 20 cm. 2s 6d. Green cloth, lettering in black.

1891.10 EDWARD KINGLAKE. *The Australian at Home: Notes and Anecdotes of Life at the Antipodes, Including Useful Hints to Those Intending to Settle in Australia.* The Leadenhall Press; George Robertson. [Oct. 1891]. T.4,570. 19 cm. 2s 6d. Brown cloth, lettering in black or (variant) purple.

1891.11 J. A. [JOHN ALEXANDER] FULLER MAITLAND AND W. S. [WILLIAM SMITH] ROCKSTRO. *English Carols of the Fifteenth Century, from a Ms. Roll in the Library of Trinity College, Cambridge.* The Leadenhall Press; Novello, Ewer; Simpkin, Marshall, Hamilton, Kent; C. Scribner's Sons. [Oct. 1891]. No job number. 32 cm. 10s. Green cloth, lettering in gilt on spine. Frontis color facsimile of Agincourt Song VII. Edited by J. A. Fuller Maitland, with added vocal parts by W. S. Rockstro.

1891.12 CHAS. [CHARLES] A. WARD. *Oracles of Nostradamus.* The Leadenhall Press; Simpkin, Marshall; C. Scribner's Sons. [Oct. 1891]. T.4,543. 19 cm. 6s. Dark blue cloth, lettering in gilt.

1891.13 ADAIR WELCKER. *Tales of the "Wild and Woolly West."* The Leadenhall Press; Simpkin, Marshall, Hamilton, Kent; C. Scribner's Sons. [Oct. 1891]. T.4,569. 17 cm. 1s. Pamphlet: cream wrappers, lettering in black.

1891.14 JOHN ASHTON [ed.]. *Real Sailor-Songs.* The Leadenhall Press; Simpkin, Marshall, Hamilton, Kent; C. Scribner's Sons; seven others. [Nov.] 1891.

---

33. *Lays of a Lazy Lawyer* is the earliest Leadenhall Press book noted with the Charles Scribner's Sons imprint. Scribner & Welford was established in 1857 as a separate company to import foreign books for the American market; in January 1891 it was absorbed into Charles Scribner's Sons, after which all business was conducted under that name. The Scribner & Welford imprint appears in some books issued in 1891 and early 1892.

No job number. 36 cm. 21s. Half vellum, blue-gray boards, lettered in red and black, coat of arms in gilt. A collection of reprints of 129 broadside ballads, many printed as broadsheets (two folding) and mounted on brown paper guards. Two hundred illustrations. Dedicated by special permission to Admiral H.R.H. the Duke of Edinburgh, K.G. (Lilly: printer's proof copy before final corrections, with revisions in an unidentified hand.)

1891.15 JOSEPH CROSS [TRANS.]. *A Daughter of the Gods: Ballads from the First, Second and Third Books of the Iliad.* The Leadenhall Press; Simpkin, Marshall, Hamilton, Kent; C. Scribner's Sons. [Nov. 1891]. T.4,557. 17 cm. 7s 6d. Vellum, lettering and vignette in gilt. With etchings by Tristram Ellis.

1891.16 YÜAN HSIANG-FU. *"Those Foreign Devils!" A Celestial on England and Englishmen.* The Leadenhall Press; Simpkin, Marshall, Hamilton, Kent; C. Scribner's Sons. [Nov.] 1891. No job number. 19 cm. 2s 6d. Dark blue cloth, lettering in gilt on spine. Translated by W. H. (William Henry) Wilkinson.

1891.17 SIR HAROLD EDWIN BOULTON, BART. *12 New Songs by Some of the Best-Known British Composers.* The Leadenhall Press; Simpkin, Marshall, Hamilton, Kent; C. Scribner's Sons. [Dec. 1891]. T.4,445. 32 cm. 12s. Brown cloth, lettering in gilt. Frontis by Frank Dicksee. With preface and poems by Boulton. Music and words. The songs were published individually by Novello.

1891.18 J. PERCY KING. *As the Wind Blows. Stray Songs in Many Moods.* The Leadenhall Press; Simpkin, Marshall, Hamilton, Kent; Scribner & Welford. [ca. Dec. 1891].[34] T.4,559. 20 cm. 5s. Light blue cloth, lettering in gilt and dark blue, short rule in gilt.

1891.19 [ANDREW TUER]. *Guess the Title of This Story! £100 for the Person Who Does.*
a. First issue: The Leadenhall Press; Simpkin, Marshall, Hamilton, Kent. [Dec.] 1891. 18 cm. 1s. No job number. Pink wrappers, lettering and blank banner outline (for correct title) in black, advertisement for Stickphast Paste on lower cover. A contest, printed in an edition of 10,000. Prize withdrawn when no one submitted the desired title: *An Eye and an I.*
b. Second issue: [Aug. 1892]. The remaining copies were issued with "1 shilling" canceled and "6d/satis superque" substituted.[35]

1891.20 HORACE STEWART. *History of the Worshipful Company of Gold and Silver Wyre-Drawers: And of the Origin and Development of the Industry Which the Company Represents.* Printed for the Company by the Leadenhall Press, 1891. R.1,259. 27 cm. Blue cloth, lettering and coat of arms in gilt. Compiled by Horace Stewart, illustrated by Estelle D'Avigdor. Initials; headpieces and tailpieces.

34. "Recent Books" listing in *Torch & Colonial Book Circular,* December 31, 1891.
35. *The English Catalogue of Books* gives the redistribution title as *Guess the Title of This Story (An Eye and an I),* but I have not located a copy with the title in this form.

1891.21 JEROME K. [KLAPKA] JEROME. *On the Stage—and Off: The Brief Career of a Would-Be-Actor. Illustrated edition.* The Leadenhall Press; Simpkin, Marshall, Hamilton, Kent; C. Scribner's Sons. [Dec.] 1891. T.4,571. 20 cm. 2s 6d. Orange-brown cloth, lettering in black. Illustrations by Kenneth M. Skeaping.

First edition: (see checklist 1885.21).

1892.1 A. C. AINGER AND SIR JOSEPH BARNBY. *Eton Songs.* The Leadenhall Press; Novello, Ewer; Simpkin, Marshall. 1891–2 [ca. Jan. 1892].[36] No job number. 32 cm. 30s (advertised in 1891 at 21s). Light blue-gray cloth, lettering in gilt. Written by A. C. Ainger, set to music by Joseph Barnby, with 35 engravings by Herbert Marshall. "Dedicated by Special Permission to Her Most Gracious Majesty the Queen." (Copies seen bound in both vellum and calf gilt.)

1892.2 "GOOSESTEP." *Splay-Feet Splashings in Divers Places.* Leadenhall Press; Scribner & Welford. [Jan., 1892]. T.4,574. 19 cm. 3s 6d. Blue cloth, lettering and vignette in black. Light verse.

1892.3 JOHN BIDDULPH MARTIN. *"The Grasshopper" in Lombard Street.* The Leadenhall Press; Scribner & Welford. [Feb.] 1892. T.4,554. 26 cm. 21s. Green cloth, lettering, and corner vignettes in gilt. A history of Martins Bank, 1483-1891: The Partners; The Business; The Premises; The Customers; Appendices.

1892.4 JAMES MEW AND JOHN ASHTON. *Drinks of the World.* The Leadenhall Press; Simpkin, Marshall, Hamilton, Kent; Scribner & Welford. [Feb.] 1892. No job number. 22 cm. 21s. Dark blue cloth, title in gilt. Numerous illustrations.

1892.5 FRED. JAMES. *Fred. James under a Spell!* The Leadenhall Press; Simpkin, Marshall, Hamilton, Kent; Scribner & Welford. [Mar. 1892]. No job number. 21 cm. 1s. Light gray card covers, title in blue. Pages printed on one side only. In verse. Illustrated by Vigne.

1892.6 JAMES MOODY LOWRY. *The Dolls' Garden Party.* The Leadenhall Press. [Apr. 1892]. T.4,583. 18 cm. 2s 6d. Quarter cream canvas, red boards, lettering in gilt. Illustrated by J. B. Clark.

1892.7 WILLIAM LUKER JR. *A Successful Picture!* The Leadenhall Press. Sept. 5, 1892. 59 cm. Price unknown. Print of four sequential drawings of an artist attempting to finish a picture of sleeping kittens, who are awakened by the dog.

1892.8 THOMAS CARLYLE. *Rescued Essays of Thomas Carlyle.* The Leadenhall Press; Simpkin, Marshall, Hamilton, Kent; C. Scribner's Sons. [Sept. 1892].[37] T.4,466. 19 cm. 2s. Quarter dark blue cloth, gray boards, printed paper label on spine. Printed on light blue paper. Edited by Percy Newberry.

36. Reviewed in February 1892 *Review of Reviews*.
37. Announced and advertised in 1890 lists and Oct. 1890 *Publishers' Circular* at the price of 1s, but no copy found issued in that year or at that price.

1892.9 JOSEPH FORSTER. *Tricks and Tricksters. Tales Founded on Fact; from a Lawyer's Note-Book.* The Leadenhall Press; Simpkin, Marshall, Hamilton, Kent; C. Scribner's Sons. [Sept.] 1892. T.4,572. 18 cm. 1s. Light gray card, title in black.

1892.10 WILFRID MEYNELL. *The Child Set in the Midst: By Modern Poets.* The Leadenhall Press. [Sept.] 1892. T.4,591. 19 cm. 6s. Black ribbed cloth, yapped fore-edges, printed paper label on spine. With facsimile of MS. "The Toys" by Coventry Patmore. Edited by Wilfrid Meynell. Includes poems by Dinah Craik, Austin Dobson, Robert Buchanan, George Meredith, Cosmo Monkhouse, D. G. Rossetti, Francis Thompson, Katherine Tynan, and earlier poets. (Private collection: Coventry Patmore's copy.)

1892.11 [SENEX]. *Counsel to Ladies and Easy-Going Men on their Business Investments, & Cautions against the Lures of Wily Financiers & Unprincipled Promoters.* The Leadenhall Press; Effingham Wilson; Simpkin, Marshall, Hamilton, Kent; C. Scribner's Sons. [Sept.] 1892. No job number. 20 cm. 3s. Quarter cream cloth, blue-gray boards, title on two cream paper labels on front.

1892.12 *The Visible to-Be. A Story of Hand-Reading.*
a. The Leadenhall Press; Simpkin, Marshall, Hamilton, Kent; C. Scribner's Sons. [Oct. 1892]. T.4,585. 19 cm. 3s 6d. Pictorial black or (variant) dark green cloth, lettering and vignette in gilt.
b. Variant: bound with *The Notions of a Nobody* (checklist 1893.7) in red or dark blue cloth, title in gilt on spine: *Palmistry. A Tale of Hand Reading.* Also reported bound with *"Those Foreign Devils!"* (checklist 1891.16).

1892.13 "THE WANDERING JEW." *The First Century and the Nineteenth. By the Wandering Jew.* The Leadenhall Press. [Oct. 1892]. T.4,609. 19 cm. 3s 6d. Black cloth, title in gilt.

1892.14 "GOOSESTEP." *Bric-à-Brac Ballads.* The Leadenhall Press; Simpkin, Marshall, Hamilton, Kent; C. Scribner's Sons. [Nov.] 1892. T.4,616. 19 cm. 1s. Red wrappers, lettering and illustration in black.

1892.15 DORA V. [VICTOIRE] GREET. *Mrs. Greet's Story of the Golden Owl.*
a. First edition: The Leadenhall Press; C. Scribner's Sons. 1892–3. [Nov. 1892]. T.4,601. 272 pp. 18 cm. 6s. Dark green cloth, brown paper labels lettered in black and the words "Golden Owl" in gilt, gold linen page marker. Printed on brown paper, illustrations by Ambrose Dudley printed on white ground. Title page with gilt-embossed owl in place of the words "Golden Owl."
b. New edition: 1893. 312 pp. 19 cm. 3s 6d. Printed on white paper.

1892.16 W. [WILLIAM] CAREW HAZLITT. *Joe Miller in Motley: (the Cream of Joe's Jests).* The Leadenhall Press; Simpkin, Marshall, Hamilton, Kent; C. Scribner's Sons. [Nov.] 1892. No job number. 19 cm. 2s. Gray boards, light gray and cream wrap-around paper labels, lettering and vignette in black. Printed on papers of different colors. Frontis and title vignette by Joseph Crawhall. Introduction by W. C. Hazlitt.

1892.17 ANDREW W. [WHITE] TUER. *The Book of Delightful and Strange Designs: Being One Hundred Facsimile Illustrations of the Art of the Japanese Stencil-Cutter to Which the Gentle Reader Is Introduced by One Andrew W. Tuer, F.S.A. Who Knows Nothing at All About It.*

a. First edition: The Leadenhall Press; Liberty & Co.; Simpkin, Marshall, Hamilton, Kent; C. Scribner's Sons; Baudry et Cie; F. A. Brockhaus. [Nov. 1892]. No job number. Obl. 20 x 23 cm. About 350 copies, 6s. Quarter cream cloth, blue-gray boards, paper labels on upper cover and spine. Original Japanese stencil plate as frontis in each copy. Introduction in English, French, and German, with separate title pages and pagination. 104 stencil plate designs printed on double leaves. Copies noted without the English introduction were most likely intended for distribution on the continent.

b. Second issue: identical to the limited issue but without the stencil plate.

Note: Republished as *Japanese Stencil Designs* by Dover Publications in 1967.

1892.18 S. [SAMUEL] GREGSON FELL [ed.]. *The Family of Darby-Coventry of Greenlands Henley on Thames.* Privately printed at The Leadenhall Press. 1892. No job number. 22 cm. With folded genealogical table and notes by S. Gregson Fell.

1892.19 MANLEY HOPKINS. *Spicilegium Poeticum: A Gathering of Verses.* The Leadenhall Press. Printed for Private Circulation. [1892]. No job number. 19 cm. 2s 6d. Full vellum with yapped fore-edge, lettering and ax cutting into bleeding heart with motto "AT AMABO" in gilt, ribbon page marker. Frontis: "E. H. after a drawing by Tony Johannot, 1848." (Princeton copy inscribed to A. B. Goulden and corrected in Hopkins' hand. NYPL copy inscribed by Hopkins.)

1892.20 CHARLES [AND MARY] LAMB. *Poetry for Children.* The Leadenhall Press. 1892. 2 vols. 15 cm. Facsimile of original published in 1809. Impression limited to 112 copies. Bound by Zaehnsdorf in brown calf, border and Grecian design with verse below in gilt.

1892.21 C. F. M. [HON. CAROLINE FULLER MAITLAND]. *How We Went to Rome in 1857, by C. F. M.* The Leadenhall Press. Printed for private circulation. 1892. T.4,583. 18 cm. Blue-gray boards, printed paper label on spine.

1892.22 HARDWICKE D. [DRUMMOND] RAWNSLEY. *The Undoing of De Harcla. A Ballad of Cumberland.* The Leadenhall Press. 1892. S.1,420. 15 cm. Price unknown. Each copy signed by the author at the end of the poem. Any profits to go to the Keswick School of Industrial Arts. Green or pink wrappers, lettered in black, with red or green ribbon ties on spine.

1893.1 MILLIE SELOUS. *The Stage in the Drawing-Room: Short One-Act Sketches for Two and Three Players.* The Leadenhall Press; Simpkin, Marshall, Hamilton, Kent; C. Scribner's Sons. [Jan.] 1893. T.4,616. 18 cm. 2s 6d. Quarter light gray cloth, gray boards, cream paper labels printed in red and black on upper cover and spine, red silk page marker.

1893.2 SIR HAROLD EDWIN BOULTON, BART. *Seven Songs to Sing.* The Leadenhall Press. [June] 1893. T.4,230. 32 cm. 6s. Blue cloth, lettering in gilt. Songs by A. J. Caldicott, L. Denza, C. Dick, M. Lawson, T. Marzials, J. L. Roeckel, Lord Henry Somerset. Edited and with words by H. Boulton. Frontispiece by Ambrose Dudley.

1893.3 PERCY [HETHERINGTON] FITZGERALD. *London City Suburbs, as They Are To-day.*

a. Regular edition: The Leadenhall Press; Simpkin, Marshall, Hamilton, Kent; C. Scribner's Sons. [June] 1893. No job number. 29 cm. 42s (21s to subscribers). Blue cloth, lettering in gilt. Photo-zincotypes from drawings by William Luker Jr., engraved by Ch. Guillaume et Cie., Paris. "By command dedicated to Her Majesty the Queen." Companion to *London City* (publisher's slip at front).

b. Large Paper edition: 33 cm. 45s.

Note: republished as *Victoria's London, Vol. 2: The Suburbs* (Alderman Press, 1984).

1893.4 LUCY ETHELDRED BROADWOOD AND J. A. FULLER MAITLAND [eds.]. *English County Songs.* The Leadenhall Press; J. Cramer; Simpkin, Marshall, Hamilton, Kent; C. Scribner's Sons. [July] 1893. No job number. 28 cm. 6s. Red or cream cloth, title and decoration in gilt, author's names in black. "Words and Music Collected and Edited by Lucy E. Broadwood and J. A. Fuller Maitland."

1893.5 JEROME K. [KLAPKA] JEROME. *Novel Notes.*

a. First edition: The Leadenhall Press; Simpkin, Marshall, Hamilton, Kent.[38] [Aug.] 1893. T.4,623. 20 cm. 3s 6d. Light brown cloth, lettering in black. With illustrations by Louis Wain, J. Gülich, Hal Hurst, Geo. Hutchinson, Miss Hammond, and others. Serialized in "The Idler."

b. Cheap edition: [Aug.] 1901. 1s. Illustrated gray-green wrappers. Ads on rear cover, inside covers, and prelims.

1893.6 R. ST. J. [Robert ST. JOHN] CORBET. *From the Bull's Point of View: The True Story of a Bull-Fight.* The Leadenhall Press; Simpkin, Marshall, Hamilton, Kent; C. Scribner's Sons. [Oct.] 1893. T.4,634. 18 cm. 6d. Red wrappers, title "The Story of a Bullfight" in black, specially designed lettering.

1893.7 T. [THOMAS] THEODORE DAHLE. *The Notions of a Nobody.* The Leadenhall Press; Simpkin, Marshall, Hamilton, Kent; C. Scribner's Sons. [Oct. 1893].

---

38. A separate edition, with different type but the same illustrations, was published in the U.S. by Henry Holt.

T.4,625. 20 cm. 2s 6d. Green cloth, lettering in black. Also seen bound together with *The Visible To-Be* (checklist 1892.11).

1893.8   Joseph Hatton. *In Jest and Earnest. A Book of Gossip*. The Leadenhall Press. [Oct.] 1893. T.4,632. 19 cm. 2s 6d. Gray or buff cloth, title in black.

1893.9   Edmund Henry Lacon Watson. *Stray Minutes: Being Some Account of the Proceedings of the Literary Club at St. Mungo-by-the-Sea*. The Leadenhall Press; Simpkin, Marshall, Hamilton, Kent; C. Scribner's Sons. [Oct. 1893]. T.4,626. 18 cm. 1s. Light gray wrappers, title and illustration of golfer in black.

1893.10   Grant Allen. *Michael's Crag*. The Leadenhall Press; Simpkin, Marshall, Hamilton, Kent. [Nov.] 1893. T.4,619. 20 cm. 3s 6d. Light gray cloth, lettering in black (variant 1: lettering in green; variant 2: light green cloth, lettering in black). "Mr. Grant Allen's new story" on cover, spine, and title page. Frontis and marginal illustrations in silhouette by Francis Carruthers Gould and Alec Carruthers Gould. (American edition published by Rand, McNally, 1893.)

1893.11   John Ashton. *A History of English Lotteries: Now for the First Time Written*. The Leadenhall Press; C. Scribner's Sons. [Nov.] 1893. T.4,630. 22 cm. 12s 6d. With 28 inserted old lottery bills in facsimile on white and colored papers. Cream cloth, printed rose paper labels, yellow silk page marker.

1893.12   The Hon. Mrs. Eleanor Frances Weston Brett. *Echoes. A Musical Birthday Book*. The Leadenhall Press; J. B. Cramer; Simpkin, Marshall, Hamilton, Kent. [Nov.] 1893. No job number. 29 cm. 12s 6d. Light green cloth, title in gilt. . Each left-hand page is a blank for two dates; each right-hand page has two pieces of music printed from engraved plates.

1893.13   Henry Sotheran [ed.]; Benjamin Rotch. *Manners & Customs of the French: Facsimile of the Scarce 1815 Edition*. The Leadenhall Press; Henry Sotheran; Simpkin, Marshall, Hamilton, Kent; C. Scribner's Sons. [Nov.] 1893. T.4,633. 22 cm. 250 copies, 16s. Half tan cloth, blue-gray boards, paper labels on cover and spine, gray silk page marker. With ten tinted illustrations, printed from the original copperplates "now destroyed." With a preface by Sotheran stating: "Who the author was is doubtful; but the writer has heard his father say that he was one Benjamin Rotch, a Middlesex Magistrate."

1893.14   [Alice B. Sargant]. *From a Yacht. King Arthur & Morgan le Fay. The Captive Bride. The Caravan and other Verses. By the Author of 'East and West.'* The Leadenhall Press. Simpkin, Marshall, Hamilton, Kent. [Dec. 1893].[39] T.4,641. 27 cm. 6s. Plain gray wrappers. "By the author of *East and West*."[40]

---

39. "Publications of the Month," *The Bookseller*, Dec. 15, 1893.
40. The author's identity is given in *The Literary Year-Book*, Vol. XVI (Routledge, 1912), p. 326. Other works include: *Endymion's Dream* (G. Bell, 1890), *The Fairy Rowke's Rade* (Elkin Mathews, 1896), and *Brownie* (J. M. Dent, 1897).

1893.15 ARCHIBALD R. [ROSS] COLQUHOUN. *Matabeleland: the War, and Our Position in South Africa.* The Leadenhall Press; Simpkin, Marshall, Hamilton, Kent. [Dec. 1893]. No job number. 18 cm. 2s 6d. White wrappers, black lettering except "WAR," in red, reproducing title page. Folding map of the country drawn by the author.

1893.16 GEORGE EDWARD STANHOPE MOLYNEUX HERBERT, EARL OF CARNARVON. *Catalogue of Books Selected from the Library of an English Amateur.*

a. For Private Circulation Only. The Leadenhall Press. 1893–97. Vol I: 1893; V.1,329. Vol. II: 1897; A.2,173. 29 cm. Plates, part mounted, 1 folding. Plain cream wrappers. 150 copies on hand-made paper. (Lilly copy of Vol. I: presentation copy from Carnarvon dated "Dec. '93.")

b. Special issue: 3 copies on vellum.

1893.17 COUNT STANISLAUS ERIC STENBOCK. *The Shadow of Death. Poems, Songs, and Sonnets.* Leadenhall Press; Simpkin, Marshall, Hamilton, Kent; C. Scribner's Sons. 1893. T.4,643. 17 cm. Price unknown. Bound in Japanese vellum paper jacket over plain white card wrappers, rectangular design of roses and thorns in red and black, title in black across banner in upper right corner.

1893.18 G. W. TAYLOR. *A Short History of St. George's Chapter (Deptford), No. 140.* The Leadenhall Press. 1893. 18 cm. Price unknown. Pamphlet. Freemasonry.

1894.1 ERNEST BRAMAH. *English Farming and Why I Turned It Up.* The Leadenhall Press; Simpkin, Marshall, Hamilton, Kent; C. Scribner's Sons. [Apr.] 1894. T.4,647. 18.5 cm. 2s 6d. Light blue-gray cloth, lettering in black and gilt. Noted by John Carter in his essay "Off-Subject Books" as one of the exemplary books in that field.

1894.2 WARWICK SIMPSON [WILLIAM PETT RIDGE]. *Eighteen of Them. Singular Stories.* The Leadenhall Press; Simpkin, Marshall, Hamilton, Kent; C. Scribner's Sons. [Apr. 1894]. T.4,645. 20 cm. 3s 6d. Light gray cloth, lettering in gilt and black.

1894.3 R. S. [ROBERT STANLEY] WARREN BELL. *The Businesses of a Busy Man.* The Leadenhall Press; Simpkin, Marshall, Hamilton, Kent; C. Scribner's Sons. [June 1894]. T.4,655. 20 cm. 1s 6d. Light blue patterned cloth, titling in gilt, central decoration and border rules in black.

1894.4 HARRY A. JAMES. *A Professional Pugilist.* The Leadenhall Press; Simpkin, Marshall, Hamilton, Kent. [June] 1894. T.4,650. 19 cm. 1s. Red illustrated wrappers printed in black. Illustrated by Kenneth M. Skeaping. (HRC copy inscribed by the author to Denis Conan Doyle.)

1894.5 SIR HAROLD EDWIN BOULTON. *Songs Sung and Unsung.* Leadenhall Press;

Simpkin, Marshall, Hamilton, Kent; C. Scribner's Sons. [June 1894]. T.4,652. 19 cm. 5s. Two parts bound *dos-à-dos* in limp light blue cloth, lettering in gilt. Covers and spines titled: *Songs Sung* and *Songs Unsung*. (Lilly copy inscribed by Boulton to Violet Spencer Churchill.)

1894.6 [JAMES FRANKLIN FULLER]. *Doctor Quodlibet. A Study in Ethics, by the Author of "Chronicles of Westerly," "John Orlebar," "Culmshire Folk" Etc.* The Leadenhall Press; Simpkin, Marshall, Hamilton, Kent; C. Scribner's Sons. [June] 1894. T.4,653. 20 cm. 3s 6d. Quarter dark blue cloth, light blue boards, lettering in gilt and black.

1894.7 MARGARET T. [MARGARET THOMSON BEVERIDGE] BELL. *Poems: and Other Pieces*. The Leadenhall Press; Simpkin, Marshall, Hamilton, Kent. [July 1894]. T.4,659. 19 cm. 5s. Green cloth, lettering in gilt, decoration in black. "Edited, with a Memoir, by her Brother" (David Beveridge).

1894.8 "DOGBERRY." *Humours and Oddities of the London Police Courts: From the Opening of This Century to the Present Time.* The Leadenhall Press; Simpkin, Marshall, Hamilton, Kent; C. Scribner's Sons. [July] 1894. T.4,640. 20 cm. 2s 6d. Blue cloth, lettering in gilt, design in black. Illustrated and edited by "Dogberry." (One illustration bears initials "J. C. K.")

1894.9 "M. H." *Socialism or Protection? Which Is to Be? A Question for the Classes and the Masses.* The Leadenhall Press; Simpkin, Marshall, Hamilton, Kent. [July 1894]. T.4,660. 18 cm. 1s. Red wrappers, lettering in black.

1894.10 [JOHN GEORGE LITTLECHILD]. *The Reminiscences of Chief-Inspector Littlechild.* The Leadenhall Press; Simpkin, Marshall, Hamilton, Kent; C. Scribner's Sons. [July] 1894. T.4,658. 20 cm. 2s 6d. Yellow cloth, rule and floral devices in black with gray printed paper labels on cover and spine.

1894.11 MRS. R. W. [CHARLOTTE ELIZABETH] WOODS. *"Have Ye Read It?" Look Sharp!* Published for the authoress by The Leadenhall Press; Simpkin, Marshall, Hamilton, Kent; C. Scribner's Sons. [July] 1894. No job number. 20 cm. 42s. Light brown cloth, lettering and decorative banners in black.

1894.12 JOHN ASHTON. *A righte Merrie Christmasse!!!: The Story of Christ-tide.*

a. Regular edition: The Leadenhall Press; Simpkin, Marshall, Hamilton, Kent; C. Scribner's Sons. [Dec. 1894]. No job number. 29 cm. 25s. Half brown sheep and red cloth boards, lettering and decorations in gilt on upper cover, gilt decoration on lower cover. Frontis etching of "The Wassail Song," by Arthur C. Behrend.

b. Special limited edition: full vellum, lettering and floral design in gilt, arabesque in gilt on lower cover, brown or green leather title label on spine, marbled endpapers, and the etching in proof state.

1894.13   Eva Boulton. *Borderland Fancies.* The Leadenhall Press; Simpkin, Marshall, Hamilton, Kent. [Dec. 1894]. T.4,661. 19 cm. 2s 6d. Tan cloth, lettering in gilt, decorative device in black. Illustrated by the author.

1894.14   "Alere Flammam."[41] *Parodies & Satires.* The Leadenhall Press. [1894]. T.4,665. 20 cm. 2s 6d. Light blue cloth, ornamental lettering in gilt and black.

1894.15   "Goosestep." *Rustling Reeds, Stirred by Goosestep.* The Leadenhall Press; Simpkin, Marshall, Hamilton, Kent; C. Scribner's Sons. 1894. T.4,663. 18 cm. Funnynym Series, no. 1. Light blue-gray illustrated wrappers. Title page printed in red and black. Cover and title page illustration by "C. W. G." Illustration for "Prelude" by K. [Kenneth] M. Skeaping. (Lilly copy inscribed by "the author.")

1894.16   W. Q. [William Quin] Warren [ed.]. *Some Reminiscences of Thomas Francis and Mary Adams and Their Family of Halstead, Essex.* Privately Printed for the Adams Family By the Leadenhall Press. 1894. 24 cm. Full brown leather, decoration and family crest in gilt, lettering in gilt on spine. Portraits of Thomas Francis and Mary Adams and 14 Etchings by F. Golden Short. Appendices including documents, letters, etc. relating to the Halstead Brewery.

1895.1   John Lascelles. *·X·Y·Z· and Other Poems.* The Leadenhall Press; Simpkin, Marshall, Hamilton, Kent; C. Scribner's Sons. [Jan. 1895]. T.4,666. 22 cm. 1s. Cream stiff wrappers, lettering and design in black, green, and yellow. Sun and Serpent Series—I (not stated but so advertised after publication of Lascelle's second book, checklist 1896.5).

1895.2   J. A. [John Alfred] Parker. *Ernest England; or, a Soul Laid Bare. A Drama for the Closet.* The Leadenhall Press; Simpkin, Marshall, Hamilton, Kent; Charles Scribner's Sons. [Apr.] 1895. T.4.664. 20 cm. 7s 6d. Brown cloth, title in gilt, black corner decorations. By the late editor of the *Indian Daily News.*

1895.3   M. J. [Martha Jane] Loftie. *Comfort in the Home.* The Leadenhall Press. [May] 1895. T.4,670. 19 cm. 1s. Wrappers, lettering, and woodcut in black.

1895.4   St. John Browne. *Master Jimmy's Fables.* The Leadenhall Press. [June 1895]. T.4,656. Obl. 13 x 21 cm. 1s. Red card covers, title in black. Illustrated by Walter Warren. Printed on one side of the leaf.

1895.5   John Ingold. *Roughly Told Stories.* The Leadenhall Press; C. Scribner's Sons. [June] 1895. 19 cm. 3s 6d. Gray cloth, lettering in black.

1895.6   Charles Newton Scott. *Laurence Oliphant: Supplementary Contributions to His Biography.* The Leadenhall Press; Simpkin, Hamilton, Marshall, Kent;

---

41. The poem "Alere Flammam" by Edmund Gosse appeared in *In Russet and Silver* (Chicago: Stone & Kimball, 1884) and in *The Yellow Book,* Vol. I (1894).

C. Scribner's Sons. [June] 1895. T.4,672. 18 cm. 1s. Gray wrappers, lettering in black.

1895.7 CHARLES C. ROTHWELL. *The Stolen Bishop.* The Leadenhall Press; Simpkin, Marshall, Hamilton, Kent; C. Scribner's Sons. [Aug. 1895]. T.4,676. 18 cm. 3s 6d. Red cloth, title and illustration of bishop's mitre in gilt, author's name and rules at top and left in black. With inserted slip printed to look like autograph note: "His Lordship writes: 'I have perused with pain and consternation this deplorable account of the manner in which I was foully kidnapped by that chit of a schoolgirl, Miss Tony Larkin, and I hereby raise my solemn protest against any vulgar hilarity which it may excite in low minds.'"

1895.8 MARGARET ELENORA TUPPER. *The Scent of the Heather: And Other Writings in Prose and Poetry.* The Leadenhall Press; Simpkin, Marshall, Hamilton, Kent; C. Scribner's Sons. 1895. No job number. 20 cm. 6s. Light brown cloth, lettering in black and gilt. Edited by Miss Bissicks. With list of original subscribers.

1895.9 MRS. R. W. [CHARLOTTE ELIZABETH] WOODS. *An Every-Day Life.* Published for the authoress by The Leadenhall Press; Simpkin, Marshall, Hamilton, Kent; C. Scribner's Sons. 1895. T.4,679. 21 cm. Tan cloth, lettering in black.

1896.1 J. K. ARTHUR. *A Bouquet of Brevities: Being Practical Maxims and Refined Sentiments, Original and Select.* The Leadenhall Press; Simpkin, Marshall, Hamilton, Kent; C. Scribner's Sons. [Feb. 1896]. T.4,682. 25 cm. 12s 6d. Red cloth, script lettering and bouquet decoration in gilt.

1896.2 *The Story of a London Clerk. A Faithful Narrative Faithfully Told.* The Leadenhall Press; Simpkin, Marshall, Hamilton, Kent; C. Scribner's Sons. [Mar. 1896]. T.4,683. 19 cm. 3s 6d. Green cloth, lettering and decoration in dark blue.

1896.3 ANDREW WHITE TUER. *History of the Horn-Book.*

a. The Leadenhall Press; C. Scribner's Sons. [Apr.] 1896. No job number. Special edition: 2 vols. 26 cm. 1,000 copies, 42s. Full vellum, lettering inside hornbook outline in gilt, leather title labels on spines. Seven facsimile hornbooks and battledores in compartments at front of both volumes. Tipped in, a notice on the use of the books. Hand-colored title vignette by Joseph Crawhall in each volume, plus illustrations and decorations by R. W. Allan, F. D. Bedford, Arthur Clay, A. Dudley, Georgie Cave France, C. M. Gere, E. Hopkins, Charles H. M. Kerr, John Leighton, Celia Levetus, Kate Light, Ida Lovering, Wm. Luker Jr., P. Macquoid, Phil May, Linley Sambourne, Miss (Maud) Sambourne, H. S. Tuke, Walter J. West, R. I. Williams and others. "Dedicated by Command to Her Majesty the Queen-Empress."

Note: The Library of Congress lists: "[Rimington, Alexander Wallace]. *Colour Music.* [London, The Leadenhall Press, Ltd., 1895]. 4 p. 25 x 19 cm." The copy is missing, however, and I have not been able to verify it as printed by the Leadenhall Press. BL lists: *Colour Music [An extract from "A New Art, 'Colour Music'."]* with no imprint, from a paper read at St. James's Hall on June 6th, 1895, which Spottiswoode printed in its entirety that year.

b. Second edition: [Oct.] 1897. 1 vol. 26 cm. 6s. With a new chapter noting 20 additional hornbooks. Three facsimile hornbooks in compartment at rear.

Note: republished by: B. Blom (New York) in 1968; S. Emmering (Amsterdam) in 1971; Arno Press (New York) in 1979.

1896.4 JAMES WOODHOUSE; REV. R. I. [REGINALD ILLINGWORTH] WOODHOUSE [ed.]. *The Life and Poetical Works of James Woodhouse, 1735–1820.* The Leadenhall Press; Simpkin, Marshall, Hamilton, Kent; C. Scribner's Sons. [June] 1896. T.4,680. 2 vols. 26.5 cm. 42s. Quarter blue cloth, light blue cloth boards, lettering in gilt and black. By James Woodhouse, Journeyman Shoemaker, edited by the Rev. R. I. Woodhouse. Frontis portrait in Vol. I engraved by Henry Cook after W. Hobday.

1896.5 JOHN LASCELLES. *The Great Drama, and Other Poems.* The Leadenhall Press; Simpkin, Marshall, Hamilton, Kent; C. Scribner's Sons. [Aug. 1896]. T.4,692. 22 cm. 1s. Cream stiff wrappers with bold design in black, green, and yellow on upper cover. Title page in red and black. Sun and Serpent Series—II.

1896.6 *Lays of the Bards. I.—the Holy Isle.* The Leadenhall Press; Simpkin, Marshall, Hamilton, Kent; C. Scribner's Sons. [Sept. 1896]. T.4,688. 18 cm. 2s 6d. Light green cloth, gilt lettering, dark green wreath and harp designs.

1896.7 LIZZIE JOYCE TOMLINSON. *A Bit of Humanity. (A Tale).* The Leadenhall Press; Simpkin, Marshall, Hamilton, Kent; C. Scribner's Sons. [Oct.] 1896. T.4,691. 18 cm. 3s 6d. Beige cloth, title with ornamental "B" and "H," author's name, leafy vignette, and bottom right corner decoration in black.

1896.8 MRS. ARTHUR [GEORGIE EVELYN CAVE FRANCE] GASKIN. *Horn-Book Jingles.* The Leadenhall Press; Simpkin, Marshall; C. Scribner's Sons. 1896–1897 [Nov. 1896]. No job number. 22 cm. 3s 6d. Green cloth, illustration and lettering in dark blue. Printed on one side only. Each leaf illustrated, hand-lettered and initialed "GECG" (Georgie Evelyn Cave Gaskin).

1896.9 PHIL [PHILIP WILLIAM] MAY. *Phil May's Gutter-snipes: 50 Original Sketches in Pen & Ink.*

a. First edition: The Leadenhall Press. [Nov.] 1896. No job number. 28 cm. 1,050 copies, 3s 6d. Green ribbed cloth, hand-lettering and illustration in gilt. "The impressions herein are extra carefully printed as proofs on fine paper." Copyright 1896 in the United States of America by the Macmillan Company (verso of t.p.).

b. Popular edition: [Nov.] 1896. 2s 6d. Illustrated stiff brown wrappers. Printed on thinner paper. Stickphast ad tipped in.

1896.10 H. [HENRY] JAMYN BROOKS. *The Mind or the Spiritual Part of Life.* The Leadenhall Press; Simpkin, Marshall, Hamilton, Kent; C. Scribner's Sons.

1896. No job number. 20 cm. 2s 6d. Gray wrappers, lettering and small fleuron in black.

1897.1 PHIL [PHILIP WILLIAM] MAY. *Phil May's A B C: Fifty-Two Original Designs Forming Two Humorous Alphabets from A to Z.*

a. First edition: The Leadenhall Press. [Mar.] 1897. No job number. 29 cm. 1,050 copies, 6s. Green ribbed cloth, hand-lettering and illustration in gilt. "The impressions herein are extra carefully printed as proofs on fine paper." Printed on rectos only. Copyright 1896 in the United States of America by the Macmillan Company (verso of t.p.)

b. Popular edition: [Oct.] 1897. 2s 6d. Illustrated stiff red wrappers. Printed on thinner paper.

1897.2 CHARLES JAMES SCOTTER. *Froggy; or, My Lord Mayor. A Story of the Trials of Office.* The Leadenhall Press; Simpkin, Marshall, Hamilton, Kent; C. Scribner's Sons. [Oct. 1897]. T.4,729. 19 cm. 3s 6d. Green cloth, lettering and decorative lily pad with two flowers in black.

1898.1 EDMOND DEMOLINS. *Anglo-Saxon Superiority: To What It Is Due ("a Quoi Tient La Supériorité Des Anglo-Saxons").*

a. First edition in English: The Leadenhall Press; Simpkin, Marshall, Hamilton, Kent; C. Scribner's Sons. [Sept.] 1898. T.4,735. 21 cm. Cream cloth, title in black. Translated by Louis Bert. Lavigne from the 10th French edition. Frontis map.

b. First popular edition: 1920. 21 cm. Brown wrappers printed in black.

1898.2 WALTER GEDDE. *A Booke of Sundry Draughtes: Principaly Serving for Glasiers: And Not Impertinent for Plasterers, and Gardiners: Be Sides Sundry Other Professions. Whereunto Is Annexed the Manner How to Anniel in Glas: And Also the True Forme of the Fornace, and the Secretes Thereof.* The Leadenhall Press; Simpkin, Marshall, Hamilton, Kent; C. Scribner's Sons. [Sept.] 1898. T.4,738. 26 cm. 6s. Vellum parchment, lettering in black and gilt, with four fore-edge leather thongs. Edited by H. (Henry) Shaw. Facsimile of: London, Printed in Shoolane, at the signe of the Faulcon, by Walter Dight. 1615.

1898.3 EDWARD KENT. *That Headstrong Boy: A Freak of His and What Came of It.* The Leadenhall Press; Simpkin, Marshall, Hamilton, Kent; C. Scribner's Sons. [Sept.] 1898. T.4,739. 20 cm. 6s. Red cloth, lettering and decoration in gilt and blind.

1898.4 MARK MUNDY. *The Vagaries of To-day.* The Leadenhall Press; Simpkin, Marshall, Hamilton, Kent; C. Scribner's Sons. [Sept. 1898]. T.4,736. 19 cm. 3s 6d. Light tan cloth, lettering and circular decoration with branching swirls in dark brown.

1898.5 MARIE PETERSEN. *The Princess Ilse: A Legend of the Harz Mountains.* The Leadenhall Press. [Sept. 1898]. T.4,732. 19 cm. 2s 6d. Scarlet cloth, lettering in gilt and black. Translated from the German by A. M. Deane.

1898.6 ANDREW WHITE TUER. *Pages and Pictures from Forgotten Children's Books.*

a. Regular issue: The Leadenhall Press; Simpkin, Marshall, Hamilton, Kent; C. Scribner's Sons. 1898–99 [Sept. 1898]. No job number. 19 cm. 6s. Navy blue cloth, title and vignette in gilt, yellow silk page marker, a square of Dutch paper mounted to page 8. "Brought Together and Introduced to the Reader by Andrew W. Tuer. Four Hundred Illustrations." Two inserted slips: a statement of first edition and a notice for the large paper issue.

b. Large paper issue: 24 cm. 112 copies, 21s. Printed on thicker and finer paper, numbered and signed by the author. Limitation slip at front.

Note: republished by: B. Blom (New York) in 1968; Singing Tree Press (Detroit) in 1969; Bracken Books (London) in 1986.

1898.7 *A Bygone Holborn.* The Leadenhall Press. 1898. C.2,111. Obl. 14 x 21.5 cm. 5,000 copies. Quarter parchment and gray paper boards, lettering and Buchanan crest in gilt. Illustrated. A history of the Holborn district of London, relating to the James Buchanan and Black Swan distilleries. (Copies located: CL, private collection.)

1898.8 WALTER NOEL HARTLEY. *Index to the Published Researches and Original Papers.* Printed at the Leadenhall Press. [1898?]. 2 vols. 23 cm. Includes articles from the *Philosophical Transactions of the Royal Society, Proceedings of the Royal Society, and Journal of the Chemical Society,* from 1873-1888. (Copy located: presentation copy to Edinburgh University Library.)

1899.1 KARL PETERS. *King Solomon's Golden Ophir: A Research into the Most Ancient Gold Production in History.* The Leadenhall Press; Simpkin, Marshall, Hamilton, Kent; C. Scribner's Sons. [Jan.] 1899. 19 cm. 2s 6d. Brown cloth, lettering in gilt. Translation from *Das goldene Ophir Salomo's,* by F. Karuth.

1899.2 PHIL [PHILIP WILLIAM] MAY. *Fifty Hitherto Unpublished Pen-and-Ink Sketches.* The Leadenhall Press. [Oct. 1899]. No job number. 20 cm. 1s. Black stiff wrappers, lettering in red. Printed on rectos only. "Mr. Phil May's original pen-and-ink drawings in this book, and others by the same gifted artist, are for sale separately. Apply to the Publishers." — pink slip tipped in after t.p.

1899.3 BASIL DAVIES AND NORMAN PRESCOTT. *The Vicar's Pups. In a Few Yelps and a Couple of Growls.* The Leadenhall Press; Simpkin, Marshall, Hamilton, Kent; C. Scribner's Sons. [Nov. 1899]. T.4,744. 20 cm. 3s 6d. Illustrated by Norman Prescott-Davies. Quarter cream cloth, pale blue-gray boards, lettering and design in black and gilt.

1899.4   EDWARD KENT. *A Lawful Crime: A Story of To-day.* The Leadenhall Press; Simpkin, Marshall, Hamilton, Kent; C. Scribner's Sons. [Nov.] 1899. T.4,747. 20 cm. 6s. Gray cloth, lettering and decoration in black. Silhouette headpiece and tailpiece illustrations.

1899.5   ANDREW WHITE TUER. *Stories from Old-Fashioned Children's Books.* The Leadenhall Press; Simpkin, Marshall, Hamilton, Kent; C. Scribner's Sons. 1899–1900. [Nov. 1899]. No job number. 19 cm. 6s. Navy blue cloth, lettering and vignette in gilt; cream dust jacket lettered in black. "Brought together and introduced to the reader by Andrew W. Tuer, F.S.A.; adorned with 250 amusing cuts."

Note: republished by: Singing Tree Press (Detroit) in 1968; Evelyn, Adams, MacKay (London) for Social Documents, Ltd., in 1969; Augustus M. Kelley (New York) in 1969; Bracken Books (London) in 1985.

1899.6   [MRS. ELIZABETH TURNER]. *The Daisy; or, Cautionary Stories in Verse. 1807.* The Leadenhall Press; Simpkin, Marshall, Hamilton, Kent; C. Scribner's Sons. [Nov.] 1899. No job number. 13 cm. 1s. Colored illustrated collage paper wrappers over thin card, printed paper labels on both covers. Illustrated Shilling Series of Forgotten Children's Books, no. 1. A facsimile reprint of the anonymous edition published by John Harris and Crosby and Co. in 1807.

1899.7   ———. *The Cowslip, or, More Cautionary Stories, in Verse. 1811.* The Leadenhall Press; Simpkin, Marshall, Hamilton, Kent; C. Scribner's Sons. [Nov. 1899]. No job number. 13 cm. 1s. Colored illustrated paper wrappers over thin card, printed paper labels on both covers. Illustrated Shilling Series of Forgotten Children's Books, no. 2. A facsimile reprint of the J. Harris edition of 1811, with 30 engravings by Samuel Williams. "By the author of that much-admired little work, entitled the Daisy" —title page.

1899.8   "JOHN-THE-GIANT-KILLER." *Food for the Mind: or, a New Riddle-Book. 1778.* The Leadenhall Press; C. Scribner's Sons. [Nov. 1899]. No job number. 13 cm. 1s. Colored illustrated paper wrappers over thin card, printed paper labels on both covers. Illustrated Shilling Series of Forgotten Children's Books, no. 3. A facsimile reprint of the original edition published by T. Carnan and F. Newbery, London, 1778.

1899.9   *The History of Little Goody Two Shoes, otherwise called, Mrs. Margery Two Shoes.* The Leadenhall Press. [1899?]. No job number. 11 cm. Colored illustrated paper wrappers over thin card, printed paper labels on both covers. Illustrated Shilling Series of Forgotten Children's Books, (no. 4?). (Copy located: Lilly, lacking the title page.)[42]

---

42. Bound in the same style as the other books in the series. Publisher's lists say: "It is intended to continue this Illustrated Shilling Series of Forgotten Children's Books. Other volumes are in preparation." No titles noted in the series after no. 3 with the possible exception of this singular copy of this title.

1899.10 [HENRY J. PFUNGST, F.S.A.]. *Descriptive Catalogue of a Small Collection Principally of Xvth and Xvith Century Bronzes.* [The Leadenhall Press]. [1899]. 33 cm. 20 copies. Pamphlet. Illustrations of 50 figures. Collection of Henry Joseph Pfungst (subsequently acquired by J. Pierpoint Morgan in 1901).

1899.11 SIR HAROLD EDWIN BOULTON, BART. *The Ballad of Thyra Lee.* Leadenhall Press. [1899]. 4 p. leaflet. Price unknown. Poetry.[43]

1900.1 EDMOND DEMOLINS. *Boers or English: Who Are in the Right?: Being the English Translation of "Boers et Anglais: où est le Droit?"* The Leadenhall Press; Simpkin, Marshall, Hamilton, Kent; C. Scribner's Sons. [Jan.] 1900. 20 cm. 1s. Pamphlet.

1900.2 JAMES FRANKLIN FULLER. *Billy. A Sketch for "the New Boy" by an Old Boy.* The Leadenhall Press; Simpkin, Marshall; Hamilton, Kent; C. Scribner's Sons. [Feb. 1900]. T.4,751. 20 cm. 3s 6d. Blue cloth, lettering in white and gilt.

1900.3 W. B. GILPIN. *Love, Sport, and a Double Event.* The Leadenhall Press; Simpkin, Marshall, Hamilton, Kent; C. Scribner's Sons. [Mar.] 1900. T.4,748. 20 cm. 3s 6d. Green cloth, lettering and sketch of two horses' heads in black.

1900.4 H. O. BLAKER. *The Principles of Warfare.* The Leadenhall Press; Simpkin, Marshall, Hamilton, Kent; C. Scribner's Sons. [June] 1900. T.4,761. 18.5 cm. 1s. Beige wrappers, titling in burgundy.

1900.5 MAX VON POCHHAMMER. *Six Stories.* The Leadenhall Press; Simpkin, Marshall, Hamilton, Kent; C. Scribner's Sons. [June 1900]. No job number. 18 cm. 3s 6d. Gray spine, white boards, lettering in burgundy. Narrated by Max von Pochhammer. With an appreciation by Evelyn Everett Green. Illustrations by Ambrose Dudley.

1900.6 CHARLES JAMES FÈRET. *Fulham, Old and New: Being an Exhaustive History of the Ancient Parish of Fulham.* Leadenhall Press; Simpkin, Marshall, Hamilton, Kent; C. Scribner's Sons. [July] 1900. T.4,749. 3 vols. 29 cm. 63s. Dark green imitation leather, lettering and parish seal in gilt. Title vignettes, nearly 500 illustrations, folding maps, plans.

1900.7 ALFRED BRAME. *The India General Steam Navigation Company, Limited.* The Leadenhall Press. 1900. T.4,758. 20 cm. Cloth, illustrations.

1900.8 JOHN MAURICE COPPEN. *The Coppyns of Kent 1300 to 1800.* Privately printed at the Leadenhall Press. 1900. E.2,345. 26 cm. Full vellum, titling and decorative border in gilt, leather label on spine.

1900.9 JOHN H. DARBY. *Report of Mr John H. Darby, M.Inst.C.E., on the Blythe River Iron Mines.*

---

43. Later turned into a dramatic scena with music composed by Reginald Somerville.

a. First edition: The Leadenhall Press. [1900]. 29 cm. Pamphlet.

b. Second edition: 1902. 25 cm. Pamphlet. "Text of report on mine in Tasmania, dated 7 December 1900, with evaluation of report by W. H. Twelvetrees. Text of report on mine in Tasmania, dated 5 June 1902, with evaluation of report by W. H. Twelvetrees."

1900.10   WILLIAM H. HORROCKS. *The Life of Sir Astley Cooper*. The Leadenhall Press. 1900. 21 cm. Pamphlet. Presidential address to the Bradford Medico-Surgical Society, 1899.

1900.11   FRANCIS W. MOORE. *Lily, of the Valley: A Play, in Three Acts*. The Leadenhall Press. [ca. 1900–1910].[44] 20 cm. "Printed as manuscript. The property of the author." Imprint from verso of title page. (Copy located: Bodleian.)

1901.1   ESTER DALE. *Madame Marie, Singer*. The Leadenhall Press; Simpkin, Marshall, Hamilton, Kent; C. Scribner's Sons. [Mar. 1901]. No job number. 20 cm. 3s 6d. Pink cloth, lettering in gilt.

1901.2   "LORD ADOLPHUS FITZDOODLE." *The Fitzdoodle Memoirs*. The Leadenhall Press. [Mar. 1901]. 19 cm. 1s. Printed paper covers.

1901.3   REV. SYDNEY [GWENFFRWD] MOSTYN. *Miss Spinney*. The Leadenhall Press; Simpkin, Marshall, Hamilton, Kent; C. Scribner's Sons. 1900 [Mar. 1901]. T.4,763. 18 cm. 2s 6d. A novel.

1901.4   LADY FLORENCE [DOUGLAS] DIXIE. *The Songs of a Child, and Other Poems by "Darling." Part I.*

a. Popular edition: The Leadenhall Press; Simpkin & Marshall, Hamilton, Kent; C. Scribner's Sons. [Dec. 1901]. T.4,783. 19 cm. 2s 6d. Tan wrappers, decorative title in blue, facsimile signature: "Florence Douglas," lettering, and fleurons in black, with decoration of heart, crown, and wings in red and gilt at upper left. Announcement of Part II at back.

b. Edition de Luxe: Vellum, 7s 6d.

c. Second edition: [Feb. 1902]. 2s 6d.

Third edition: see checklist 1903.4.

1901.5   CHARLOTTE THORPE. *The Children's London*.

a. Regular edition: Leadenhall Press; Simpkin, Marshall, Hamilton, Kent; C. Scribner's Sons. [Nov. 1901]. T.4,760. 26 cm. 10s 6d. Gray cloth spine, burgundy cloth bevelled boards, lettering and decorations in gilt. Illustrations by William Luker Jr.

b. Large paper edition: 29 cm. 250 copies, price unknown.

---

44. Year range from Bodleian. I have not been able to establish the exact year of publication.

1901.6　EDWARD TESCHEMACHER. *Songs of the Morning. Lyrics for Music.* The Leadenhall Press; Simpkin, Marshall, Hamilton, Adams; C. Scribner's Sons. [1901]. T.4,779. 20 cm. 2s 6d. Gray cloth, title in gilt, each word on its own line underlined in gilt, with the periods justifying the title block.

1902.1　COLIN SMITH, WRITER ON BRIDGE. *Bridge Condensed.* The Leadenhall Press; Simpkin, Marshall, Hamilton, Kent; C. Scribner's Sons. [Jan.] 1902. 13.5 cm. 1s. Blue paper wrappers with dark blue title and rules.

1902.2　PHILIP SIDNEY, F.R. HIST. SOC. [ed.]. *Abou-Hamed: Being Some Account of Its Battle and Its Ghost Story.* The Leadenhall Press. [June 1902]. No job number. 19 cm. 2s 6d. Dark blue-green cloth, title in gilt, border rule in blind. With a memoir of Major Sidney.

1902.3　FREDERICK HITCHIN-KEMP. *A General History of the Kemp and Kempe Families of Great Britain and Her Colonies: With Arms, Pedigrees, Portraits, Illustrations of Seats, Foundations, Chantries, Monuments, Documents, Old Jewels, Curios, Etc.* The Leadenhall Press; C. Scribner's Sons. [Oct. 1902]. T.4,753. 6 parts in 1 vol. 29 cm. 42s. Red cloth, lettering and coat of arms in gilt. Facsimiles, genealogical tables, portraits. With a Supplement "privately printed for subscribers."

1902.4　FREDERICK HITCHIN-KEMP. *Ye Legende of Ye Kempes.* Leadenhall Press. [1902]. Obl. pamphlet. A poem. (Copy located: BL.)

1903.1　LADY FLORENCE DIXIE. *The Story of Ijain, or, the Evolution of a Mind.*

　　　　a. First edition: The Leadenhall Press; Simpkin, Marshall, Hamilton, Kent; C. Scribner's Sons. [Jan. 1903]. T.4,801. 20 cm. 5s. Green or red cloth, lettering in gilt. Color frontis portrait of the author at nineteen. With an epilogue by "Saladin" (William Stewart Ross, Secularist). Written over a period of twenty-five years and first published in installments in *The Agnostic Journal,* beginning May 3, 1902.

　　　　b. Second edition: [June 1903]. 4s.

1903.2　N. B. GAZDER. *Streamlets from the Fount of Poesy.* The Leadenhall Press; C. Scribner's Sons. [Mar. 1903]. 20 cm. 3s 6d.

1903.3　LADY FLORENCE [DOUGLAS] DIXIE. *Isola, or the Disinherited: A Revolt for Woman and All the Disinherited.*

　　　　a. The Leadenhall Press; C. Scribner's Sons. [June 1903]. T.4,783. 19 cm. 3s 6d. Dark blue cloth, lettering in silver. Verse drama. "With remarks thereon by George Jacob Holyoake." Date attributed by Bodleian. Written in 1877, first published in serial form in *Young Oxford* in 1902.

　　　　b. Second edition: [1903 or 1904]. 3s 6d.

1903.4   LADY FLORENCE [DOUGLAS] DIXIE. *Part I and Part II of The Songs of a Child and Other Writings by "Darling."* The Leadenhall Press; Simpkin & Marshall; C. Scribner's Sons. [1903]. T.4,788. 2 parts in 1 vol.: third edition of Part I, first edition of Part II. 19 cm. 5s. White boards, facsimile signature: "Florence Douglas," decorative title, lettering, and fleurons in gilt, decoration of heart, crown, and wings in red and gilt at upper left. Edited by G. L. D.

1903.5   HERBERT DE ROUGEMENT. *A Century of Lloyd's Patriotic Fund, 1803–1903.*

a. First edition: Printed at the Leadenhall Press. [1903]. 18 cm. White wrappers with black title underlined in red.

b. Second issue: [1914] as *A history of Lloyd's Patriotic Fund, from its foundation in 1803.* 20 cm. Printed for the Committee for Managing the Patriotic Fund.

1904.1   LADY FLORENCE DIXIE. *Eilabelle; or, the Redeemed. A Drama.* The Leadenhall Press; Simpkin, Marshall, Hamilton, Kent; C. Scribner's Sons. 1904. 20 cm. 3s 6d. Frontis portrait of the author as war correspondent of the *Morning Post.*

1904.2   J. WOOD. *Imaginary Conversations of Three White-Letter Days in the Anglo-Saxon Cloisters.* The Leadenhall Press. 1904. T.4,805. 20 cm. 300 copies. Price unknown. Green linen, lettering in gilt. A revised edition of *Voices of the Past.*

1905.1   FREDERICK PAGE BARTON. *Bridge Simplified . . . with Remarks on the New Laws Ab Ovo Usque ad Mala.* The Leadenhall Press. [Jan.] N.2,010. 1905. 16 cm. 2s 6d. Red cloth.

1905.2   STEPHEN SYEDS [MRS. GRAIN]. *Mohammed Aben Alamar, or, the Invention of the Moorish Arch: A Legend.* The Leadenhall Press; C. Scribner's Sons. 1905. No job number. 19 cm. Green boards, lettering and decoration in gilt. Illustrations by M. Alison Atkins. Title within decorative red and black architectural borders. Printed in red and black. (Copy in private collection inscribed by "Mrs. Grain," with a line through "Stephen Syeds" on title page, and "Mrs. Grain" substituted.)

1905.3   R. I. [REGINALD ILLINGWORTH] WOODHOUSE. *A Brief Guide to Merstham Parish Church, Surrey.* The Leadenhall Press. 1905. 25 cm. Pamphlet. Compiled by the Rev. R. I. Woodhouse. Illustrated.

1909.1   [LEADENHALL PRESS LIMITED]. *Types and Types of Beauty from the Leadenhall Press.* The Leadenhall Press. [ca. 1909]. 22 cm. 1s. Gray-blue paper wrappers with type and decorations printed in black and brown. Type specimens. (Later issued with "50 Leadenhall Street" struck out and Southwark address stamped below.)

1909.2   [LEADENHALL PRESS, LIMITED]. *Estimate of the Numbers Engaged in the Trades and Professions in the United Kingdom and Colonies.*

a. First edition: The Leadenhall Press. [1909]. 18 cm.

b. Revised edition: [1919].

1911.1   J. J. [JOHN JAMES] PILLEY. *The Progress Book: An Illustrated Register of Development from Birth Till Coming of Age and After.*

a. First edition: The Leadenhall Press; Simpkin, Marshall. [June] 1911. No job number. 21 cm. Blue cloth, title in gilt. Sections for: weight, birth and baptismal registration, vaccination, teeth, mental progress, educational record, religious progress, recreation, annual autograph, fingerprints, and photographs. With tables on average heights and weights for males and females.

b. Revised, enlarged edition: [Nov.] 1913. "Specially printed for Mellin's Food, Limited" —t.p.; with Mellin's Food ads on most versos. Green cloth, upper cover ruled in blind and lettered in gilt. Reissued in 1923 and 1925.

1913.1   JOHN GALSWORTHY. *The Slaughter of Animals for Food.*

a. First edition: RSPCA and the Council of Justice to Animals; The Leadenhall Press Ltd. [inside back cover]. [1913]. No job number. 22 cm. 1d. White wrappers, lettering in black with red rules. Reprinted from *The Daily Mail*. Plus: "A claim on humanity. The Meat Trade and Mr. Galsworthy; a rejoinder.—The Meat Trade and its Defence; a criticism, by A. Lee. (Lee of Fareham, Arthur Hamilton Lee, Viscount). Issued by the Royal Society for the Prevention of Cruelty to Animals and the Council of Justice to Animals.

b. Second edition: Republished in 1922, with RSPCA only on cover, and first paragraph of p. 2: "The thing is horrible, but is it necessary?" omitted.

A Selection of Examples in Color, 1869-1905

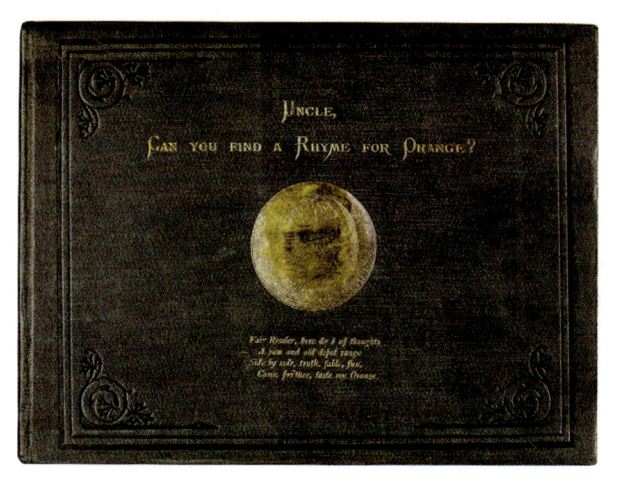

Field & Tuer's first book as primary publisher. Checklist 1869.1.
(Courtesy, Trustees of the National Library of Scotland.)

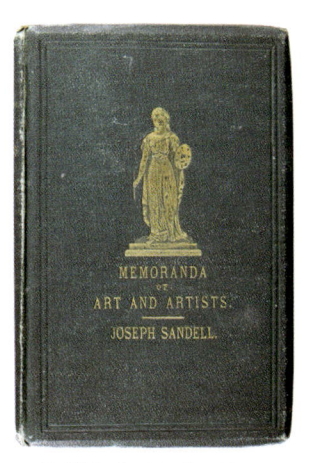

Published with Simpkin & Marshall. Checklist 1871.2.

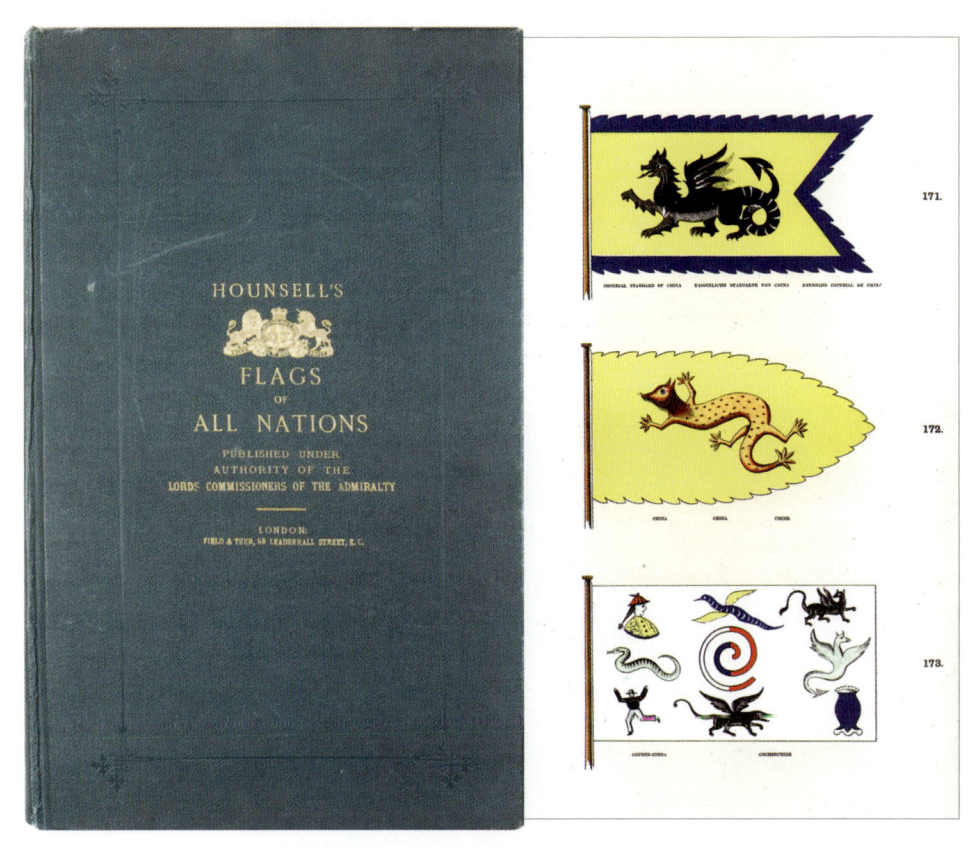

With 188 chromolithographed and tinted plates. Checklist 1873.2.
(Courtesy, Lilly Library, Indiana University, Bloomington, IN.)

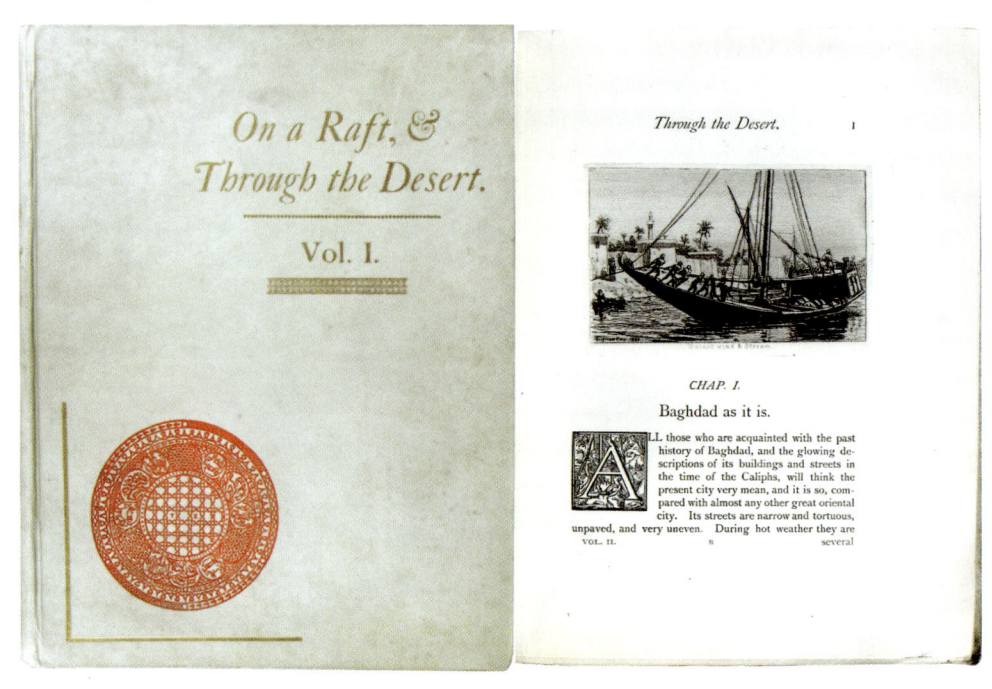

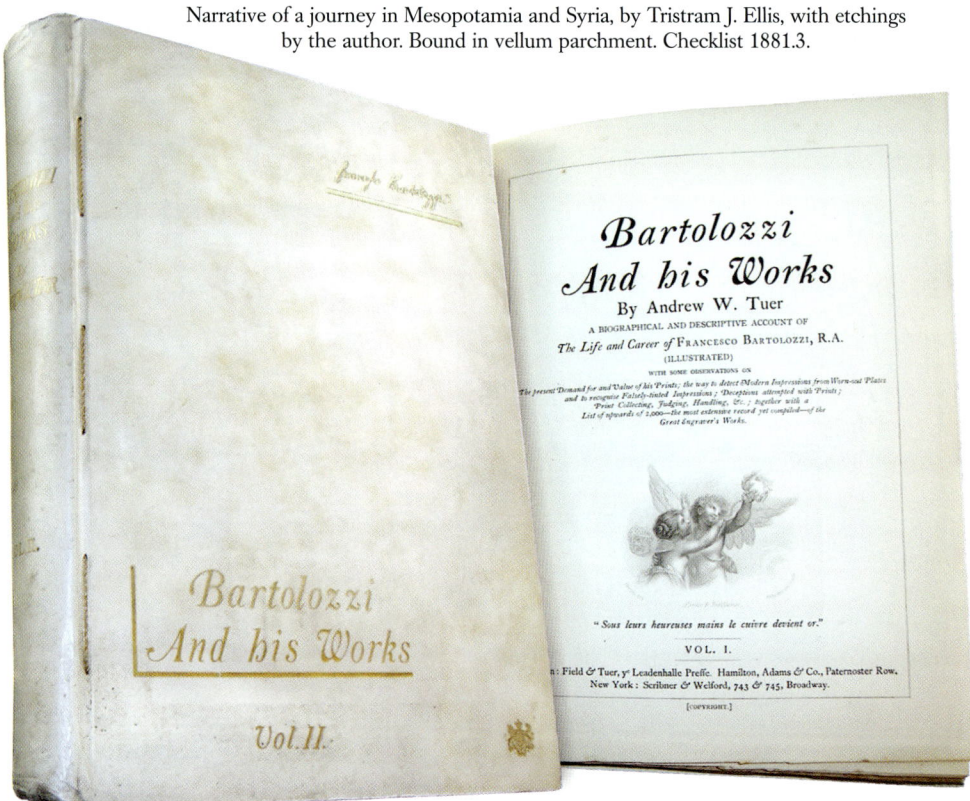

Narrative of a journey in Mesopotamia and Syria, by Tristram J. Ellis, with etchings by the author. Bound in vellum parchment. Checklist 1881.3.

First edition in two volumes, with a biography, illustrations, and a list of over 2000 engravings. Checklist 1882.1.

Chromolithographed plate from *Glass in the Old World* by Madeline Anne Wallace-Dunlop. Checklist 1882.8.

When Is Your Birthday? 12 designs and sonnets by Edwin J. Ellis, with suede slip-cover and box. Checklist 1883.12. (Courtesy, Trustees of the National Library of Scotland.)

With mounted illustrations and historiated initials in sepia. In folding box. Checklist 1883.14.

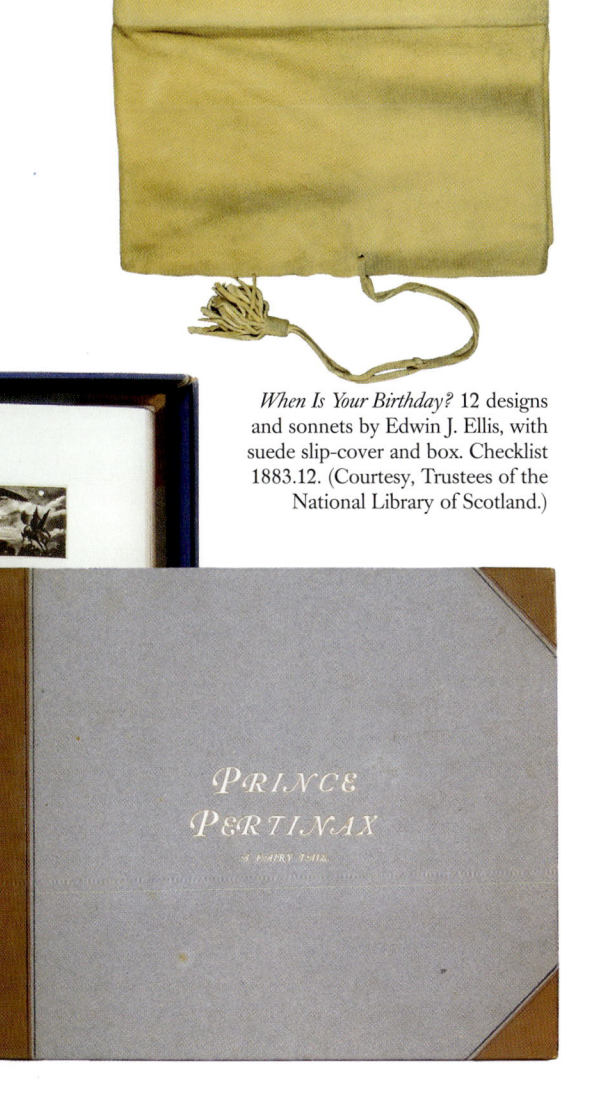

The three collections of old ballads and tales illustrated with woodcuts by Joseph Crawhall II.

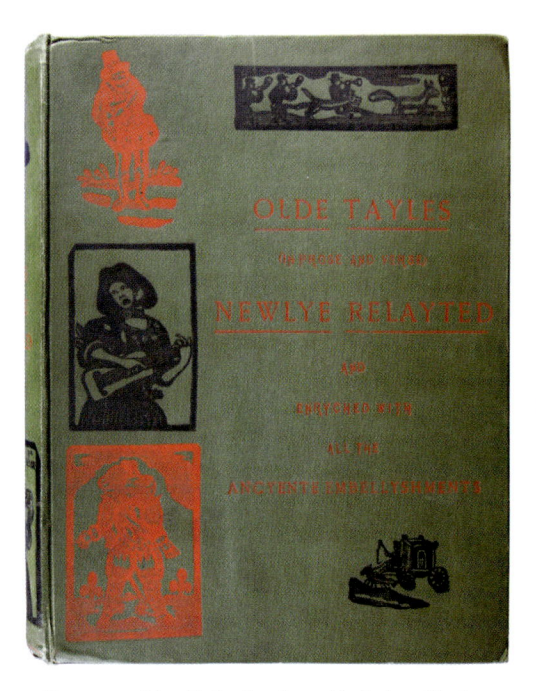

Fourteen of the 17 chapbooks and ballads, with the illustrations in black and white. Checklist 1883.4.

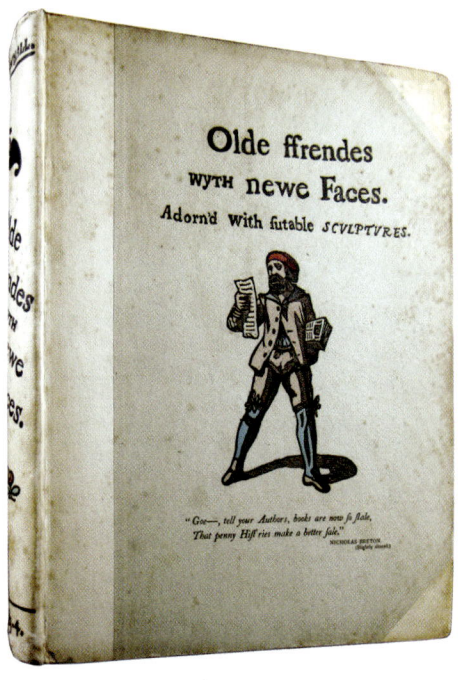

The companion volume to *Crawhall's Chap-book Chaplets*, containing nine ballads. Checklist 1884.5.

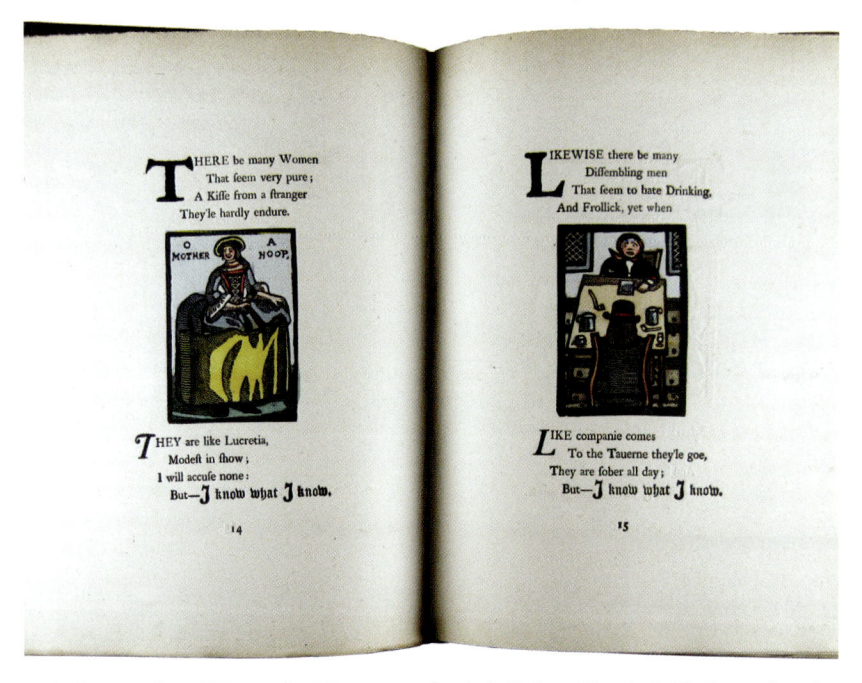

Left: pages from *I Know what I Know*, one of eight ballads in *Chap-book Chaplets*, each with its own colored wrappers. Checklist 1883.15. Right: printed dust wrapper for *Chap-Book Chaplets* (courtesy Richard Landon).

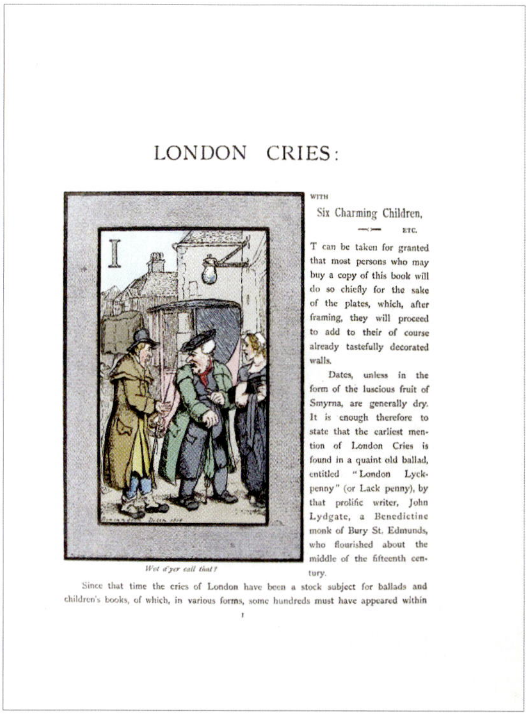

Page 1 of *London Cries,* with 15 hand-colored illustrations and six stipple engravings on plates. Checklist 1883.25.

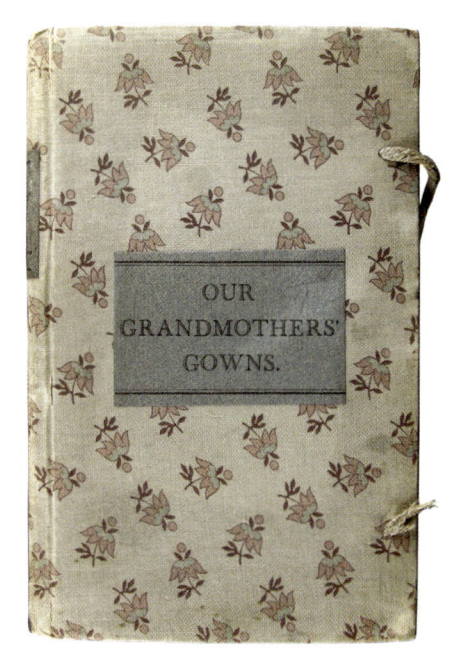

By Mrs. Alfred W. Hunt, with hand-colored illustrations by George Halkett. Bound in printed cloth. Checklist 1884.37.

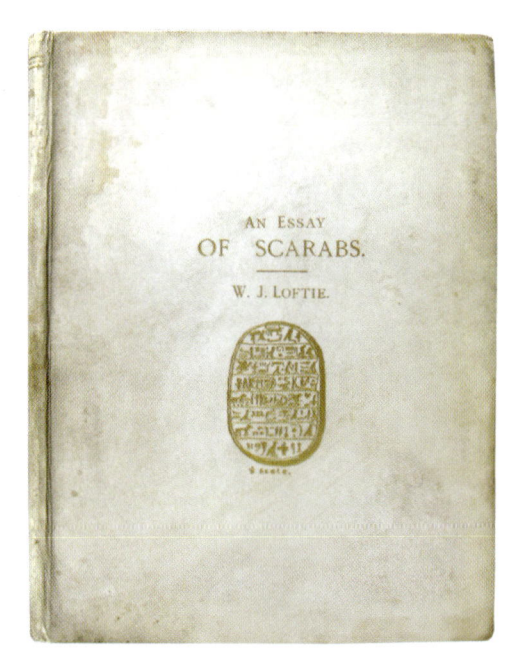

With the catalogue of a collection of Egyptian amulets, illustrated by W. M. Flinders Petrie. Checklist 1884.39.

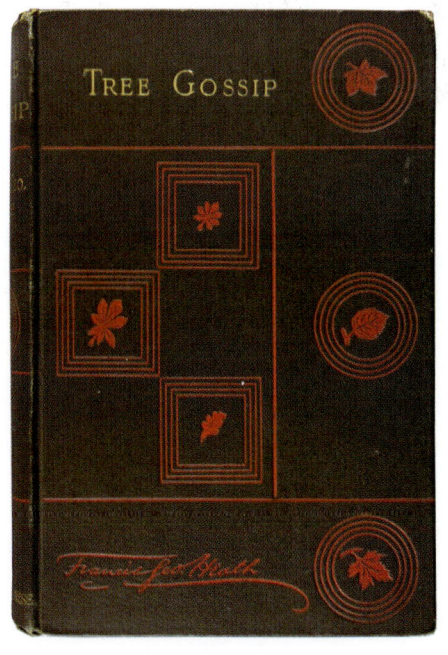

Sylvan facts and lore, by botanist Francis George Heath. Checklist 1885.5.

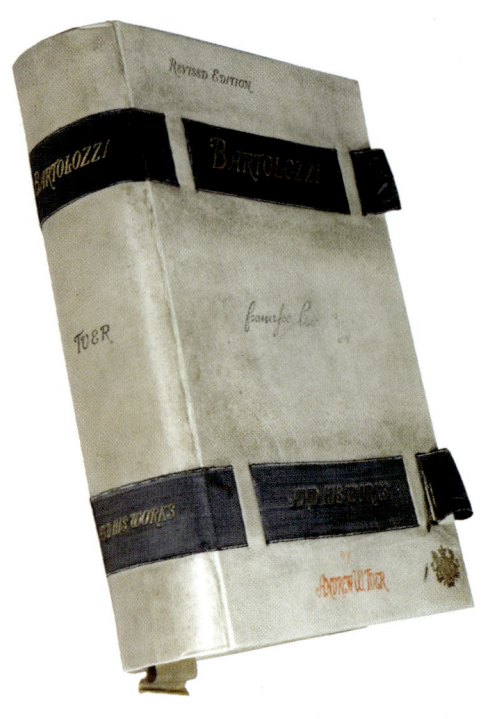

Bartolozzi and His Works, second edition in one volume, full vellum with silk bands. Checklist 1885.35. (Courtesy, Lilly Library, Indiana University, Bloomington, IN.)

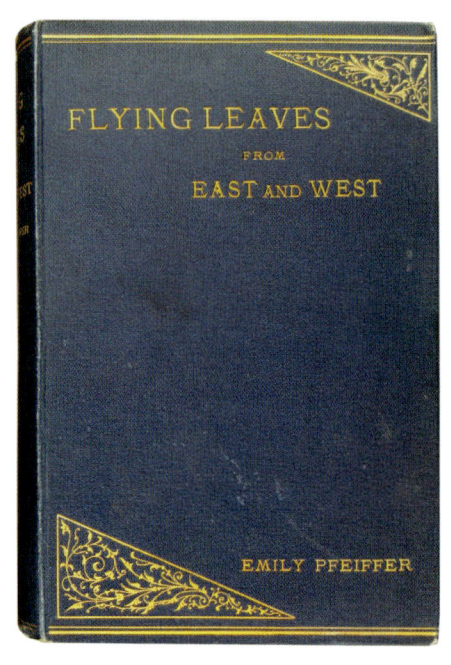

A book of travels in the Mediterranean, Near East, and America, by poet and feminist Emily Jane Pfeiffer. Checklist 1885.37.

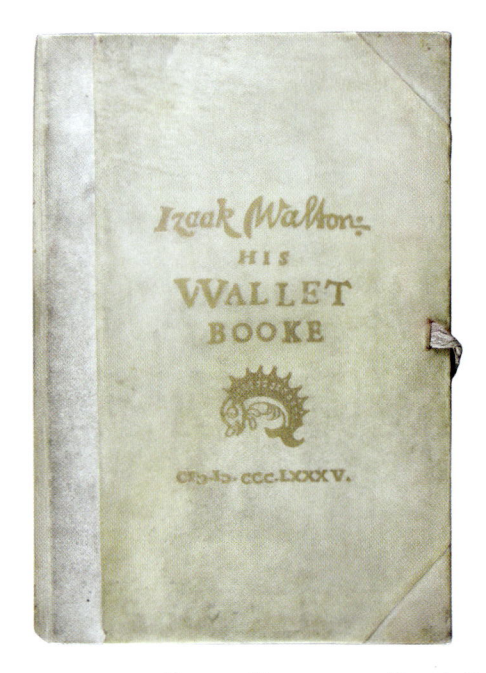

Upper and lower covers of Joseph Crawhall's *Izaak Walton, His Wallet Booke,* large paper edition bound in parchment and vellum. Checklist 1885.36.

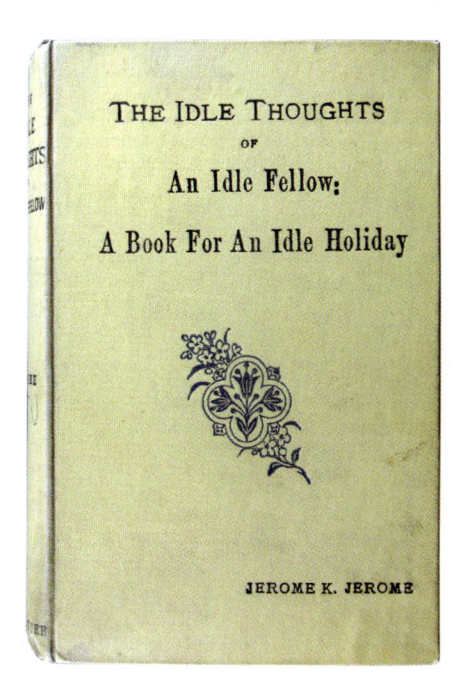

Jerome K. Jerome's second book "... sold like hotcakes," he recalled. Checklist 1886.9.

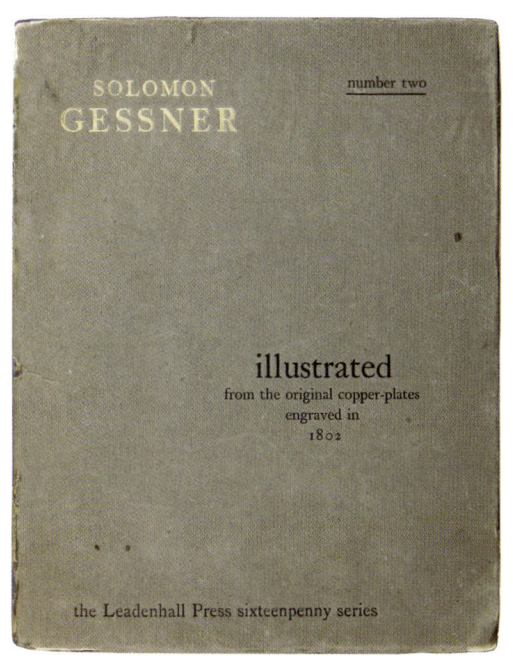

One of four books in the Sixteenpenny Series, with illustrations from original copperplates. Checklist 1886.12.

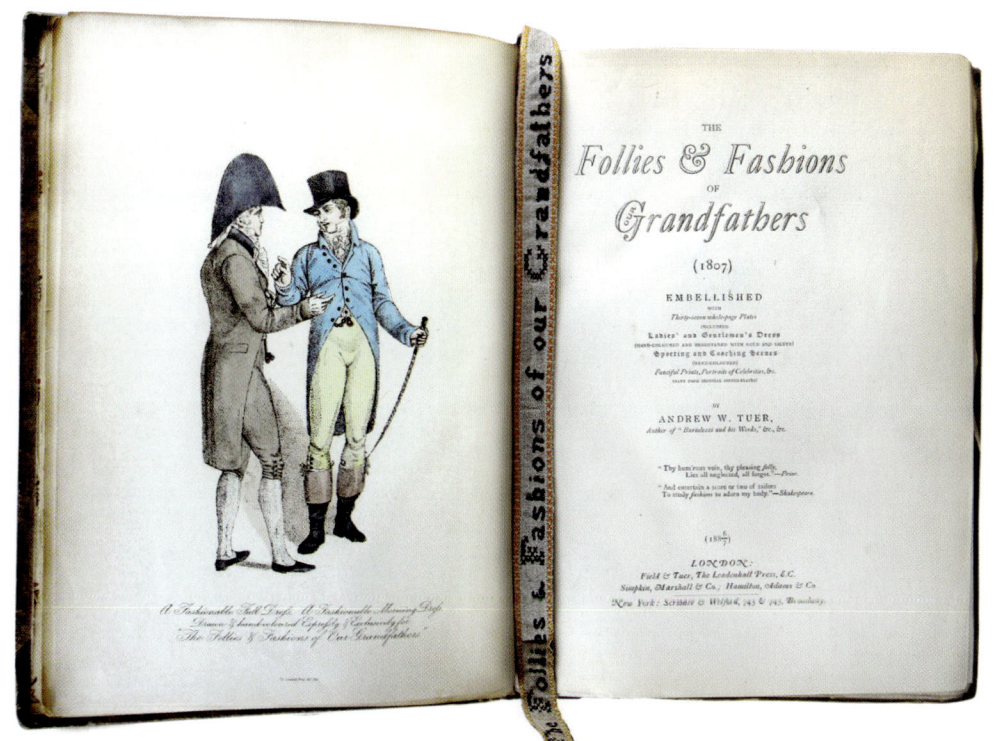

Hand-colored illustrations, and embroidered labels and page marker. The Special Large Paper edition consisted of three copies only. Checklist 1886.17.

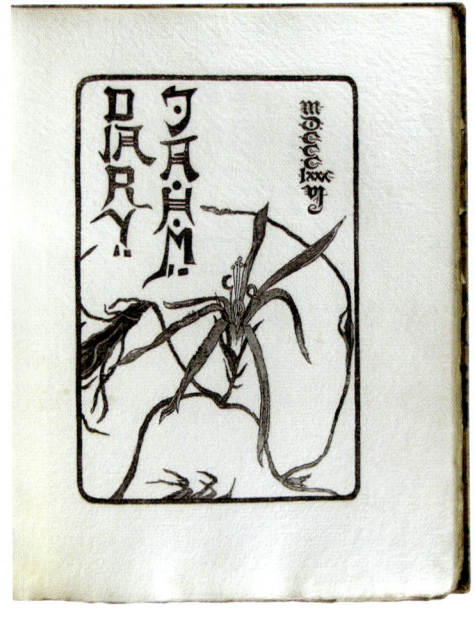

Diary J.A.H.M. by Jessie A. H. Muir, bound in Japanese-style velvet, printed on handmade paper, with a woodblock title page. Checklist 1886.24.

"Dedicated to the Brewers of the United Kingdom and all Who Value Honest Malt Liquor." Checklist 1886.22.

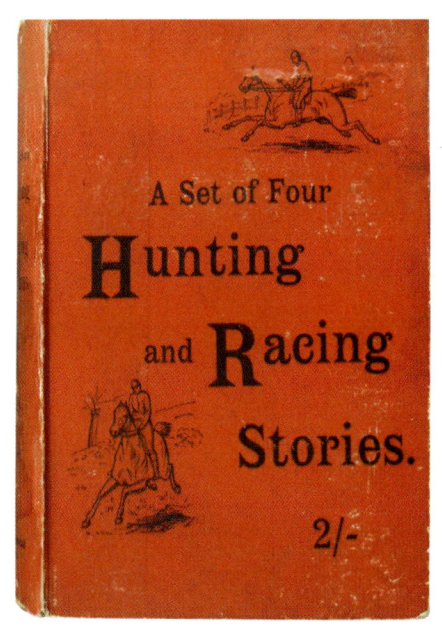

By W. B. Gilpin. Ad for Cooper Cooper & Co. Tea on lower cover. Checklist 1887.4.

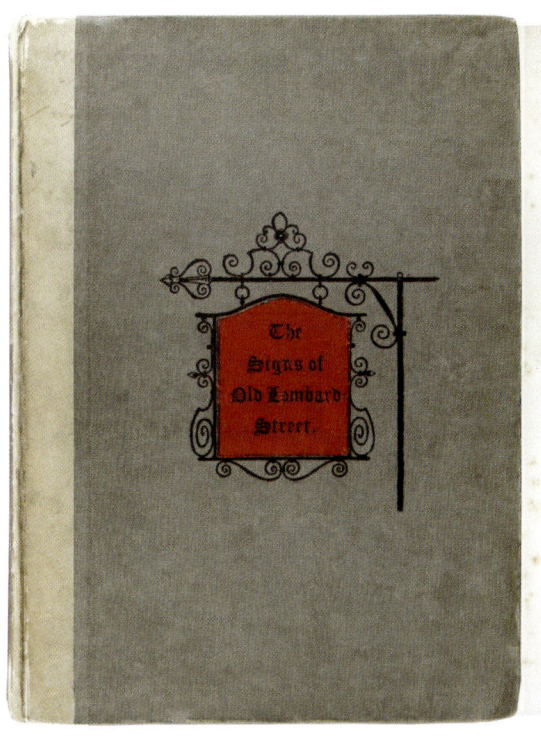

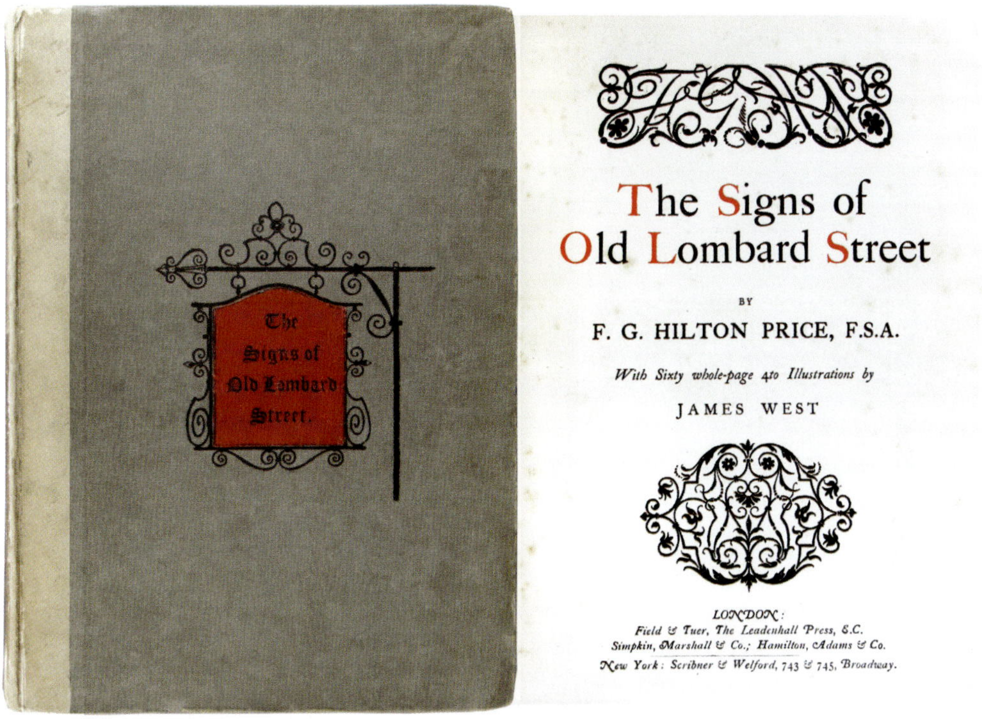

Descriptions and illustrations of 109 historic trade signs of the goldsmiths of old London. Checklist 1887.15.

From *The Gaping, Wide-mouthed, Waddling Frog*, with hand-colored illustrations. Price: one shilling. Checklist 1887.18.

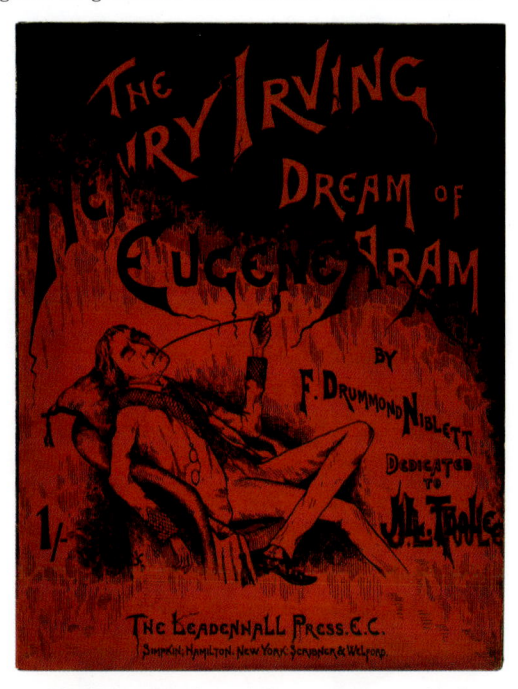

Blocked in "Mephistophilian sanguine on a black ground" (double impression of "J. L. Toole" by design). Checklist 1888.6.

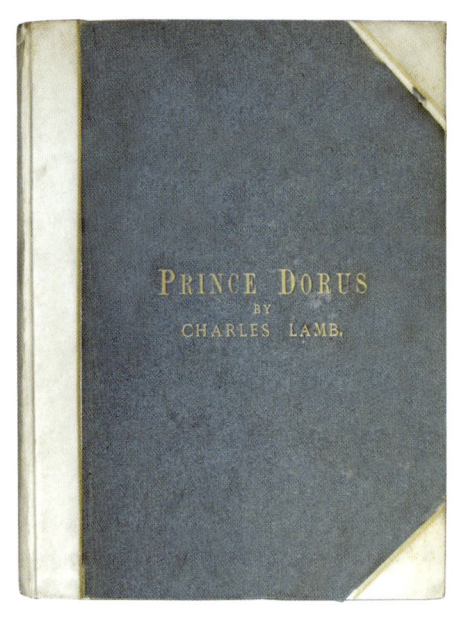

Proof copy issue, with nine hand-colored illustrations. Checklist 1889.10.

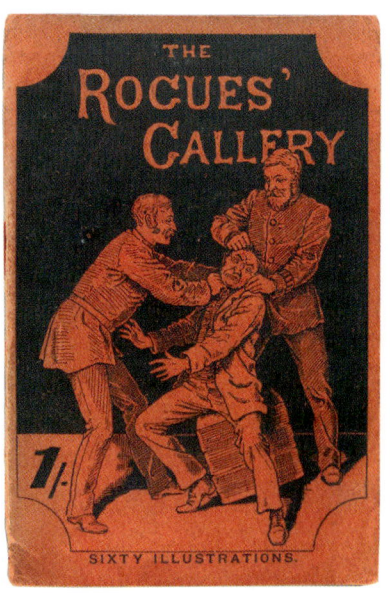

By Charles T. Clarkson and Joseph H. Richardson, illustrated by Harry Parkes. Checklist 1890.6.

Left: fore-edge painting by William Luker Jr., proof issue of *Kensington Picturesque & Historical*. Checklist 1888.21b.

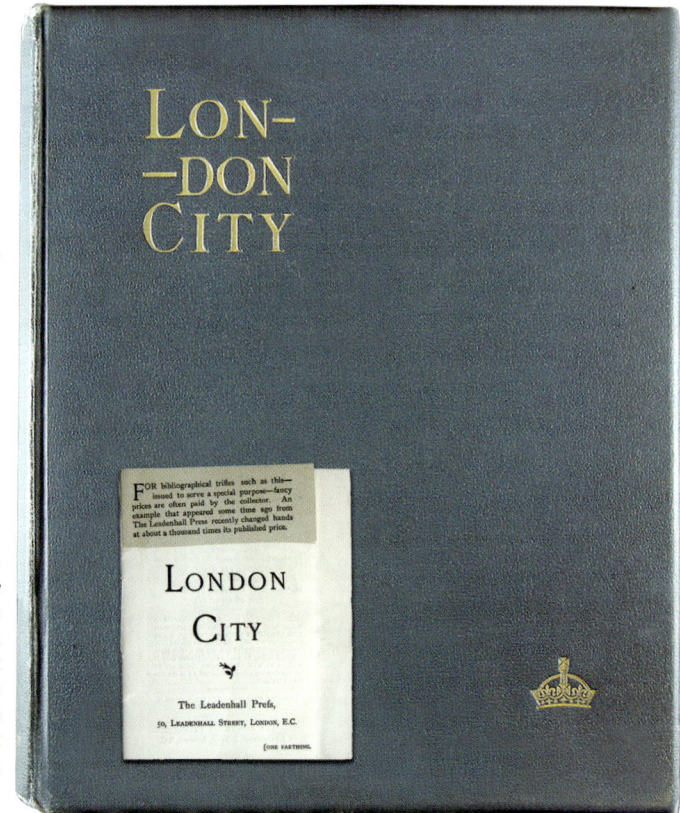

Right: *London City* (checklist 1891.2) with copyright pamphlet to secure title (checklist 1890.10).

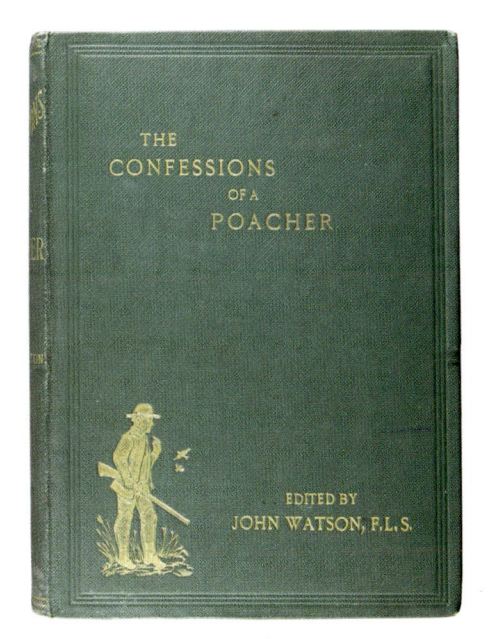

Illustrated by James West. First issue, followed by a cheap edition in illustrated wraps. Checklist 1890.27.

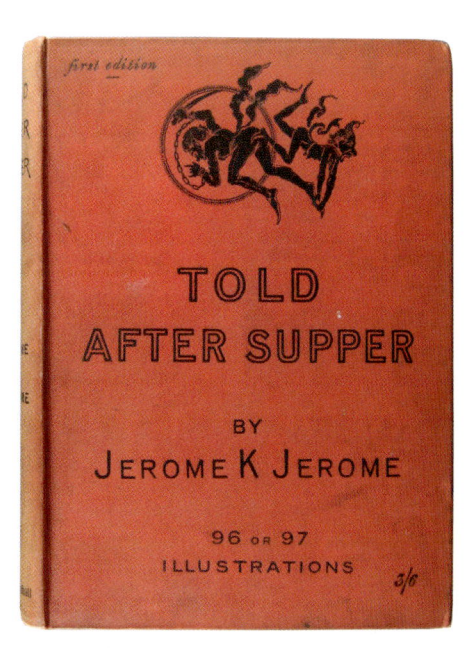

Printed in dark blue ink on light blue paper, with illustrations by Kenneth Skeaping (97, including cover). Jerome did not like the production. Checklist 1890.25.

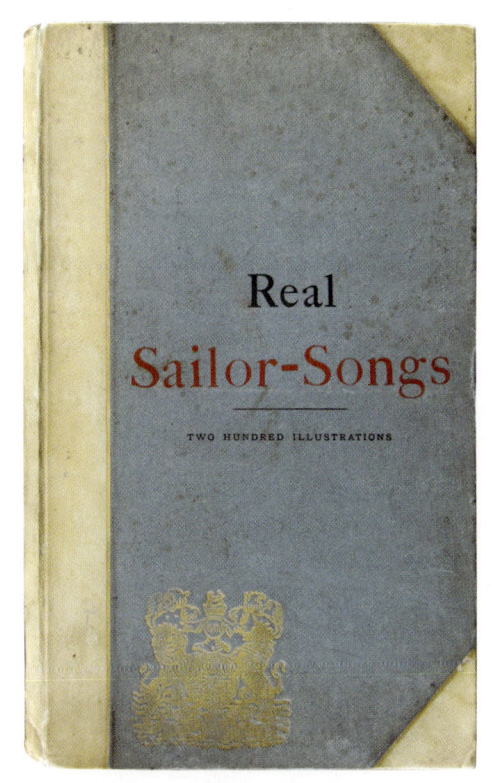

Broadside ballads collected by John Ashton, many as broadsheets mounted on guards. Checklist 1891.14.

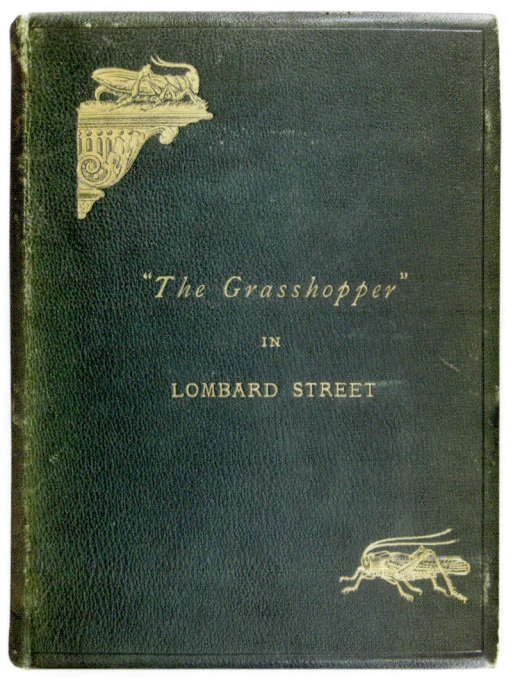

A history of Martins Bank and London banking in general from 1483 to 1891. Checklist 1892.3.

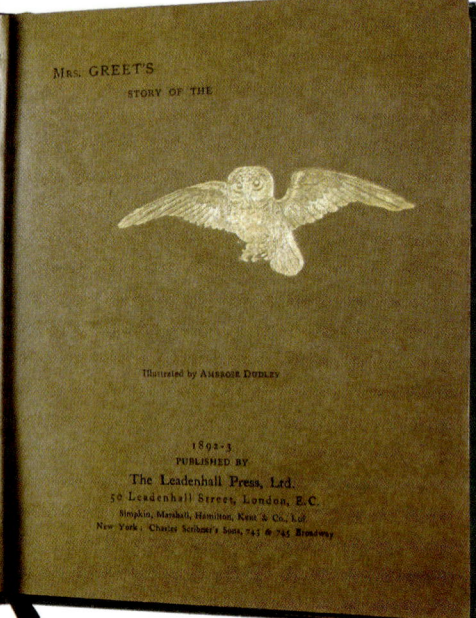

Mrs. Greet's Story of the Golden Owl was printed on brown paper, with illustrations by Ambrose Dudley on white ground. Checklist 1892.15.

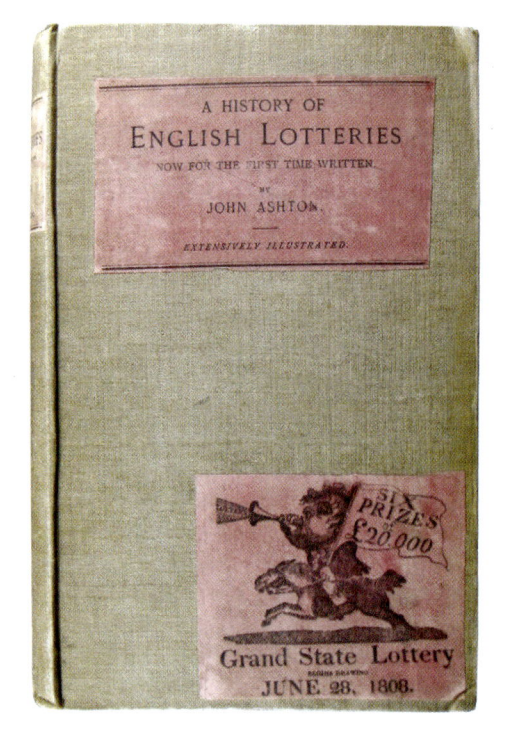

A History of English Lotteries by John Ashton, with 28 old lottery bills in facsimile printed on white and colored papers. Checklist 1893.11.

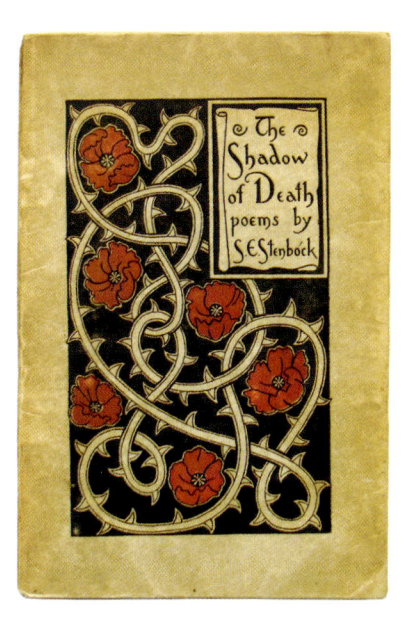

By Count Stanislaus Eric Stenbock. Artist unknown. Checklist 1893.17. (Courtesy, Clark Library, UCLA.)

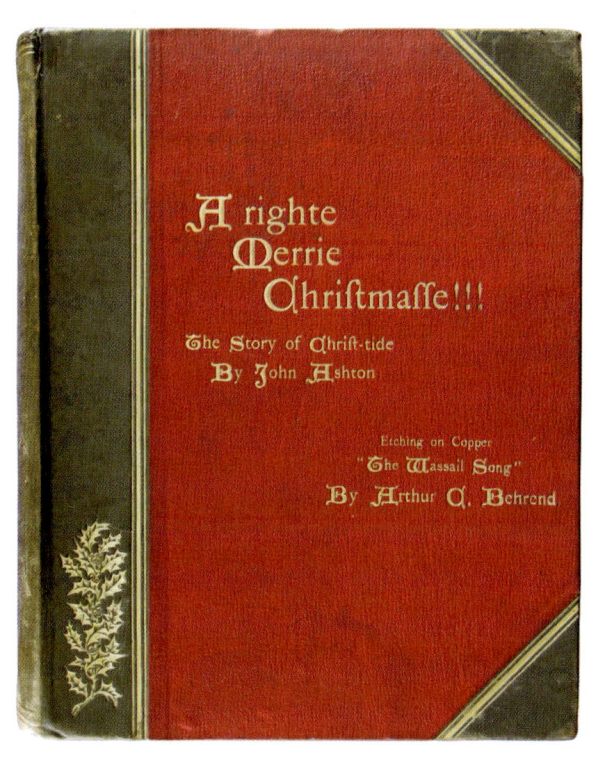

An elaborate gift book; a special edition was issued in full vellum with a different cover design. Checklist 1894.12.

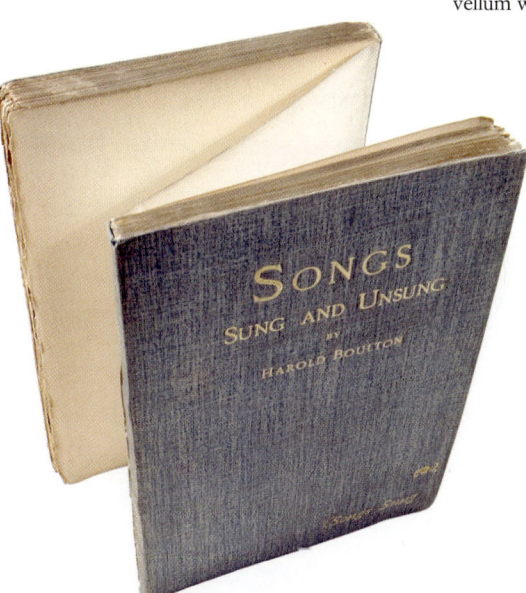

Bound *dos-à-dos*, with *Songs Sung* on one side, *Songs Unsung* on the other. Checklist 1894.5. (Courtesy, Lilly Library, Indiana University, Bloomington, IN.)

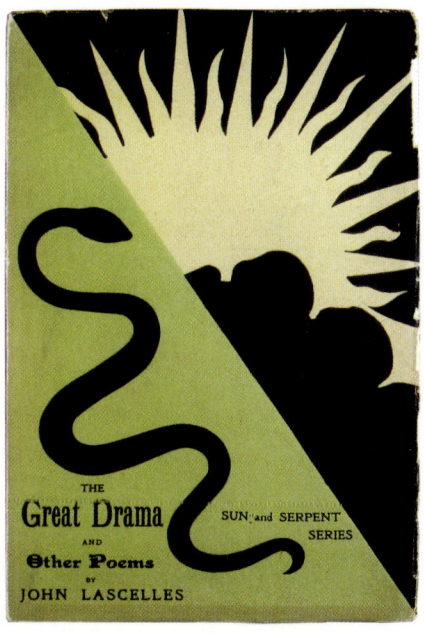

The second book in the Sun and Serpent Series by John Lascelles. Artist unknown. Checklist 1896.5.

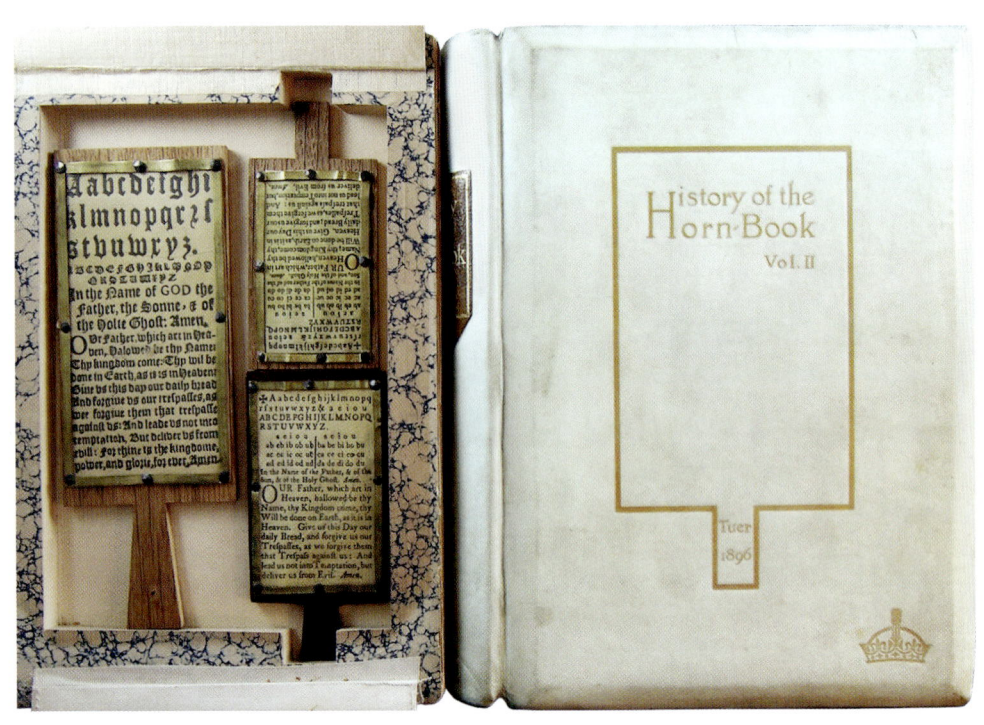

Andrew Tuer's *History of the Horn-Book,* in full vellum, with seven facsimile hornbooks in compartments. Checklist 1896.3.

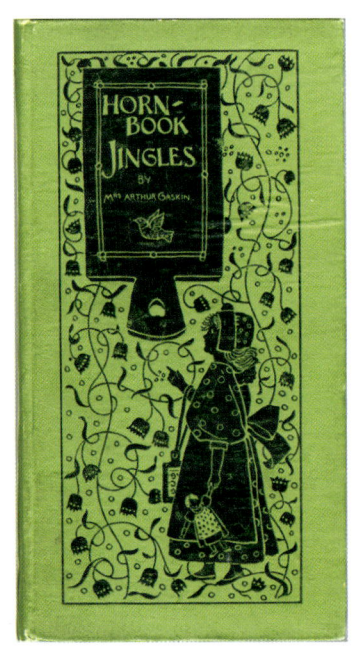

Illustrated and lettered by Georgie Gaskin. Checklist 1896.8. (Courtesy, Lilly Library, Indiana University, Bloomington, IN.)

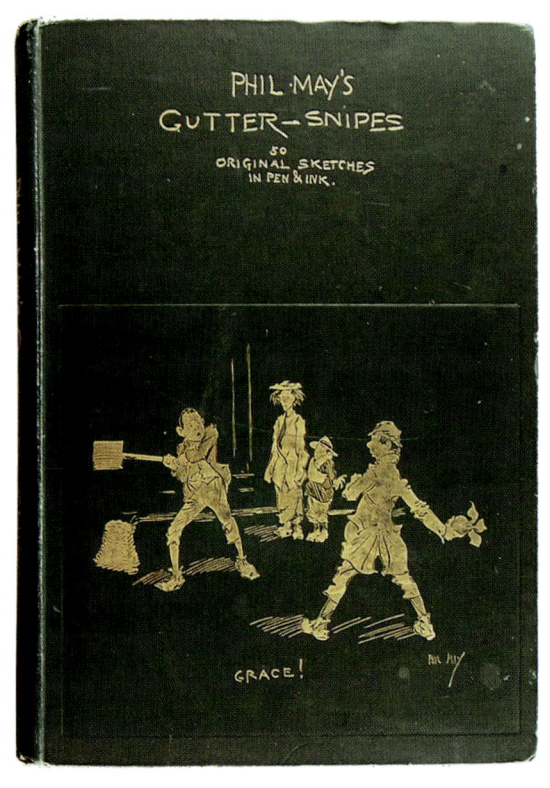

One of three books by Phil May. Checklist 1896.9.

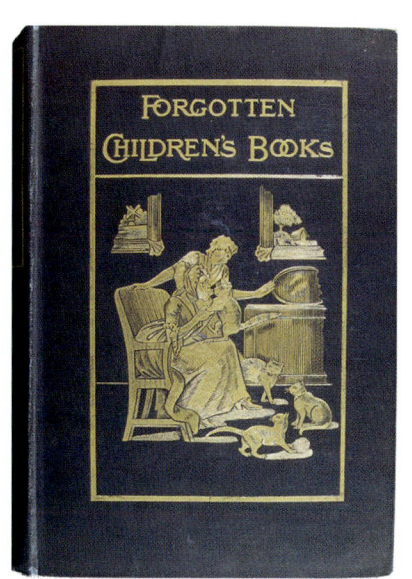

The first of two books of old children's stories collected and introduced by Andrew Tuer. Checklist 1898.6.

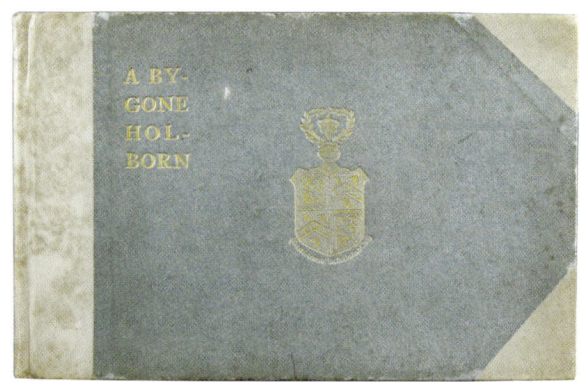

A history of the James Buchanan and Black Swan distilleries. Checklist 1898.7.

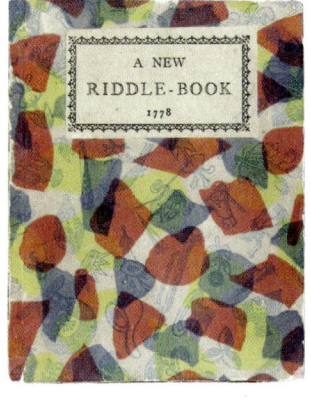

One of the facsimile titles from the Illustrated Shilling Series of Forgotton Children's Books. Checklist 1899.8.

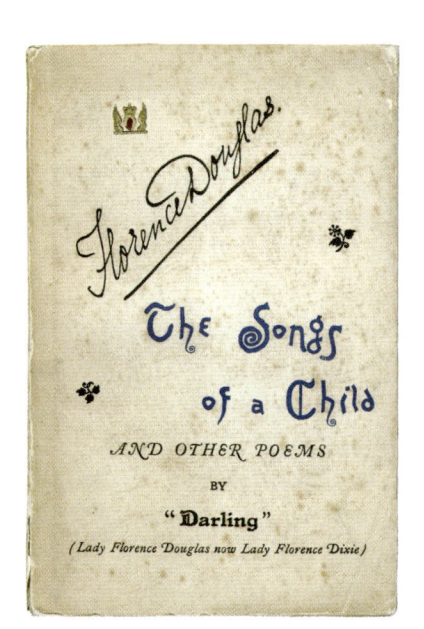

By the sister of the Marquis of Queensbury. Checklist 1901.4. (Courtesy, Lilly Library, Indiana University, Bloomington, IN.)

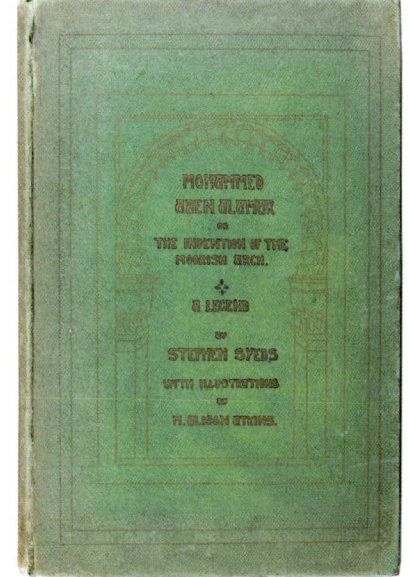

One of the last books published by the Leadenhall Press. Checklist 1905.2.

Advertising insert ca. 1897. Checklist EPH.50.

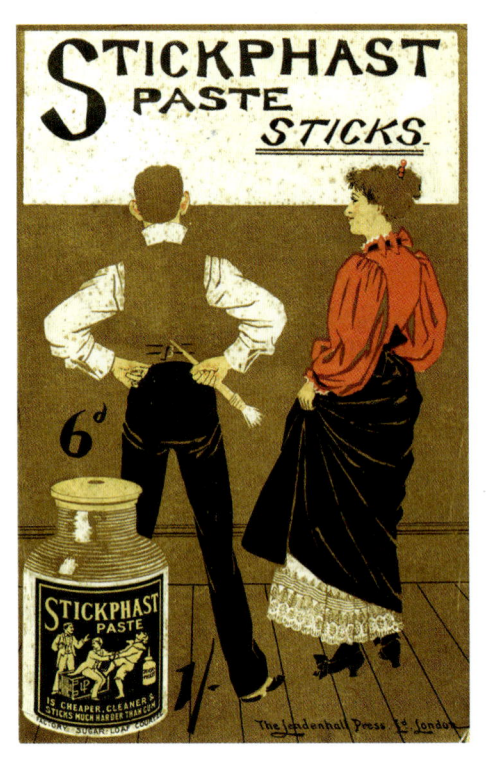

Advertising insert ca. 1894. Checklist EPH.43.

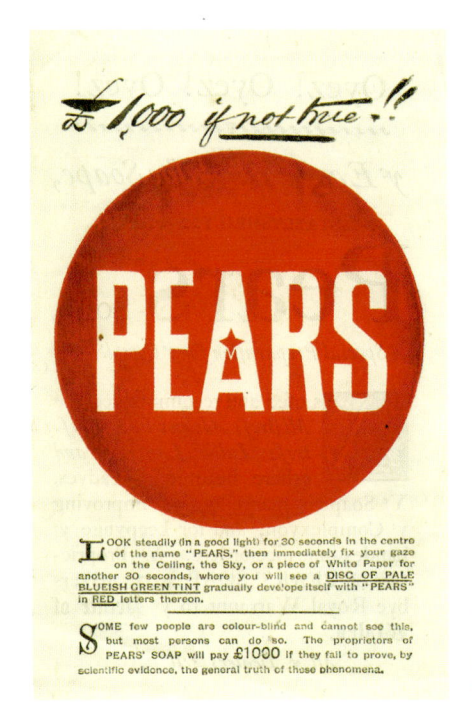

Optical illusion advertisement for Pears' Soap ca. 1887. Checklist EPH.30.

Advertising insert ca. 1894. Checklist EPH.44.

Appendix A
Checklist of Andrew W. Tuer

❧ *Author, compiler*

AWT.1   *Luxurious Bathing: A Sketch by Andrew W. Tuer with Twelve Folio Etchings, Initials, Etc. by Sutton Sharpe.* 1879. (Checklist 1879.1)

AWT.2   *Luxurious Bathing: (Second Edition) A Sketch by Andrew W. Tuer with Eight Etchings by Tristram Ellis.* 1880. (Checklist 1880.1)

AWT.3   *Bartolozzi and His Works. Biographical & Descriptive Account of the Life & Career of Francesco Bartolozzi, R.A.*
   a. First edition: [1882]. 2 vols. (Checklist 1882.1)
   b. Second edition: 1885. 1 vol. (Checklist 1885.35)

AWT.4   *List of the Works of Bartolozzi (Arranged under Heads).* [1882]. Offprint from *Bartolozzi and His Works.* (Checklist 1882.2)

AWT.5   *The Kaukneigh Awlminek, 1883.* [1882]. (Checklist 1882.7)

AWT.6   *London Cries: with Six Charming Children.* 1883. (Checklist 1883.25)

AWT.7   *Quads for Authors, Editors, & Devils.* 1884. (Checklist 1884.25)

AWT.8   *John Bull's Womankind. (Suggestions for an Alteration in the Law of Copyright in the Titles of Books).* [1884]. (Checklist 1884.28)

AWT.9   *Old London Street Cries and the Cries of To-day.* 1885. (Checklist 1885.29)

AWT.10 *The Follies & Fashions of Our Grandfathers (1807).* 1886–1887. (Checklist 1886.17)

AWT.11 *1,000 Quaint Cuts from Books of Other Days.* [1886]. (Checklist 1886.19)

AWT.12 *The First Year of a Silken Reign (1837–8).* 1887. Written with Charles Edward Fagan. (Checklist 1887.6)

AWT.13 *"Thenks Awf'lly!" Sketched in Cockney . . .* 1890. (Checklist 1890.8)

AWT.14 "The Art of Silhouetting," in the *English Illustrated Magazine,* No. 82, Vol. 7, July 1890, p. 747–752.

AWT.15 *London City.* The Leadenhall Press. [1890]. Pamphlet to secure the title of W. J. Loftie's *London City.* (Checklist 1890.10)

AWT.16 *Told After Supper.* The Leadenhall Press. [1890]. Pamphlet to secure the title of Jerome K. Jerome's *Told After Supper.* (Checklist 1890.19)

AWT.17 *Guess the Title of This Story!* 1891. (Checklist 1891.19)

AWT.18 *The Book of Delightful and Strange Designs.* [1892]. (Checklist 1892.16)

AWT.19 *History of the Horn-Book.*
a. First edition: 1896. 2 vols. (Checklist 1896.3)
b. Second edition: 1897. 1 vol. (Checklist 1896.3)

AWT.20 *Pages and Pictures from Forgotten Children's Books.* 1898–99. "Brought Together and Introduced . . . by Andrew W. Tuer, F.S.A." (Checklist 1898.6)

AWT.21 *Stories from Old-Fashioned Children's Books.* 1899–1900. "Brought Together and Introduced . . . by Andrew W. Tuer, F.S.A." (Checklist 1899.5)

Editor, contributor

AWT.22 *The Paper & Printing Trades Journal.* 1872-1891. Editor, contributor. (Checklist 1872.3)

AWT.23 *The Printers' International Specimen Exchange.* Volumes I–VIII: 1880–1887. Editor, introduction. (Checklist 1880.3)

AWT.24 *Catalogue of a Loan Collection of Engravings & Etchings by Francesco Bartolozzi, R.A. . . .* 1883. Introduction. (Checklist 1883.1)

AWT.25 JOHN HOPPNER AND CHARLES WILKIN. *Bygone Beauties.* [1883]. Annotations. (Checklist 1883.22)

AWT.26 INCORPORATED SOCIETY OF AUTHORS. *The Grievances between Authors & Publishers.* 1887. Appendix. (Checklist 1887.13)

AWT.27 [RICHARD SCRAFTON SHARPE; MRS. PEARSON]. *Dame Wiggins of Lee and her Seven Wonderful Cats.* 1887. Introduction. (Checklist 1887.17)

AWT.28 *The Gaping, Wide-mouthed, Waddling Frog.* 1887. Preface. (Checklist 1887.18)

AWT.29 *Deborah Dent and Her Donkey.* 1887. Introduction. (Checklist 1887.19)

AWT.30 CHARLES LAMB. *Prince Dorus.* 1889. Introduction. (Checklist 1889.10)

Bookplates and cards

AWT.31 *Ex Libris Andrew White Tuer [Pierrot suspended from the gallows]* [bookplate]. 1881. 8 cm. Illustration of two devils hanging Pierrot from a gibbet, roasting him over a burning book on a pitchfork. Cautionary verse in French on scroll across bottom left corner. Motto "Dum Spiro Spero" on floating ribbon. Art by William Harcourt Hooper, with his initials and date in stippled border.

AWT.32 *AWT. Steale not thisse boke for feare of shame...* [bookplate]. [ca. 1881].[1] 6 cm. Outline initials "AWT" with motto "Dum Spiro Spero" on stippled background. Warning to book thieves on separate panel. Art attributed to William Harcourt Hooper (unsigned).

AWT.33 *A•Oner for A•Tuer* [bookplate]. [ca. 1881]. 5 cm. Illustration of scissors with letters "AWT" in front of a bottle of Stickphast Paste, on stippled background. Lettering: "STICK-PHAST" and "The Paper & Printing Trade hys Journal." Design and art attributed to William Harcourt Hooper (unsigned).

AWT.34 ANDREW W. TUER. *[4 Cards Illustrating Horn-Books]*. The Leadenhall Press. [ca. 1894]. Each card with "Andrew W. Tuer, The Leadenhall Press, 50 Leadenhall Street, London, E.C." (Appendix B: EPH.45)

AWT.35 *Ex Libris And: W. Tuer* [bookplate]. [1893]. 9.5 cm. Illustration of a girl sitting under a tree reading a book with a hornbook suspended from her girdle. Lettering in scrolls. Design and art by Georgie Cave France, sent to Tuer as a Christmas card.[2] Signed in the border: "G. Cave. France."

Bookplate by Ambrose Dudley and Andrew Tuer. Bookplate by Georgie Cave France.

Note: A Tuer pictorial bookplate was listed for 1887 in *Dated Book-Plates (Ex Libris) with A Treatise on their Origin and Development* by Walter Hamilton (London: A. & C. Black, 1895). Its design was not pictured or described, no bookplate with that date has been located, and its existence has not been verified.

1. Date from *The Book-Plate Collector's Miscellany* for 1890-91.
2. *Ex Libris Journal*, Vol. IV, Part 2, Feb. 1894, p. 25, and *History of the Horn-Book*, Vol. II, p. 75.

AWT.36   *Andrew Double U Tuer hys . . .* [bookplate]. 1895. 7 cm. Illustration of book on chipped blue china plate. "Andrew Tuer thoughtitout 1895 Ambrose Dudley drewitout" in the decorations on the china plate.

AWT.37   *Ex Libris Collectanea [bookplate].* 1895. Obl. 6.5 x 14 cm. Illustration of sideboard with teapot, cups, candles, mouse, eight blue china plates, and open book propped up at front. Letters "BOOK" across pages of book, "P-L-A-T-E-S" on six of the plates, "Ex Libris Collectanea" on edge of counter, and "Andrew Tuer thoughtitout 1895 Ambrose Dudley drewitout" across base of sideboard.

AWT.38   *Andrew Double U Tuer Hys Booke 19 Hundred [bookplate].* 1900. Illustration of a cheval glass reflecting a hand holding a card, on which the inscription appears in reverse. (Not located.)[3]

Andrew W. Tuer sale catalogues

AWT.39   SOTHEBY, WILKINSON & HODGE. *Catalogue of the Well-Known Collection of Children's Books of the XVIIth, XVIIIth and XIXth Centuries, and the Valuable Series of Horn-Books, of the late A. W. Tuer, Esq. F.S.A. &c.* July 17, 1900. Included: specimen covers to novels by Surtees, Lever, Dickens, and others; advertisements, 1743–1813, in 7 volumes; printing exhibition catalogues; books on bank notes; books on the Lancashire dialect; children's books of the 17th, 18th, and 19th centuries; battledores and hornbooks; original art for *Horn-Book Jingles* (G. E. C. Gaskin) and *Prince Pertinax* (M. Hooper); engravings, etchings, woodcuts, drawings, and prints.

AWT.40   SOTHEBY AND CO. *Catalogue of the Valuable Printed Books, Illuminated & Other Manuscripts, Autograph Letters and Historical Documents, etc. comprising . . . The Property of the Late Andrew W. Tuer, Esq.* June 27, 1927. Included: office copies of Leadenhall Press books; autograph letters; original art; proofs; type specimens; books and periodicals; ballads; bank notes; bookplates; designs for woven fabrics; Christmas cards and valentines; lottery advertisements, ballads, engravings, tickets, and other ephemera; miniature books and bookcases; ornamental alphabets; silhouettes; fashion plates and trade cards.

---

3. Described and pictured "Andrew White Tuer and His Bookplates" by J. P. T. Bury, *The Bookplate Journal*, Vol. 6, Number 1, March 1988, pp. 11–12. Also described in "The Late Andrew W. Tuer and His Book-plates," *Ex Libris Journal*, Vol. X, Part 9, September 1900.

Appendix B
Ephemera

This list of 53 items, while representative, is very far from comprehensive. I have not, for instance, included items from *The Printers' International Specimen Exchange* not found separately, although many are clearly samples of actual prospectuses and commercial work. It is my hope that more ephemera surviving in libraries, private collections, and dealers' stock will be brought to light.

My guideline for this list was that to qualify as ephemera, a piece must have been printed as advertising (except for publisher's book lists), for a single event or holiday, or with the expectation that it would be discarded after use. By those criteria, a pamphlet to secure copyright for a book is placed in the general list, while a prospectus for the same book is classed as ephemera. Likewise, a single-sheet poem begins the main checklist, while the 50-page *Author's Paper Pad* resides here. Job numbers, where I have been able to find them, are noted. Two additional location abbreviations are used: JJ-Bodleian (John Johnson Collection of Printed Ephemera, Bodleian Library, Oxford) and JS-Iowa (John Springer Collection of Printing Ephemera, University of Iowa Library).

EPH.1   WHITELOCK & SON. *Price List of Ladies' under Clothing, India Outfits, and Wedding Outfits from Whitelock & Son, India and General Outfitters, 166, Strand, London, Opposite the Church near Somerset House.* "Ex officina Field & Tuer, 136 the Minories, London." —back cover. [ca. 1862–1867]. 17 cm. Pamphlet. (Copy located: Harvard.)

EPH.2   [JAMES KENDREW]. *Valentines* [facsimiles]. [Jonathan King; Field & Tuer, the Leadenhall Press]. [ca. 1868–1880].

a. *The Comet Changed to a Valentine for the 14th of February.* 26 cm. Facsimile reprint of an original engraving by James Kendrew of York, ca. 1835, showing two lovers surrounded by cherubs. Inspired by Halley's Comet in 1835.

b. *You sniveling wretch of a lover give o'er your raptures . . .* 26 cm. Facsimile reprint of an engraving by James Kendrew of York, ca. 1820–1830, showing a clothed man in a tub surrounded by three women washing him down. A comic verse warns him to "check the o'erflowings of love or be dub'd by the mop, and sous'd well by the pail."

Note: Andrew Tuer produced reprints from 13 original copperplates in his collection for the valentine maker and collector Jonathan King to sell to other collectors. One of those copperplates is now in the Hallmark Historical Collection.[4] I have not identified the other copperplates or reprints.

---

4. Frank Staff, *The Valentine & Its Origins* (New York: Praeger, 1969), pp. 54, 56.

EPH.3   PURE ICE MANUFACTURING COMPANY. *Cold: A New Manufacture.* The Pure Ice Manufacturing Company; printed by Field and Tuer, ye Leadenhalle Presse. 1878. 25 cm. Refrigeration machinery, ice, etc. (Copy located: TCD.)

EPH.4   TAYLOR BROTHERS. *Paris Exhibition, 1878.* Taylor Brothers; printed by Field and Tuer, ye Leadenhalle Presse. 1878. C.4,613. Folder announcing bronze medal award for excellence of manufacture. (Copy located: JS-Iowa.)

EPH.5   BLYTH & SONS. *Designs of Cabinet Furniture, Chimney Glasses, Draperies, &C. Manufactured by Blyth & Sons.* A. McGregor; printed by Field & Tuer. 1879. Lithographed plates. With *Price List of Modern Furniture,* also bearing the imprint of Field & Tuer. (Copy located: BL.)

EPH.6   MESSRS. PUTTICK & SIMPSON, AUCTIONEERS. *Formerly the Mansion of Sir Joshua Reynolds, P.R.A.* [trade card]. Engraved and printed by The Leadenhall Press. [ca. 1878–1882]. "Books; pictures; engravings; china (antique); furniture (antique); plate; jewellery; coins; postage stamps; musical instruments." (Copy located: JJ-Bodleian.)

EPH.7   [ANDREW WHITE TUER]. *Bartolozzi and His Works* [prospectus]. Field & Tuer, the Leadenhall Press. [1881]. 23 cm. Single sheet printed on both sides. Recto: "In the Press," with description of the book and its contents. Verso: complimentary quote from the *Academy.*

EPH.8   FIELD & TUER. *Choice Art Books* [order forms]. [1882]. Folder of leaves advertising four new publications, with order forms at bottom. Titles: *Journals and Journalism, My Ladye and Others, Six Etchings of Well-Known Views,* and *On a Raft and Through the Desert.* (Copy located: JS-Iowa.)

EPH.9   *Hanworth Park, April 25th 1882. Programme [of an Amateur Concert] and Analytical Remarks.* Field & Tuer, ye Leadenhalle Presse. [April 1882]. Copy located: BL.)

EPH.10 SAVAGE CLUB. *Savage Club 25th Anniversary Dinner. Saturday, February 11th, 1882* [menu]. Ye Leadenhalle Presse. 1882. T.3,067. "Sir Philip Cunliffe-Owen K.C., M.C., C.B., &c., in the Chair." (Copy located: JJ-Bodleian.)

EPH.11 [WINDSOR GALLERY]. *Exhibition of Engravings by Francesco Bartolozzi* [announcement]. Field & Tuer. [1882]. 25 m. Printed on one side in black and red. An announcement of the intended exhibition, with a description of the intended goals, and an invitation for contributions: "General Directions for intending Exhibitors." (Copy located: Winterthur.)

EPH.12 [WINDSOR GALLERY]. *Bartolozzi Exhibition Under the Patronage of Her Majesty the Queen* [invitation]. Field & Tuer. [ca. Nov. 1882]. 15 cm. Featuring "An impression from a copper-plate engraving by Bartolozzi" depicting two children and a harp. (Copies located: Winterthur.)

a. Private Press View: Engraving at center of invitation. At bottom: "Mr. E. Barrington Nash presents his compliments to _____ and begs the honour of a Visit at the Private Press View on Friday, December 8th, 1882."

b. Private View: Engraving at top of invitation. At bottom: "Mr. E. Barrington Nash presents his compliments to _____ and begs the honour of a Visit at the Private View on _____."

EPH.13 *Ye Openynge of ye Reading Room atte ye Halsteade Brewehouse* [handbill]. [Aug.] 1883. Single sheet. Ornamental border and type. "On Tuesdaye, ye Twenty-eighth daye of August, Anno Domini MDCCCLXXXIII, atte VIII of ye clocke inne ye evenynge." (Copy located: private collection.)

EPH.14 WORKINGMEN'S INSTITUTE, AT BARNES. *Bill of the Play: The Rivals: En Pension: Number One Round the Corner.* Ye Leadenhalle Presse. [Sept.] 1883. G.2,059. Obl. 15 x 19.5 cm. Leaflet. Ornamental type, borders, vignettes. October 1, MDCCCLXXXIII at foot of front cover. "The audience are requested not to laugh *too* loud at the jokes, and to wake *gently* any one who may happen to snore during the performance." — p. 4. (Copy located: private collection.)

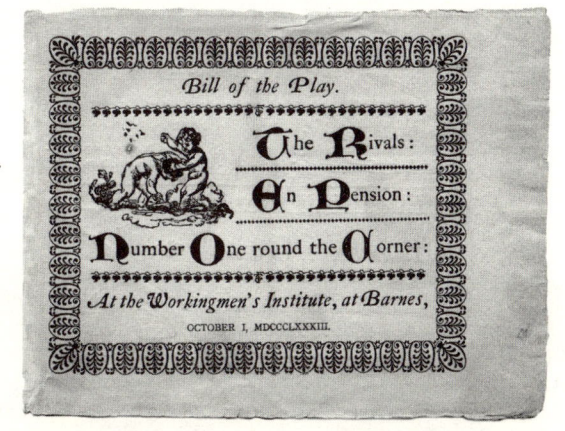

EPH.15 FIELD & TUER, THE LEADENHALL PRESS. *The Author's (Hairless) Paper-Pad.*

a. *The Author's Paper Pad.* Field & Tuer, the Leadenhall Press. [1883–1890]. 23 cm. Fifty ruled blank sheets preceded and followed by identically printed cover sheets. (Not located.)

b. *The Author's Hairless Paper Pad.* [1890–1913?]. The Leadenhall Press. Fifty sheets mounted on a new base of thick blotting paper. New accessory: the "Author's Paper Pad Holder." (Not located.)

c. *The Author's Hairless Paper Pad.* [ca. 1913–1927]. "The Leadenhall Press, Ltd.: 24–27, Garden Row, Southwark, S.E. 1" on cover. (Copy located: Lilly, bearing endorsement by "the late Sir F. C. Burnand of *Punch*," who died in 1917, implying variations in the covers.)

EPH.16 [JOSEPH CRAWHALL]. *Prospectus. Crawhall's Chap-book Chaplets.* Field & Tuer. [1883]. 29 cm. With hand-colored woodcut and order form. Also bound in at rear of *Olde ffrendes wyth newe Faces.* (Copy located: Durham.)

EPH.17 [ANDREW WHITE TUER]. *Prospectus. Olde ffrendes wyth newe Faces.* Field & Tuer. [1883]. 29 cm. With hand-colored woodcut and order form. Also bound in at rear of *Crawhall's Chap-book Chaplets.* (Copy located: Durham.)

EPH.18 [ANDREW WHITE TUER]. *Prospectus. (1) Quads, (2) Quads (enlarged edition), (3) Quads within Quads.* Field & Tuer, ye Leadenhalle Presse. [1883]. 11 cm. Leaflet describing in amusing detail the complexities of the editions. Often seen tipped to front endpaper of enlarged edition.

EPH.19 [FIELD & TUER, THE LEADENHALL PRESS]. *Memento Imprynted yn Ye Olde Streete of London Towne ye Greate Attraction yn Ye Health Exhibition, South Kensyngton, Anno Domini 1884.* Field & Tuer, ye Leadenhall Presse. [July] 1884. 29 cm. Leaflet. A list of books published by Field & Tuer: "Tarry a while faire Mistresse and gentle Sir: step in and freely examine without stinte ye quainte and curious bookes set forth below. Have ye half-an-hour to spare, ye reading of them will pleasure ye greatlie."; ads for Stickphast Paste and the Author's Paper Pad; "Some Printers' Jokes!"; facsimile page from *Old Aunt Elspa's ABC.*

EPH.20 [FREDERICK YORK & SON]. *Duc De Sully's House, ye Olde London Street, International Health Exhibition, South Kensington* [handbill]. Ye Leadenhalle Presse. [July 1884]. G.2,128. 27 cm. Handbill announcing an "Antiente Cloke" said to have belonged to Guy Fawkes, made by Joseph Knibb of London, "still in perfect going order." At foot: "Exhibited by Messrs. Frederick York & Son, Dealers in all Antiquities, 3, Horsemarket, Kettering, Northamptonshire." (Copy located: private collection.)

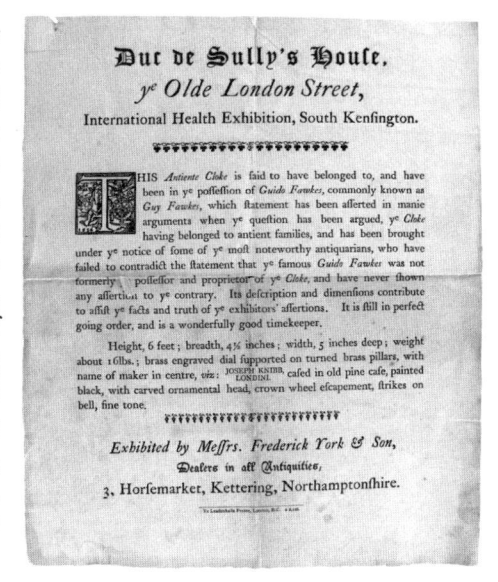

EPH.21 [JOSEPH CRAWHALL]. *Prospectus: Izaak Walton: His Wallet Booke Being the Songs in "the Compleat Angler" Newly Set Forth and Illustrated by Joseph Crawhall.* Imprinted at The Leadenhall Press. [1884]. 29 cm. Prospectus for the forthcoming publication, with order form. Hand-painted woodcut of an angler. (Copy located: Durham.)

EPH.22 THE LEADENHALL PRESS. *Memento: Inventions Exhibition, South Kensington, 1885.* Ye Leadenhall Press. [Aug. 1885]. 20 cm. Recto: Engraving in brown ink captioned "'Our Grandmothers' Prints' in Ye Olde London Streete," signed: F. Bartolozzi Sc. 1763. Below: "Bartolozzi Prints, Republished at Ye Leadenhalle Presse." Verso: "Inventions Exibition.—'Our Grandmothers' Prints' in old-fashioned frames. Prospectus free. Copper-plate printing shewn as practised 100 years ago." (Copies located: Lilly, Wellcome.)

EPH.23 *The Happy Blend; or, How John Bull Was Suited to a T [handbill].* Ye Leadenhalle Presse. [1885]. 22 cm. Leaflet. An illustrated advertisement for tea-blenders.

EPH.24 [CITY OF LONDON CORPORATION]. *Banquet at Guildhall on Monday, November 10th, 1884. The Right Honourable George Swan Nottage, Lord Mayor. James Whitehead, Esquire (Alderman) and George Faudel Phillips, Esquire, Sheriffs.* Field & Tuer, the Leadenhall Press. [Nov. 1884]. T.3,416. 24 cm. Souvenir program, mainly devoted to a description of Guildhall. Beige card wrappers with title inside elaborate heraldic frame printed in brown. The Right Honourable George Swan Nottage, Lord Mayor, etc. (Copy located: NYPL.)

EPH.25 ——. *Banquet at Guildhall, Nov. 10, 1884* [menu]. Field & Tuer, the Leadenhall Press. [Nov. 1884]. 18 cm. Engraving signed: F. Bartolozzi, 1763. "After the banquet there will be dancing in the library, and a selection of instrumental music will be performed in the new council chamber." (Copy located: NYHS.)

EPH.26 [A. F. PEARS]. *Nice Hands! Good Complexion! And Healthful Skin.* [advertisement for Pears' Soap]. [Field & Tuer, the Leadenhall Press]. 1884. Lithograph. "I have found Pears' Soap, as recommended by Professor Sir Erasmus Wilson, matchless for the hands and complexion." (Copy located: JJ-Bodleian.)

EPH.27 ——. *Don't Destroy This!!! It Is Printed on a Japanese Handkerchief* [advertisement for Pears' Soap]. [Field & Tuer, the Leadenhall Press]. [ca. 1885]. 36 cm. Printed on rice paper. (Copy located: JJ-Bodleian.)

EPH.28 ——. *Curious advertisement of 100 years ago. Pears' Soap 1879.* [Field & Tuer, the Leadenhall Press]. [ca. 1885]. 21 cm. Illustration of mother bathing infant, with lettering by Joseph Crawhall, in black, green, yellow, and red. (Copy located: Newcastle.)[5]

---

5. The Newcastle copy is mounted, matted, and framed so that any imprint (if present) is hidden, but it seems unlikely that this advertisement could have been produced by anyone other than the Leadenhall Press.

EPH.29 ——. *If you look at the above star for 30 seconds and then at the star in the blank space below* . . . [advertisement for Pears' Soap]. 1887. Chromolithograph optical illusion. (Copy located: JJ-Bodleian.)

EPH.30 ——. *£1,000 if not true!! PEARS* [advertisement for Pears' Soap]. The Leadenhall Press. [ca. 1887]. 22 cm. Large red circle with white "PEARS" and small red star at center. "Look steadily. . . in the centre of the name 'PEARS,' then immediately fix your gaze on the Ceiling, the Sky, or a piece of White Paper . . . where you will see a disc of pale blueish green . . . with 'PEARS' in red lettering thereon." Verso: "Oyez! Oyez! Oyez! ye Earlie Englyshe Soape, Establyshed 100 Years, Pears' Soap." (Copy located: private collection.)

EPH.31 ——. *Curious & beautiful optical illusion presented by the proprietors of Pears' Soap.* [advertisement]. The Leadenhall Press. [ca. 1887]. 22 cm.

a. Chromolithograph: Two sets of seven concentric circles (one blue, one red) side by side. "Strobic Circles Invented by Professor Silvanus P. Thompson, D.Sc., B.A. Give this a slight but rapid circular twisting motion thus [spiral], when each circle will separately revolve on its own axis."

b. Printed in black. Instructions begin: "Hold this Diagram by the right-hand bottom corner and give it a slight but rapid circular twisting motion . . ."

EPH.32 ——. *Curious & beautiful optical illusion. Strobic Circles Invented by Professor Silvanus P. Thompson, D.Sc., B.A.* [advertisement for Pears' Soap]. The Leadenhall Press. [ca. 1888]. 22 cm.

a. Chromolithograph: Six blue and red double circles surrounding a blue circle with cogs pointing inwards. "Give this a slight but rapid circular twisting motion thus [spiral], when each circle will separately revolve on its own axis. The inner cogged wheel will be seen to revolve in an *opposite direction*."

b. Printed in black. Instructions begin: "Hold this Diagram by the right-hand bottom corner and give it a slight but rapid circular twisting motion . . ."

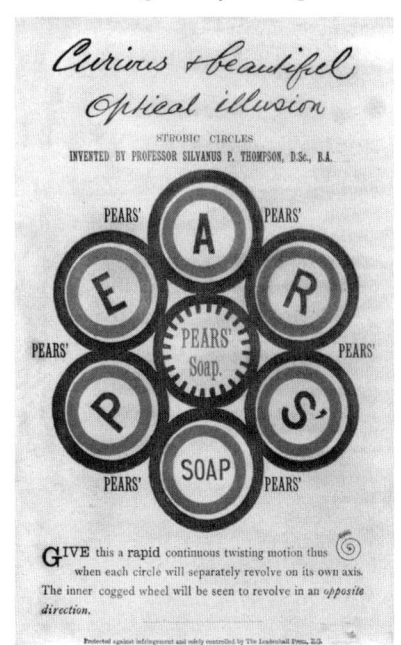

EPH.33 *Types from the Leadenhall Press.*

a. Field & Tuer, The Leadenhall Press. [ca. 1888]. 28 cm. Single sheet printed on both sides: the center spread from publisher's lists. Recto: 13 rows of alphabets in increasing sizes and various fonts, one row each of numerals and ornaments, one initial, one vignette. Verso: pages 3 and 6 of *Extracts from Field & Tuer's List, The Leadenhall Press* (checklist 1884.44b), 1888–90.

b. The Leadenhall Press. [1891]. Recto: wording changes to *Specimens of Types from the Leadenhall Press, Ltd.* Verso: pages 7 and 8 of publisher's ads from *Extracts from The Leadenhall Press Book List* (checklist 1884.44c), 1891–92.

EPH.34 EDWIN FOX AND BLOUSFIELD, AUCTIONEERS. *The New River: Unique Auction, May, 1890.* Printed at the Leadenhall Press. [ca. May 1890]. N.1,622. 29 cm. Cream stiff wrappers, lettering in black. "Biddings at the Auction Mart on the 21st May 1890 for one whole & undivided King's Share in the New River Company" (leaflet, tipped to p. [2] of wrappers). "Introductory Remarks," reprinted from original, attached to Particulars of Sale issued "on the occasion of their selling by auction in July last an entire Adventurers' Share." (Copy located: JJ-Bodleian.)

EPH.35 CLARKE, NICKOLLS, COOMBS, LTD. *French, American and English Confectionery: Specialities for Hotels, Restaurants, Pastrycooks, and Bakers.* The Leadenhall Press. [1890]. J.1,612. 22 cm. Price list pamphlet. Illustration of the Clarke, Nicholls & Coombs buildings on back cover.

EPH.36 [W. J. LOFTIE]. *London City Prospectus.* [ca. 1889]. 29 cm. Leaflet. "To be published at 42/-; Price to subscribers 21/- nett; Large-paper copies, of which not a single copy will be printed beyond those actually subscribed for, 45/- nett. *London City,* a large, thick quarto . . . will be perhaps the most beautifully and profusely illustrated art book ever attempted."

EPH.37 *London City* [prospectus for] *The City, by W. J. Loftie; illustrated by W. Luker.* The Leadenhall Press. 1890. 13 cm. Pamphlet. (Copy located: UL.)

EPH.38 *"London City" by W. J. Loftie* [advertisement]. Field & Tuer, The Leadenhall Press. [1890]. 20 cm. Pamphlet. (Copy located: Glasgow.)

EPH.39 *Received of ____ the Sum of ____ for ____ of "London City" To be delivered when Published* [subscription receipt]. The Leadenhall Press. 1890. 28 cm. Single sheet. Receipt for order of a copy of *London City.* The top half is devoted to an illustration of a coach-filled street by William Luker Jr.

EPH.40 [PERCY HETHERINGTON FITZGERALD]. *London City Suburbs (as They Are To-day)* [prospectus]. The Leadenhall Press. [1892]. 28.5 cm. Pamphlet. "To be published at 42/-; Price to subscribers 21/- nett; Large-paper copies . . . 45/- nett. (Copy located: NLS.)

EPH.41 [A. F. PEARS]. *Pears' Soap a Specialty for Children.* [advertisement]. The Leadenhall Press. [ca. 1892]. Illustration of mother bathing infant.

EPH.42 [ANDREW WHITE TUER]. *The Stinks in Leadenhall Street.* The Leadenhall Press. 1894. 42 cm. Broadside. Notice issued by the Leadenhall Press, complaining of the "stinks" in the neighborhood.

EPH.43 [FIXOL & STICKPHAST, LTD]. *Stickphast Paste Sticks.* [advertising insert]. The Leadenhall Press. [ca. 1894]. 22 cm. Single sheet of brown paper printed on both sides. Recto: illustration (unsigned) printed in white, black, red, and flesh tone of man in shirtsleeves, seen from the rear, holding large brush, hands on hips, observed admiringly by a woman. Verso: in black type, "[Other side, please] STI C.K.P.H. AST PAS T: EST I.C.K.S.," with endorsement from actress Ellen Terry.

EPH.44 ———. *STUCK IN WITH STICKPHAST PASTE LOOK HOW IT STICKS!* [advertising insert]. The Leadenhall Press. [ca. 1894]. Z.70,400. Obl. 17 x 14 cm. Illustrated title border[6] printed in black and red, title lettered in black. "'I always stick in my scraps and papers with STICKPHAST PASTE.' –Ellen Terry." (Copy located: private collection, tipped into *A New Shilling Book of Alphabets.*)

EPH.45 ANDREW W. TUER. [4 Cards Illustrating Horn-Books]. The Leadenhall Press. [ca. 1894]. Each card with "Andrew W. Tuer, The Leadenhall Press, 50 Leadenhall Street, London, E.C." (Only copies located: Princeton.)

a. *Flemish Horn-Book.* 13 cm. Illustration of hornbook with alphabet in Flemish script under variant of Maltese cross.

b. *A B C Ballbrett.* Illustration of hornbook shape used in Germany (Bohemia), Sweden, Norway, and Denmark.

c. *[Untitled].* 13 cm. Illustration of untitled female figure, seen from the rear, studying a horn-book.

d. *[Untitled].* 11.5 cm. Woodcut illustration of horn book with alphabet followed by "AMEN." Text: "Mr. Andrew W. Tuer, of the Leadenhall Press, 50 Leadenhall Street, E.C. is engaged on a little work on Horn-Books, and desires it to be known that he will be grateful for references to material and examples. —*Athenaeum.*"

EPH.46 [ANDREW WHITE TUER]. *Prospectus: History of the Horn-Book.* The Leadenhall Press. [ca. 1895]. Pamphlet. Title page of book as p. 1, publisher's note p. 2–3, with 5 half-tone reproductions and 3 woodcuts. (Not located.)

EPH.47 [MRS. ARTHUR (GEORGIE EVELYN CAVE FRANCE) GASKIN]. *Prospectus for Horn-Book Jingles.* 24.5 cm. Single sheet printed on one side. With illustration by G. E. C. Gaskin. (Not located.)

---

6. Possibly by Georgie Cave France Gaskin or R. I. Williams, judging by their contributions to *History of the Horn-Book. The Studio* of October 1894 awarded prizes for (among other things) a design for a small show card for Stickphast Paste. Awards went to H. Dawson and H. C. Graff, but the winning designs were not pictured.

EPH.48   THE LEADENHALL PRESS, LTD. *Manifold Papers* [samples]. The Leadenhall Press. [ca. 1895–1900]. 19 cm. White card covers printed in black, with 8 paper samples. Front cover: price list of eight papers lettered A–H ("New Perfection," "Gossamer," "South Kensington Tracing Paper," etc.), and two "Double Crown" sizes.[7] Rear cover: ads for Stickphast Paste and "Indentures for Printers' Apprentices." (Copy located: Lilly.)

EPH.49   [FIXOL & STICKPHAST, LTD]. *Stickphast Paste Sticks*. [advertising insert]. The Leadenhall Press. [ca. 1896]. 19 cm. Illustration by Phil May of rear view of a rumpled man, with raised brush in one hand and bucket in the other, next to a dapper lad.

EPH.50   ——. *These two sheets of paper (forming one leaf) are stuck together with Stickpaste Paste* [advertising insert]. The Leadenhall Press. [ca. 1897]. 22 cm. Two leaves glued together: one pink, one white, printed in black and red, two opposite corners folded one to each side reading: "see underneath." Illustration on both sides printed in black and red: "May Old Friends [Stickphast Paste bottle]." (Date from insertion in *The Art Journal*, 1897.)

EPH.51   [ANDREW WHITE TUER]. *Prospectus: Pages and Pictures from Forgotten Children's Books*. The Leadenhall Press. [ca. 1898]. 20 cm. Pamphlet. Title page of book as p. 1, publisher's note p. 2–3, with 5 half-tone reproductions and 3 woodcuts. (Copy located: NYHS.)

EPH.52   THE LEADENHALL PRESS, LTD. *What Grade to Use: ...* [Price List, Etc. Of Fixol]. The Leadenhall Press. [ca. 1914]. (Copy located: St. Bride.)

EPH.53   BARRY JACKSON AND BASIL DEAN. *Yuletide at the Scala Theatre* [playbill]. The Leadenhall Press. 1919. "Fifinella"—a musical fantasy by Messrs. Barry Jackson and Basil Dean, Scala Theatre, Saturday, December 20th, 1919. (Copy located: Bodleian.)

---

7. Advertisements for several of the same papers appeared in *The Printers' Universal Book of Reference and Every-hour Office Companion. An Addendum to "The Printers', etc., Business Guide."* (London: J. Haddon, 1875), suggesting that earlier versions of *Manifold Papers* samplers were issued.

THE LEADENHALL PRESS SIXTEENPENNY SERIES.

Illustrated Gleanings from the Classics.

No. 1.—SIR CHARLES GRANDISON,
by SAMUEL RICHARDSON. With Six Illustrations from the original copper-plates engraved in 1778 by ISAAC TAYLOR: and a Preface by JOHN OLDCASTLE.

No. 2.—SOLOMON GESSNER,
"The Swiss Theocritus." With Six Illustrations and extra Portrait from the original copper-plates engraved in 1802 by ROBERT CROMEK from Drawings by THOMAS STOTHARD, R.A.: and a Preface by JOHN OLDCASTLE.

No. 3.—THE SEASONS,
by JAMES THOMSON. With Four Illustrations and extra Portrait printed direct from the original copper-plates engraved in 1792: and a Preface by JOHN OLDCASTLE.

No. 4.—TRISTRAM SHANDY,
by LAURENCE STERNE. With Six unpublished Illustrations in aquatint from the original copper-plates engraved in 1820: and a Preface by JOHN OLDCASTLE.

☞ The Publishers regretfully announce that No. 4, TRISTRAM SHANDY, finishes the series, which, for lack of further material in the way of original copper-plates, they are unable to continue. *(see p. 6.)*

(4)

CRAWHALL'S
Chap-book
Chaplets.

I. *The Barkeshire Lady's Garland.*
II. *The Babes in the Wood.*
III. *I Know what I Know.*
IV. *Jemmy & Nancy of Yarmouth.*
V. *The Taming of a Shrew.*
VI. *Blew-cap for me.*
VII. *John & Joan.*
VIII. *George Barnewel.*

LONDON:
Field & Tuer.   Simpkin, Marshall & Co.
Hamilton, Adams & Co.
NEW YORK: Scribner & Welford.

The
Vellum-Parchment Shilling Series
OF
Miscellaneous Literature.

No. i.
"ENGLISH AS SHE IS SPOKE: OR A JEST IN SOBER EARNEST."
"*Excruciatingly funny.*"—*The World.*

No. i a.
"ENGLISH AS SHE IS SPOKE: OR, A JEST IN SOBER EARNEST."
"HER SECONDS PART." (NEW MATTER.) *As funny as the first part.*

No. ii.
The Story of a Nursery Rhyme, By C. B.,
with numerous whole-page illustrations, by Edwin J. Ellis. The text, which is set *entirely* in the very beautiful and artistic type which heads this notice, and the illustrations, are printed throughout in a new shade of blue ink.

No. iii.
HENRY IRVING, ACTOR AND MANAGER: A Critical Study. By WILLIAM ARCHER.

No. iv.
CHRISTMAS ENTERTAINMENTS, illustrated with many diverting cuts—a reprint of the very amusing and scarce 1740 edition, an original copy of which would now command more than twice its weight in gold.

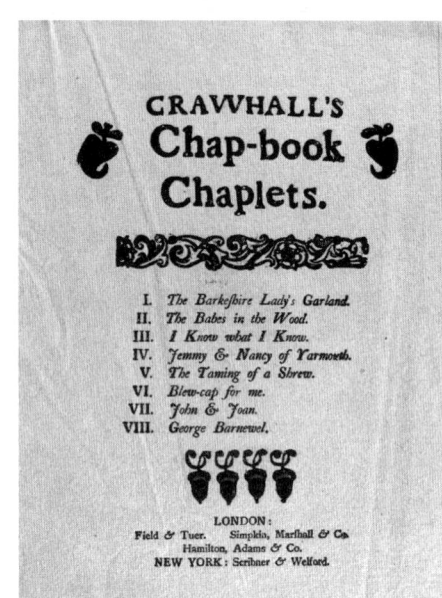

The Leadenhall Press Series
OF
Forgotten Picture Books for Children.
ONE SHILLING EACH.
with numerous elegantly coloured engravings.

i.
Dame Wiggins of Lee & her Seven Wonderful Cats. A humorous Tale. Written principally by a Lady of Ninety. Embellished with Sixteen Beautifully Coloured Engravings.

ii.
The Gaping, Wide-mouthed, Waddling Frog. A new and entertaining Game of Questions and Commands. With proper directions for playing the Game and crying Forfeits. Embellished with Thirteen Beautifully Coloured Engravings.

iii.
Deborah Dent and her Donkey. A humorous Tale. Embellished with Ten Beautifully Coloured Engravings.

[OTHERS IN THE PRESS]

Appendix C
Series

Andrew Tuer entertained many ideas for ongoing series, some of which never went beyond the first title. Others, such as the "Parchment Paper Series" and the "White Parchment Series," which occasionally appeared in announcements and reviews, were never implemented or perhaps were intended simply to associate a book with the familiar format of the popular Vellum-Parchment Shilling Series of Miscellaneous Literature.

Field & Tuer's Series of English Re-prints

1. *An Account of the Methods Whereby the Charity Schools Have Been Erected & Managed* (1871.3)

Vellum-Parchment Shilling Series of Miscellaneous Literature

List in *The Truth About Tonquin* (1884.6):

1. *English as She Is Spoke: Or, a Jest in Sober Earnest* (1883.5)

1a. *English as She Is Spoke . . . Her Seconds Part* (1883.23)

2. *The Story of a Nursery Rhyme* (1883.8)

3. *Henry Irving, Actor and Manager, a Critical Study* (1883.9)

4. *Christmas Entertainments* (1883.16)

5. *Are We to Read ?SDRAWKCAB* (1884.1)

6. *Ye Oldest Diarie of Englysshe Travell* (1884.2)

7. *Reasonable Apprehensions and Reassuring Hints* (1883.6b)

8. *One Hundred and Forty-Two Selected Texts from The Imitation of Christ* (1884.3)

9. *You Shouldn't. Being Hints to Persons of Aristocratic Instincts* (1884.8)

10. *The Truth About Tonquin*

Variant list in *Don't: A Manual of Mistakes and Improprieties* (1883.26):

Deleted: *You Shouldn't*

9. *Don't* (List does not include number 10.)

Variant list in *Ethics of Some Modern Novels* (1884.16):

Deleted: *You Shouldn't*

9. *The Truth About Tonquin*

10. *Ethics of Some Modern Novels*

Variant list, ad for "Printed on Vellum," *Recent Books and Something About Them*:

Deleted: *The Story of a Nursery Rhyme* and *Christmas Entertainments*

Included in unnumbered list: *You Shouldn't*, *Don't*, and *The Truth About Tonquin*

Crawhall's Chap-book Chaplets (1883.15)
1. *The Barkeshire Lady's Garland*
2. *The Babes in the Wood*
3. *I Know What I Know*
4. *Jemmy & Nancy of Yarmouth*
5. *The Taming of a Shrew*
6. *Blew Cap for Mee*
7. *John & Joan*
8. *George Barnewel*

Olde ffrendes wyth newe Faces (1884.5)
1. *Ye Loving Ballad of Lorde Bateman*
2. *A True Relation of the Apparition of Mrs. Veal*
3. *The Long Pack: a Northumbrian Tale*
4. *The Sword-Dancers*
5. *John Cunningham, the Pastoral Poet*
6. *Ducks & Green Peas, or, the Newcastle Rider: a Tale in Rhyme*
7. *Ducks & Green Peas; a Farce*
8. *Andrew Robinson Stoney Bowes Esquire*
9. *The Gloamin' Buchte*

"The Perfect Way" Shilling Series
1. *How the World Came to an End in 1881* (1884.4)

Ye Leadenhalle Presse Pamphlets
1. *History of the Decline and Fall of the British Empire* (1884.7)
2. *Can Parliament Break Faith?* (1884.10)

Ye Leadenhalle Presse Oblong Shilling-Series
1. *John Oldcastle's Guide for Literary Beginners* (1884.11)
2. *Journalistic Jumbles; or, Trippings in Type* (1884.12)
3. *Decently and in Order* (1884.13)

Historical Sporting Series
1. *Foot-Ball: Its History for Five Centuries* (1885.8)

Plays for Young People
1. *The Foster-Brother and The Creoles* (1886.21)
2. *The Prime Minister and Tom* (1887.8)

The Leadenhall Press Sixteenpenny Series: Illustrated Gleanings from the Classics
    1. *Sir Charles Grandison* (1886.11)
    2. *Solomon Gessner: "The Swiss Theocritus"* (1886.12)
    3. *The Seasons* (1888.2)
    4. *Tristram Shandy* (1888.3)

The Leadenhall Press Series of Forgotten Picture Books for Children
    1. *Dame Wiggins of Lee* (1887.17)
    2. *The Gaping, Wide-mouthed, Waddling Frog* (1887.18)
    3. *Deborah Dent and Her Donkey* (1887.19)
    4. *The Dame and Her Donkeys Five* (1888.9)

Bind Me As You Please Series
    1. *A Life's Reminiscences of Scotland Yard* (1890.13b)

Curatica, or Leaves from a Curate's Note-book
    1. *My First Curacy* (1891.4)

Funnynym Series
    1. *Rustling Reeds, Stirred by Goosestep* (1894.15)

Sun and Serpent Series
    1. *·X·Y·Z· and Other Poems* (1895.1)
    2. *The Great Drama, and Other Poems* (1896.4)

Illustrated Shilling Series of Forgotten Children's Books
    1. *The Daisy; or, Cautionary Stories in Verse* (1899.6)
    2. *The Cowslip, or, More Cautionary Stories, in Verse* (1899.7)
    3. *Food for the Mind: or, a New Riddle-Book* (1899.8)
    4. *The History of Little Goody Two Shoes* (1899.9)

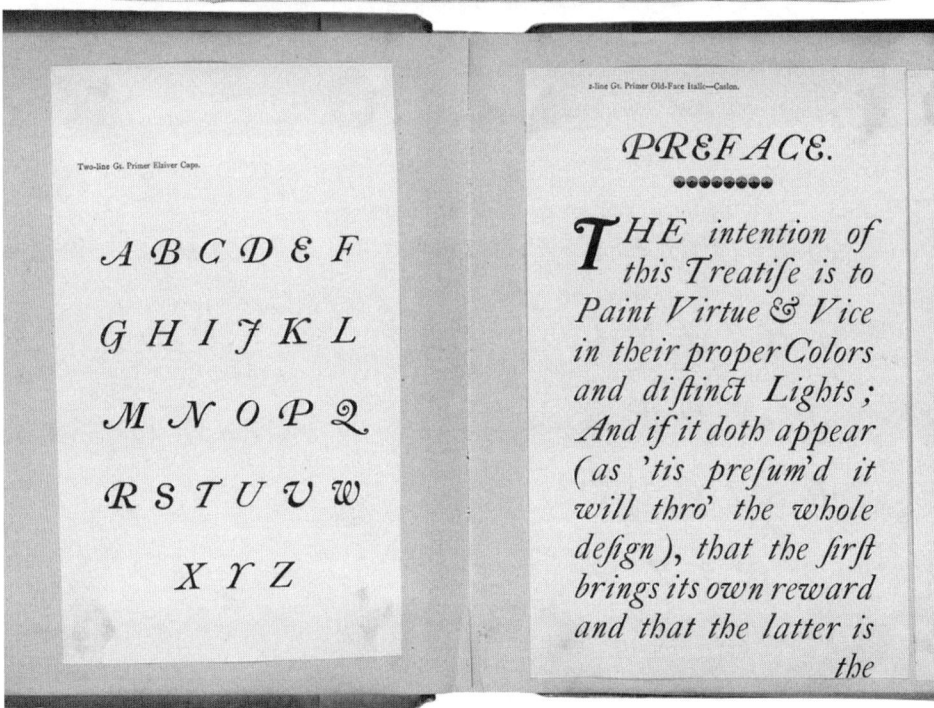

Specimens of Type. Field & Tuer [ca. 1885], TypTs 805 85.392 v.2 F, Houghton Library, Harvard University.

Appendix D
Collections

The most extensive collections of books published by Field & Tuer and the Leadenhall Press are at the six Legal Deposit Libraries in the UK: the British Library, the Bodleian Library (Oxford), Cambridge University Library, the National Library of Scotland, Trinity College Dublin Library, and (to a lesser extent) the National Library of Wales. The City of London Libraries (primarily St. Bride and Guildhall), and many university libraries in the UK have significant holdings.

In North America, the Lilly Library at Indiana University has the largest collection of books and other important items (see below). The Library of Congress and the New York Public Library each have more than 100 titles, as well as American editions of titles with separate copyrights. Many major university and public libraries have significant holdings, including limited editions and interesting association copies (sometimes found in general circulation).

The National Library of Australia, the National Library of New Zealand, and the University of Sydney have a number of titles, and there are scatterings of books in European and other libraries around the world.

To locate copies of books in libraries, search WorldCat (worldcat.org) and Copac (copac.ac.uk). Many titles have been digitized and can be viewed online at Internet Archive (archive.org) and Google Books (google.com/books). Archives can be searched through WorldCat, the National Union Catalog of Manuscripts Collections (loc.gov/coll/nucmc), and ArchiveGrid (archivegrid.org).

Special collections of note:

BEINECKE RARE BOOK AND MANUSCRIPT LIBRARY, YALE UNIVERSITY. **Betsy Beinecke Shirley Collection of American Children's Literature:** Four letters from Alice Morse Earle to Andrew Tuer, 1899–1900, one with manuscript transcript, possibly by Tuer.

THE BODLEIAN LIBRARY, OXFORD UNIVERSITY. **John Johnson Collection of Printed Ephemera:** Advertisements, playbills, programs, prospectuses, cards, and menus printed by Field & Tuer and the Leadenhall Press, and two Tuer bookplates.

THE BRITISH LIBRARY. **Gordon Papers (Bell Collection):** Letter from Field & Tuer to Sir H. W. Gordon, 1885. **Shaw Papers:** Letter from Field & Tuer to G. B. Shaw, 1889. **Gladstone Correspondence:** Letter from Andrew Tuer. **Hazlitt Correspondence:** Letters from Andrew Tuer to essayist William Hazlitt. **Leadenhall Press v. Messrs. G. Mellin:** Correspondence with the Society of Authors relating to a case against Mellin & Co., 1895.

DETROIT PUBLIC LIBRARY. **Kate Greenaway Collection:** Two letters to Andrew Tuer.

UNIVERSITY OF GLASGOW LIBRARY. **Correspondence of James McNeill Whistler:** Letters from Field & Tuer to Whistler's lawyers, from Andrew Tuer to Whistler, between Whistler and Albert Maeterlinck, and from Whistler to George Henry Lewis, regarding Sheridan Ford's attempts to publish without permission letters that subsequently appeared in *The Gentle Art of Making Enemies* (London: Heinemann, 1890).

THOMAS FISHER RARE BOOK LIBRARY, UNIVERSITY OF TORONTO. **Nineteenth century Scottish chapbooks collection:** Twenty-six volumes from the library of Joseph Crawhall, some with his manuscript notes, containing approximately 600 chapbooks, mainly from the first half of the nineteenth century, some earlier, most printed in Scotland, some in England, many illustrated. Also **a copy of Crawhall's** *Olde ffrendes wyth newe Faces.*

GETTY RESEARCH LIBRARY, LOS ANGELES, CA. **John Saddler letters to Andrew White Tuer, 1881–88:** Eight letters concerning stipple engravers, work in progress, book illustration, and the lack of demand for line engraving.

HOUGHTON LIBRARY, HARVARD UNIVERSITY. **Specimens of Type, Field & Tuer:** [ca. 1885]. 2 vols. Vellum, lettered in gilt. Vol. 1: 31 cm. 207 mounted leaves, some folded. Vol 2: 29 cm. 172 mounted specimens, some folded. Founders include: Stephenson & Blake, Figgins, McKellar, Smiths & Jordan, Bruce, Zeese, Gerbach, Schmittner, Miller & Richard, Sir C. Reed & Sons, Day & Collins, and Central Type Foundry. Also included are a Field & Tuer device, "The New Steam Compositor," and several Japanese woodcuts.

THE LILLY LIBRARY, INDIANA UNIVERSITY (BLOOMINGTON). An extensive collection of Field & Tuer and Leadenhall Press publications, as well as items from Andrew Tuer's personal collection, including publisher's copies, presentation copies, original art, and *Dover's Annalia Dubrensia: a reprint*, a presentation copy from Thomas Hailing. **Tuer MSS., 1879–1918:** Letters to Andrew W. Tuer and his wife, Thomasine Louisa (Louttit). Correspondents: Walter Besant, Max O'Rell (Paul Blouët), Walter Crane, Joseph Crawhall (with original drawings), Frank Dicksee, Robinson Duckworth, John Galsworthy, Jerome K. Jerome, Charles Samuel Keene, Joseph Knight, Andrew Lang, John Leighton, Norman MacColl, Alice Meynell, W. M. Flinders Petrie, Harry Quilter, John Richard Robinson, John Ruskin, Owen Seaman, and Linley Sambourne. **Blouët MSS., 1887–1896:** Letters and postcards from Paul Blouët ("Max O'Rell") to Andrew Tuer and to Field and Tuer. **Hornbooks, ca. 1550-1986:** Includes even original hornbooks formerly owned by Tuer and described and illustrated in *History of the Horn-Book*.

THE MORGAN LIBRARY, NEW YORK, NY. **Album: London, 1890:** Signed and dated by Joseph Crawhall. Among the contents: bookplates by Thomas Bewick (one of 14 printed on vellum) and Bilibald Pirckheimer (designed by Albrecht Dürer); pen drawing and watercolor sketch by Crawhall; letters from artists, writers, publishers, and engravers, including Charles M. Adamson, Jane Bewick, Robert Chambers, William Chappell, Myles Birket Foster, James Guthrie, George James Howard, Charles S. Keene, Cecil G. Lawson, Frederick Conway Montagu, William Bell Scott, and Andrew Tuer.

NEWCASTLE CITY LIBRARY. **The Crawhall Collection:** Books, impressions from wooden blocks on card mounted in album with letters from Andrew Tuer.

THE NEW YORK PUBLIC LIBRARY RARE BOOK COLLECTION. Haldane Macfall. *Some Thoughts Suggested by the Art of Joseph Crawhall. Illustrated with Woodcuts, the Presence of which is due to the Courtesy of the Leadenhall Press.* [n.p., n.d.]. 28cm. Printed on one side of leaf. Author's presentation copy to publisher Morgan Shepard.

PATERNO LIBRARY, PENNSYLVANIA STATE UNIVERSITY. **Grant Allen Literary Manuscripts and Correspondence:** Autograph manuscript of *Michael's Crag* with corrections and revisions, 1893; original ink-and-gouache silhouette illustrations for *Michael's Crag* by F. Carruthers Gould, mounted in an album. **Mortlake Collection of English Life and Letters:** correspondence from George Augustus Sala to Tuer.

PRINCETON UNIVERSITY LIBRARY. **Walter Besant Correspondence, 1876-1901:** Includes letters written to Besant, in his capacity as one of the founders (1884) of the Society of Authors, from various correspondents, including Andrew Tuer. **Archives of Charles Scribner's Sons:** Includes a folder of letters written in 1884 to Scribner's from Max O'Rell and Field & Tuer concerning American rights to *John Bull and His Island* and the forthcoming English translation of *Les Filles de John Bull.* Also Scribner & Welford archives and correspondence between London and New York offices.

ROBINSON LIBRARY, NEWCASTLE UNIVERSITY. **Joseph Crawhall Collection:** Inscribed books, letters to and from Andrew Tuer, original art, original woodblocks.

WINTERTHUR LIBRARY, WINTERTHUR, DELAWARE. **The Guercino Etchings Dispute** [scrapbook]: 34 cm. Vellum, titling in gilt. 37 letters and several clippings relating to a review of *Bartolozzi and His Works* in the *Athenaeum* of Sept. 9, 1882. Also included: a copy of *Catalogue of a Loan Exhibition of Engravings and Etchings by Francesco Bartolozzi,* two invitations, and an announcement. Correspondents include: W. C. Alexander, George Cook, J. Cotton, George Doo, Louis Fagan, J. Deffett Francis, P. G. Hamerton, R. H. Holmes (Royal Librarian, Windsor Castle), C. H. Middleton-Wake, Bernard Quaritch, Lawrence Hilliard (for John Ruskin), John Saddler, and W. B. Scott.

WOODSON RESEARCH CENTER, FONDREN LIBRARY, RICE UNIVERSITY. **Letters to Andrew Tuer, 1880-1897:** Correspondents: W. C. Adams, Grant Allen, J. Ashby-Sterry, J. Kent Ballard, F. C. Barnum, P. T. Barnum, Robert Barr, W. F. Blake, F. Boughton, E. A. Walls Budge, Buffalo Bill's Wild West Co., W. T. Byron, Charles Dickens Jr., R. Duckworth, Amelia B. Edwards, Th. Fales, Percy Fitzgerald, Myles Birket Foster, Alfred Scott Gatty, E. C. Glyn, Walter F. Godley, Sir Henry Gordon, Walter F. Gordon, J. O. Hallwell-Phillips, W. E. Henley, John Hollingshead, Marcus B. Huish, Jerome K. Jerome, Charles S. Keene, Joseph Knight, Sir E. Ray Lankester, Percy Macquoid, W. C. Meberghurten, Mortimer Menpeg, Lady Dorothy Nevill, Edward A. Parry, J. Humphreys Parry, Alfred Parsons, Howard Paul, Emily Pfeiffer, Sir Henry Ponsonby (for Queen Victoria), F. G. Hilton Price, Compton Reade, and Edward Yates.

YOUNG RESEARCH LIBRARY, UNIVERSITY OF CALIFORNIA, LOS ANGELES. **Joseph Crawhall Papers, 1864–1890:** Proof copies, scrapbooks, and limited editions; letters, one from Andrew Tuer. **Marie Corelli Papers:** Includes letters from Field & Tuer and Andrew Tuer. **Henry Stevens Papers, 1819–1886:** Letters from Andrew Tuer and Field & Tuer.

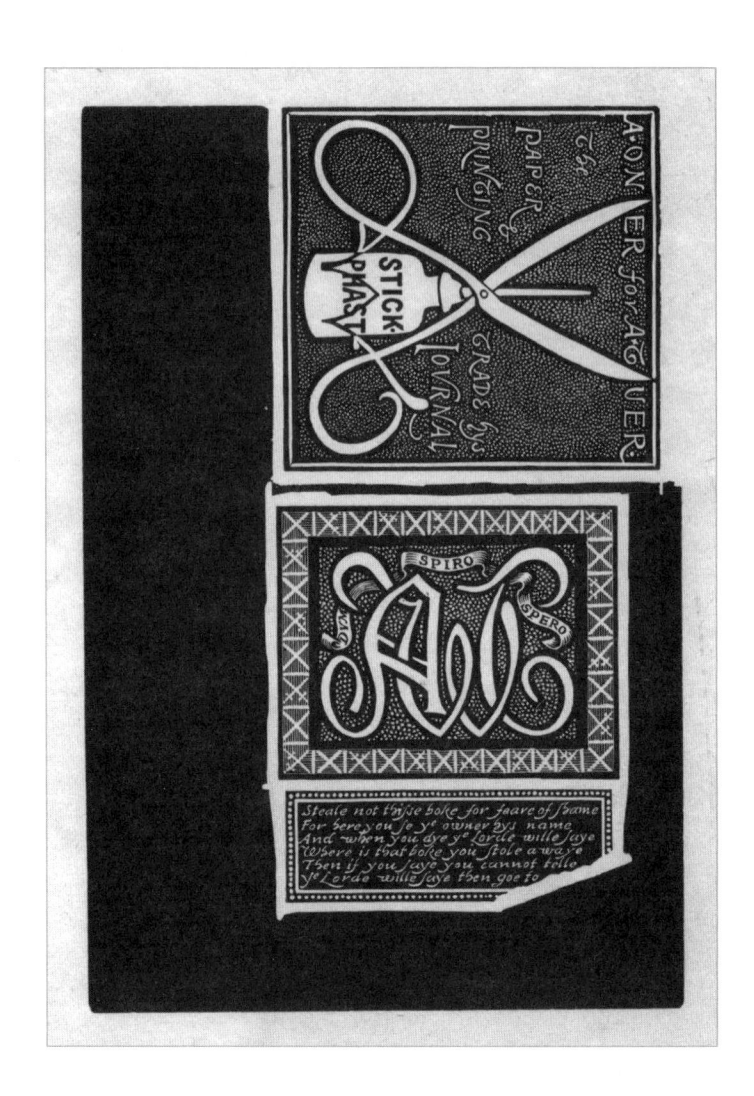

Proof of designs for two bookplates attributed to W. H. Hooper (see page 107).

Bibliography

Some of the sources listed below are included more for context than for how much they have to say about Field & Tuer and the Leadenhall Press. Curious readers are encouraged to search out Andrew Tuer's many contributions and letters to *Notes and Queries,* the *Athenaeum,* the *Pall Mall Gazette* and other journals and newspapers, as well as contemporary articles and letters by others about Tuer and the Leadenhall Press.

Anderson, Patricia J., and Jonathan Rose. *British Literary Publishing Houses, 1820–1880.* Detroit: Gale Research, 1991: 171-2.

"Andrew W. Tuer." *The British Printer,* Vol. IV, No. 34, July–August, 1893: 225–226.

"Andrew White Tuer," *Printing Review—Magazine of the Printing Industry,* Number 54, Summer 1950: 39-40.

Bigmore, E. C., and C. W. H. Wyman. *A Bibliography of Printing,* London: Bernard Quaritch, 1883-1886: Vol. II: 182, 374; Vol. III: 24–26.

Bullen, George, Esq., F.S.A. *Caxton Celebration 1877. Catalogue of the Loan Collection of Antiquities, Curiosities and Appliances connected with the Art of Printing.* London: N. Trübner & Co., 1877.

Bury, J. P. T. [John Patrick Tuer]. "A. W. Tuer and the Leadenhall Press." *The Book Collector,* Volume 36, No. 2, Summer 1987: 225–243.

Bury, J. P. T. "Andrew White Tuer and His Bookplates." *The Bookplate Journal,* Vol. 6, Number 1, March 1988: 5–14.

DeVinne, Theodore L. "The Chap-book and Its Outgrowths." *The Literary Collector: An Illustrated Monthly Magazine of Book-Lore and Bibliography,* November, 1902: 1-5.

"The Horn-Book in Ex Libris." *Ex Libris Journal (Journal of the Ex Libris Society),* Vol. IV, Part 2, Feb. 1894: 25

"The Late Andrew W. Tuer and His Book-Plates." *Ex Libris Journal (Journal of the Ex Libris Society),* Vol. X, Part 9, September 1900: 132.

Felver, Charles S. *Joseph Crawhall: the Newcastle wood engraver : 1821–1896.* Newcastle upon Tyne: F. Graham, 1973.

Hailing's Circular. (Cheltenham: Thomas Hailing, Oxford Printing Works). Vol. I: No. 1, November 1877 through No. 10, Spring 1882.

Hudson, Graham. "Artistic Printing: A Re-evaluation." *Journal of the Printing Historical Society, New Series 9,* Spring 2006: 39–63.

Jennett, Sean. "Printers' International Specimen Exchange." *Print IX: 4,* March–April, 1955: 17–18.

Johnson, A. F. "Old-Face Types in the Victorian Age," *The Monotype Recorder,* Sept.-Dec. 1931: 5–14.

Johnson, Dr. John. "The Development of Printing, other than Book Printing." *The Library,* Fourth Series, XVII-1, 1936. pp. 22–35.

Joyner, George. *Fine Printing: Its Inception, Development, and Practice.* (London: Cooper and Budd, 1895): 26-28.

Kuzmanovic, N. Natasha. *John Paul Cooper, Designer and Craftsman of the Arts and Crafts Movement.* (Stroud: Sutton Publishing, 1999): 20–21, 70–72, 74.

Lewis, John. *Printed Ephemera: The Changing Uses of Type and Letterforms in English and American Printing.* (Ipswich: W. S. Cowell, 1962): 12–13.

McLean, Ruari. *Victorian Book Design and Colour Printing.* Second edition, enlarged and revised. (London: Faber & Faber, 1972).

Meynell, Francis. *English Printed Books.* (London: Collins, 1946).

Myers, Robin. *The British Book Trade from Caxton to the Present Day: A Bibliographical Guide.* (London: Andre Deutsch, 1973).

Peltz, Lucy. "Tuer, Andrew White (1838–1900)." *The Oxford Dictionary of National Biography.* Oxford: Oxford University Press, 2004. (Also: the entry signed "C. D." in *The Dictionary of National Biography.*)

Peterson, William S. *The Kelmscott Press, A History of William Morris's Typographical Adventure.* (Berkeley: University of California Press, 1991).

Ray, Gordon Norton. *The Illustrator and the Book in England from 1790 to 1914.* (New York: Pierpont Morgan Library; London: Oxford University Press, 1976).

Rickards, Maurice and Michael Twyman, eds. *Encyclopedia of Ephemera. A Guide to the Fragmentary Documents of Everyday Life for the Collector, Curator and Historian.* (London: Routledge, 2000).

Ridler, Vivian. "Artistic Printing: A Search for Principles." *Alphabet and Image 6,* 1948: 4–17.

Shattock, Joanne, ed. *The Cambridge Bibliography of English Literature, Vol. 4, 1800–1900 (3rd Edition).* (Cambridge: Cambridge University Press, 1999).

Shepard, Leslie. *The History of the Horn Book: a Bibliographical Essay.* ([Cambridge]: Rampant Lions Press for the Broadsheet King, 1977).

Southward, John. *Catalogue of the William Blades Library.* (London: printed for the Governors of the St. Bride Foundation Institute by Bradbury, Agnew & Co., 1899).

White, Gleeson. "Children's Books and Their Illustrators." *The International Studio,* Special Winter Number, 1897-8: 3–68.

Index

Titles are in italics. Illustrations and collections are not indexed.

A. Y. D.: *The Owls of Olynn Belfry* 67
Abbey, Edwin A.: *Selections from the Hesperides* (illust.) 46
A B C Mariners' Guide, The (R. T. Stevens) 39, 41, 44, 44*n*, 53
Abou-Hamed: Being Some Account of Its Battle and Its Ghost Story (Sidney) 102
Academy, The (periodical) 24*n*, 53*n*, 83*n*
Account of the Methods Whereby the Charity Schools Have Been Erected & Managed, An 39
Adams, Francis O.: *The Grievances between Authors & Publishers* (contr.) 73
Addy, George Henry: *A Song of Love and Liberty* 72
Æsop Redivivus (Boyle) 81
Age of Marie Antoinette, The (Scott) 80
Ainger, A. C.: *Eton Songs* 87
Aird & Coghill (printers) 10
Al-So. *See* Somers, Alexander
Allan, R. W.: *History of the Horn-Book* (illust.) 95
Allan, Wilfrid: *Weather Wisdom* 80
Allen, Grant 25, 26; *Michael's Crag* 25, 26, 91
Amateur Tommy Atkins (Watkins-Pitchford) 63
Amongst the Shans (Colquhoun) 61
Anderson, Joseph: *The Winter's Tale* (illust.) 78
Anderson, Mary: *The Winter's Tale* (arr.) 78
Andrew Robinson Stoney Bowes Esquire (Crawhall) 47, 55, 120
Angier Bros.: *A Handbook of Freight Tables and Tonnage Schedules* 41; *Comparative Rates of Freight* 41
Anglo-Saxon Superiority (Demolins) 97
Antony & Cleopatra (Shakespeare) 29, 83
Archer, James: *Songs of the North* (illust.) 64
Archer, William: *Henry Irving, Actor and Manager* 49
Are We to Read ?SDRAWKCAB (Millington) 16, 48*n*, 53, 119
"Art of Silhouetting, The" (Tuer) 12, 105
Art Embroidery in the Sewing Machine 58
Arthur, J. K.: *A Bouquet of Brevities* 95
Art of Making and Selling Butter, The ("E. M.") 78
Arts of Ancient Egypt, The (Petrie) 60
Ashton, John: *Men, Maidens and Manners a Hundred Years Ago* 27, 77; *Real Sailor-Songs* 27, 85; *Drinks of the World* 87; *A History of English Lotteries* 16, 27, 91; *A righte Merrie Christmasse!!!* 27, 93
A Song of the Wind (Stout) 38
Aspects of Fiction (Laffan) 62
As the Wind Blows. Stray Songs in Many Moods (King) 86
Athenaeum, The 14, 25, 32, 33, 116
Atkins, M. Alison: *Mohammed Aben Alamar* (illust.) 103
Australian at Home, The (Kinglake) 85

Author's (Hairless) Paper Pad 6, 33, 109, 111–112
Author, The (periodical) 19*n*
"B.": *A Political Catechism* 78; *Palaver; the Fairy Genius of Atlantis* 81; *The Truth About Democracy* 84
Babes in the Wood, The (Crawhall) 47, 50, 120
Baby's Record (R. I. Woodhouse) 79
Baglioni, A Tragedy, The (Cartwright) 77
Bagshaw, Samuel. *See* Watkins-Pitchford, Walter M.
Bairns' Annual, The (Corkran) 26, 67
Balguy, Guy: *The Bantams of Sheffield* 85
Ballad of Thyra Lee, The (H. Boulton) 100
Ballads of Schiller No. 1. The Diver (Harford) 41
Banquet at Guildhall: menu 113; program 113
Bantams of Sheffield, The (Balguy) 85
Barkeshire Lady's Garland, The (Crawhall) 47, 50, 120
Barnby, Sir Joseph: *Eton Songs* 87
Barnum, P. T. 30
Bartolozzi and His Works (Tuer) 14, 33, 36, 44, 66
Bartolozzi Exhibition [invitation] 111
Barton, Frederick Page: *Bridge Simplified* 103
Beauty and the Beast (Lamb) 25, 73
Bedford, Francis D.: *History of the Horn-Book* (illust.) 95
Beerbohm, Max 2
Behrend, Arthur C.: *A righte Merrie Christmasse!!!* (illust.) 93
Bell, Margaret T.: *Poems: and Other Pieces* 93
Bell, R. S. Warren: *The Businesses of a Busy Man* 92
Besant, Walter: *The Grievances between Authors & Publishers* (contr.) 73
Besemeres, John Daly: *No Actress. A Stage Doorkeeper's Story* 38
Bewick, Thomas 18, 62, 77
Bewicke, Alicia E. Neva: *Mother Darling!* 64
Bewick Memento (Robinson) 18, 62
Bianca Capello, A Tragedy (Cartwright) 69
Bickerdyke, John. *See* Cook, Charles Henry
Bickers & Son, publishers 12
Bill of the Play: The Rivals: En Pension 111
Billy. A Sketch for "the New Boy" by an Old Boy (Fuller) 100
Bind Me As You Please Series 82, 121
Birmingham Group 3, 28
Bit of Humanity, A (Tomlinson) 96
Blackburn, Douglas: *Thought-Reading or Modern Mysteries Explained* 57
Blackburn, Jemima: *Songs of the North* (illust.) 64
Blackwood's Edinburgh Magazine 73
Blades, William: Caxton Exhibition 8*n*, 40*n*; *The Life and Typography of William Caxton* 40*n*

Blake, William 29
Blaker, H. O.: *The Principles of Warfare* 100
Blew Cap for Mee (Crawhall) 47, 50, 120
Blomfield, Rev. F. G: *How Is the Gospel to Be Preached to the Poor?* 39
Blots & Blemishes 79
Blouët, Madame: *The Dear Neighbours!* (trans.) 67
"Blue Peter": *A Week in a Wherry on the Norfolk Broads* 83
Boers or English: Who Are in the Right? (Demolins) 100
Book-Plate Collector's Miscellany, The 107n
Book of Delightful and Strange Designs, The (Tuer) 1, 31, 89
Book of Japanese Designs (import) 35
Book of Jousts, A (Lowry) 25, 75
Booke of Sundry Draughtes, A (Gedde) 97
Bookplate Journal, The 2, 108
Bookseller, The (periodical) 21, 36, 91n
Bookworm, The (periodical) 31
Borderland Fancies (E. Boulton) 94
Boulton, Eva: *Borderland Fancies* 94
Boulton, Sir Harold Edwin: *Ballad of Thyra Lee* 100; *Seven Songs to Sing* 90; *Songs of the North* (ed.) 64–65; *Songs Sung and Unsung* 21, 92; *12 New Songs by Some of the Best-Known British Composers* 86
Bouquet of Brevities, A (Arthur) 95
Boyle, Mary: *Æsop Redivivus* 81
Bramah, Ernest: *English Farming and Why I Turned It Up* 92
Brame, Alfred: *The India General Steam Navigation Company* 100
Brand, Wilhelm Ferdinand: *London Life Seen with German Eyes* 72
Brett, Eleanor Frances Weston: *Echoes. A Musical Birthday Book* 91
Bric-à-Brac Ballads ("Goosestep") 88
Bridge Condensed (C. Smith) 102
Bridge Simplified (Barton) 103
Brief Guide to Merstham Parish Church, A (R. I. Woodhouse) 103
British Printer, The ii, 11, 15, 42n
British Railways and Canals ("Hercules") 63
British Sugar and French Bounties (Lubbock, W. H. Smith) 40
British Sugar Industries and Foreign Export Bounties (Ohlson) 42
British Typographia 11
Broadwood, A. Hennen: *Ye Gestes of Ye Ladye Anne* (illust.) 59
Broadwood, Lucy Etheldred: *English County Songs* (ed.) 90
Brooks, Henry Jamyn: *The Mind or the Spiritual Part of Life* 96
"Brother Bob": *You Shouldn't* 19, 55

Browne, St. John: *Master Jimmy's Fables* 94
Browning, Robert 29, 58
Brownrig, Ralph: *Sermons in Sentences* 58
Buchanan, Robert: *The Child Set in the Midst: by Modern Poets* 25, 88
Buffalo Bill's Wild West Co. 30
Bullen, George: *Caxton Celebration 1877. Catalogue of the Loan Collection of Antiquities, Curiosities, and Appliances Connected with the Art of Printing* 9n
Bunce, Oliver Bell: *Don't* 19, 53
Burke, Ulick Ralph: *Business and Pleasure in Brazil* 55
Burma and the Burmans (Colquhoun) 63–64
Burne, F. S. Janet: *Sybil's Dutch Dolls* 73
Burne-Jones, Edward: *Songs of the North* (illust.) 3, 28, 64
Bury, John Patrick Tuer: "Andrew W. Tuer and the Leadenhall Press" in *The Book Collector* 1–2, 1n; "Andrew White Tuer and His Bookplates" in *The Bookplate Journal* 2, 108n
Business and Pleasure in Brazil (Burke, Staples) 55
Businesses of a Busy Man, The (R. Bell) 92
Butterfly's Ball and the Grasshopper's Feast, The (Roscoe) 51
Bygone Beauties (Hoppner, Wilkin, Tuer) 51–52
Bygone Holborn, A 98
"C. B.": *The Story of a Nursery Rhyme* 44, 49
Caird, James Tennant: *A Celebrity at Home* 75
Caldecott, Randolph: *The Owls of Olynn Belfry* (illust.) 28, 67
Caldicott, Alfred James: *Seven Songs to Sing* (contr.) 90
Canada's Poet (Gay) 57
Can Parliament Break Faith? ("W") 55, 120
Cantlie, Sir James: *Degeneration Amongst Londoners* 63
Cargo Book (Field & Tuer) 37
Carlyle, Thomas: *A Pearl of English Rhetoric. Thomas Carlyle on the Repeal of the Union* 78; *Rescued Essays of Thomas Carlyle* 87
Carolino, Pedro: *English as She Is Spoke* 48; *English as She Is Spoke…Her Seconds Part* 52
Carruthers Gould, Alec and Francis: *Michael's Crag* (illust.) 26, 91
Carter, R. Brudenell: *Are We to Read ?SDRAWKCAB* (introd.) 53
Cartwright, Sir Fairfax Leighton: *The Baglioni, A Tragedy* 77; *Bianca Capello, A Tragedy* 69; *The Emperor's Wish, A Play* 63; *Lorello, A Play* 64
Catalogue of a Loan Collection of Engravings & Etchings by Francesco Bartolozzi (Tuer) 46–47, 106
Catalogue of Books Printed for Private Circulation (Dobell) 36
Catalogue of Books Selected from the Library of an English Amateur (Herbert) 92
Catalogue of the Second Exhibition … of Engravings & Etchings by Francesco Bartolozzi (Nash) 47

Caxton Celebration 2-3, 15, 24, 40
Caxton Celebration 1877. Catalogue of the Loan Collection 9, 9n
Celebrity at Home, A. (Caird) 75
"Censor." *See* Bunce, Oliver Bell
Century of Lloyd's Patriotic Fund, A (Rougement) 103
Chambers, Robert: *Illustrations of the Author of Waverley* 56
Chapters from "The Perfect Way." The Nature and Constitution of the Ego (Kingsford) 76
Charles Dickens Sale, The 38
Charles Scribner's Sons 52, 52n, 58n, 85n
Ch. Guillaume et Cie (engravers): *Kensington Picturesque & Historical* 78; *London City* 84; *London City Suburbs* 90
Child Set in the Midst: by Modern Poets, The (W. Meynell) 13, 25, 88
Children's London, The (Thorpe) 101
Chinese Painted by Themselves, The (Tcheng-Ki-Tong) 63
Chiswick Press 15
Choice Art Books (Field & Tuer) 110
Christmas Box, or New Year's Gift, The 77
Christmas Entertainments 50–51, 119
Clark, J. B.: *The Dolls' Garden Party* (illust.) 87
Clarkson, Charles Tempest: *Police!* 79; *The Rogues' Gallery* 81
Clay, Arthur: *History of the Horn-Book* (illust.) 95
Clayton's Annual Register of Shipping 7, 37
"A Clergyman": *Decently and in Order* 48, 56, 120
Coghlan, Charles: *Antony & Cleopatra* (actor) 83
Cold: A New Manufacture (Pure Ice Mfg. Co.) 110
Cole, Emma: *Respectfully Inscribed to Mr. G. Ridler* 36
Collectors' Marks (Fagan) 27, 49–50; expanded edition (Einstein and Goldstein, eds., 1918) 27n, 49–50
Colquhoun, Archibald Ross: *Amongst the Shans* 61; *Burma and the Burmans* 63; *English Policy in the Far East* 27, 65; *Matabeleland: the War, and Our Position in South Africa* 27, 92; *The Opening of China* 60; *The Truth about Tonquin* 27, 55
Comfort in the Home (M. J. Loftie) 94
Comparative Rates of Freight (Angier) 41
Confessions of a Poacher, The (J. Watson) 84
Contemporary Notices of Charles Lamb (Moxon) 85
Conversion and Unification of the Spanish Debt, The ("A Castillian") 43
Conway, Hugh. *See* Fargus, Frederick John
Cook, Charles Henry (pseud. John Bickerdyke): *The Curiosities of Ale & Beer* 71
Cooper, John Paul 32
Coppen, John Maurice: *The Coppyns of Kent* 100
Coppyns of Kent, The (Coppen) 100
Corbet, Robert St. John: *From the Bull's Point of View* 90; *The Handsome Examiner* 81
Corelli, Marie 30, 60

Corkran, Alice: *The Bairns' Annual* 26, 67
"*Cornered*" (Porritt) 84
Corporation of London: *Some Rules for the Conduct of Life* 40
Corpse in the Copse or the Perils of Love, The (Lorraine) 68
Counsel to Ladies and Easy-Going Men on their Business Investments ("Senex") 88
Cowslip, The (Turner) 99, 121
Cradle of the Shan Race, The (Lacouperie) 61
Craik, Dinah: *The Child Set in the Midst: by Modern Poets* 88
Crane, Walter 11, 24
Crawhall's Chap-book Chaplets 17, 47, 47n, 50, 54, 120
Crawhall, Elspeth 17, 50, 58, 61
Crawhall, Joseph, II: artistic style 16; relationship with Andrew Tuer 16, 17, 18; contributes jokes to Charles Keene 18; and the Leadenhall Press 28
Crawhall, Joseph, II, works of: *Olde Tayles Newlye Relayted* 16, 17, 47; *Crawhall's Chap-book Chaplets* 17, 47, 47n, 50, 54, 120; *Olde ffrendes wyth newe Faces* 1, 17, 47, 47n, 50, 54, 120; *Andrew Robinson Stoney Bowes Esquire* 47, 55, 120; *The Babes in the Wood* 47, 50, 120; *The Barkeshire Lady's Garland* 47, 50, 120; *Blew Cap for Mee* 47, 50, 120; *Ducks & Green Peas, or, the Newcastle Rider* 55, 120; *Ducks & Green Peas; a Farce* 47, 55, 120; *George Barnewel* 47, 50, 120; *The Gloamin' Buchte* 47, 54, 55, 120; *I Know What I Know* 47, 50, 120; *Jemmy & Nancy of Yarmouth* 47, 50, 120; *John & Joan* 47, 50, 120; *John Cunningham, the Pastoral Poet* 47, 55, 120; *The Long Pack: a Northumbrian Tale* 47, 54, 120; *The Sword-Dancers* 47, 54, 120; *The Taming of a Shrew* 47, 50, 120; *A True Relation of the Apparition of Mrs. Veal to Mrs. Bargrave* 47, 54; *Ye Loving Ballad of Lorde Bateman* 47, 54, 120; *London Cries* (illust.) 52; *Old Aunt Elspa's ABC* 17, 57; *Old Aunt Elspa's Spelling Bee* 17, 60; *Old London Street Cries and the Cries of To-day* (illust.) 65; *Izaak Walton: His Wallet Booke* 17, 66; *Joe Miller in Motley* (illust.) 89; *History of the Horn-Book* (illust.) 24, 95
Crawhall, Joseph, III: *Olde ffrendes wyth newe Faces* (illust.) 54
Creighton, Trevor: *Ethics of Some Modern Novels* 56, 119
Crickmore, Hovell: *Ye Foure Etchynges By Maister H. Crickmore* 66
Cross, Joseph: *A Daughter of the Gods* (trans.) 86
Cruikshank, George 15, 52
Cundall, Joseph 2
Curatica, or Leaves from a Curate's Note-book 84, 121
Curiosities of Ale & Beer, The (Cook) 71
Curious Old Cookery Receipts 85
"Cylinder" 19: *Prince Bismarck's Map of Europe* 76

Dahle, Thomas Theodore: *The Notions of a Nobody* 90
Daisy, The (Turner) 99, 121
Dale, Ester: *Madame Marie, Singer* 101
Dame and Her Donkeys Five, The 76, 121
Dame Wiggins of Lee (Sharpe, Pearson) 14, 74, 106, 121
Danby, Thomas William: *Practical Guide to the Determination of Minerals by the Blowpipe* 40
Daniel, Rev. C. H. O. 2
Darby, John H.: *Report of Mr. John H. Darby, M.Inst. C.E., on the Blythe River Iron Mines* 100
"Darling". *See* Dixie, Lady Florence
Daughter of the Gods, A (Cross) 86
Davidson, Gwendoline: *Kitten's Goblins* 26, 78; *A Story of Stops* 26, 83
Davies, Basil: *The Vicar's Pups* 98
Davies, Edward W. L.: *Our Sea-Fish and Sea-Food* 73
D'Avigdor, Estelle: *History of the Worshipful Company of Gold and Silver Wyre-Drawers* (illust.) 86
Davy, J. & Sons, the Dryden Press 10
Dawn of the Twentieth Century, The 75
Dean & Munday 14, 14n, 74, 76
Dear Neighbours!, The (O'Rell) 67
Deborah Dent and Her Donkey 74, 106, 121
Decently and in Order ("A Clergyman") 48n, 56, 120
Degeneration Amongst Londoners (Cantlie) 63
Delamar's Fetich. A Story of the Riviera 76
Demolins, Edmond: *Anglo-Saxon Superiority* 97; *Boers or English: Who Are in the Right?* 100
Denham-Smith, Sir James (pseud. J. W. Gilbart-Smith): *My Ladye and Others: Poems* 43
Dent, J. M. 32, 34
Denza, Luigi: *Seven Songs to Sing* (contr.) 90
Descriptive Catalogue of a Small Collection Principally of Xvth and Xvith Century Bronzes (Pfungst) 100
Designs of Cabinet Furniture . . . (Blyth & Sons) 110
Devil's Acres, The 84
De Vinne, Theodore Low 16, 48: "The Chap-book and Its Outgrowths" in *The Literary Collector* 16n
Dexter, John F.: *Dickens Memento* 63
Diary J.A.H.M. (Muir) 21, 71–72
Diary of Eve in Eden, A.M. I 82
Dick, C.: *Seven Songs to Sing* (contr.) 90
Dickens Memento (Dexter, A. Meynell) 13, 38, 63
Dicksee, Frank: *12 New Songs by Some of the Best-Known British Composers* (Illust.) 86
Disraeli, Benjamin: *Lord Beaconsfield on the Constitution* 57
Dixie, Lady Florence 26: *The Songs of a Child, Part I* 101, 103; *The Story of Ijain, or, the Evolution of a Mind* 26, 102; *Isola, or the Disinherited* 26, 102; *The Songs of a Child, Part II* 103; *Eilabelle; or, the Redeemed. A Drama* 103
Dixon, J. M.: *The Curiosities of Ale & Beer* (contr.) 71

Dobell, Bertram: *Catalogue of Books Printed for Private Circulation* 36
Dobson, Austin: *The Child Set in the Midst: by Modern Poets* 25, 88
Doctor Quodlibet. A Study in Ethics (Fuller) 93
"Dogberry": *Humours and Oddities of the London Police Courts* 19, 93; clues to identity of 19n
Dolls' Garden Party, The (Lowry) 87
Don't (Bunce) 48, 53, English rights 53n, 119
Dorset, Catherine Ann: *The Lion's Masquerade* 51; *The Peacock at Home* 51
Douglas, Lady Florence. *See* Dixie, Lady Florence
Drat the Boys! (O'Rell) 71
Drinks of the World (Mew, Ashton) 87
Duc De Sully's House, International Health Exhibition 112
Ducks & Green Peas, or, the Newcastle Rider (Crawhall) 55, 120
Ducks & Green Peas; a Farce (Crawhall) 47, 55, 120
Dudley, Ambrose (illustrator): *A Life's Reminiscences of Scotland Yard* 28, 82; *Mrs. Greet's Story of the Golden Owl* 21, 88; *Seven Songs to Sing* 90; *History of the Horn-Book* (illust.) 95; *Six Stories* 100; bookplate designs for Andrew Tuer 107-108
Du Maurier, George 18, 29
Duties and Conduct of Nurses in Private Nursing, The (Richardson) 74
"E. M.": *The Art of Making and Selling Butter* 78
Earhart, J. F. (printer) 10
Eccles, Charlotte O'Connor (pseud. "A Modern Maid"): *Modern Men. By a Modern Maid* 73
Echoes. A Musical Birthday Book (Brett) 91
Echoes of Memory (Furlong) 25, 61;
Eighteen-Eighty-Five ("A Civil Servant") 62–63
Eighteen of Them. Singular Stories (Simpson) 92
Eight Tales of Fairyland (Poirez) 26, 73
Eilabelle; or, the Redeemed. A Drama (Dixie) 103
Elephant's Ball and Grand Fête Champetre, The ("W. B.") 51
Ellis, Edwin John (illustrator) 28; *Some Well-known "Sugar'd Sonnets" by William Shakespeare* 29, 45; *"C. B." The Story of a Nursery Rhyme* 49; *When Is Your Birthday?* 49; *The Winter's Tale* 78; *Antony & Cleopatra* 29, 83
Ellis, Tristram James (illustrator) 28: *Luxurious Bathing* 13, 29, 42, 105; *On a Raft, and Through the Desert* (author, illust.) 13, 15, 29, 43; *Six Etchings of Well-Known Views in Kensington Gardens* 29, 45; *Some Well-Known "Sugar'd Sonnets" by William Shakespeare* 29, 45–46; *Echoes of Memory* 61; *Diary J.A.H.M.* 72; *A Daughter of the Gods* 86
Emperor's Wish, A Play, The (Cartwright) 63
English as She Is Spoke (Carolino) 48, 48n, 119
English as She Is Spoke . . . Her Seconds Part (Carolino) 48n, 52, 119

English Carols of the Fifteenth Century (J. Maitland, Rockstro) 85
English Catalogue of Books 36, 48, 53*n*, 86*n*
English County Songs (L. Broadwood, J. Maitland) 90
English Farming and Why I Turned It Up (Bramah) 92
English Illustrated Magazine, The 12
English Policy in the Far East (Colquhoun) 27, 65
Ennui De Voyage (Windt) 80
Ephemera: Essays on Various Subjects (E. Watson) 82
Epigrams: Original and Selected (Standring) 41
Ernest England; or, a Soul Laid Bare (Parker) 94
Essay of Scarabs, An (Loftie) 60
Estimate of the Numbers Engaged in the Trades and Professions 33*n*, 103–104
Ethics of Some Modern Novels (Creighton) 56–57, 119
Eton Songs (Ainger, Barnby) 87
Evans's Music and Supper Rooms (Townsend) 38
Every-Day Life, An (Woods) 95
"*Evidence*" (Noel) 69
Ex-M.P.: *A Radical Nightmare* 67
Exhibition of Engravings by Francesco Bartolozzi 111
Ex Libris Journal 28, 33*n*, 107*n*; 108*n*
Ex Libris Society 32
Extracts from Field & Tuer / The Leadenhall Press Book List 61
Facta Non Verba. An Examination of the Figures and Statements Published as the Result of the Analyses of Professor Frankland (Ω [Omega]) 41
Fagan, Charles E.: *The First Year of a Silken Reign* 72
Fagan, Louis: *Collectors' Marks* 27, 49
Family of Darby-Coventry, The (Fell) 89
Fargus, Frederick John (pseud. Hugh Conway): "*Somebody's*" *Story* 68
Fell, Samuel Gregson: *The Family of Darby-Coventry* 89
Felver, Charles S. 48; *Joseph Crawhall The Newcastle Wood Engraver* 48*n*
Fennell, J. G.: *The Curiosities of Ale & Beer* (contr.) 71
Fèret, Charles James: *Fulham, Old and New* 100
Ffoulkes, L. Florence: *Short Poems in Sunlight and Shade* 72
Field & Tuer (1862-78): formation of 5; stationery business 5, 37; manufacturing 6; move to Leadenhall Street 7; first published books 7, 35; imprint 35; Caxton Celebration, 1877 8–9
Field & Tuer, the Leadenhall Press, E.C. (1879-92): 1884 International Health Exhibition 9*n*; typography 15; auction of remainders 25; imprint 35; Max O'Rell and Scribner's 52*n;* Sheridan Ford and Whistler's letters 30
Field & Tuer's Series of English Re-prints 39, 119
Field, Abraham: biographical information 5–6; retirement and death 31
Fiennes, Celia: *Through England on a Side Saddle* 26, 77

55 Guineas Reward (Milford) 70
Fifty Hitherto Unpublished Pen-and-Ink Sketches (May) 98
'*Fining Down' on Natural Principles without Banting* (Millington) 57
First Century and the Nineteenth, The ("The Wandering Jew") 88
First Year of a Silken Reign, The (Tuer, C. Fagan) 72, 105
"Fitzdoodle, Lord Adolphus": *The Fitzdoodle Memoirs* 101
Fitzdoodle Memoirs, The ("Fitzdoodle") 101
Fitzgerald, Percy Hetherington: *London City Suburbs* 29, 90, 115; *The Story of "Bradshaw's Guide"* 81
Fixol & Stickphast, Limited 31, 33
Flags and Signals of All Nations (Hounsell) 39
"Flammam, Alere" 19; *Parodies & Satires* 94
Fleuron, The (periodical) 15
Florian, Alphonse de: *Holy Blue!* 56
Flower, Desmond 1
Flying Leaves from East and West (E. Pfieffer) 26, 67
Follies & Fashions of Our Grandfathers, The (Tuer) 22, 70, 105
Fonseca, José da: *English as She Is Spoke* 48
Food for the Mind: or, a New Riddle-Book ("John-the-Giant-Killer") 99
Foot-Ball: Its History for Five Centuries (Shearman, Vincent) 62, 120
Footman, Henry: *The Nature and Prevalence of Modern Unbelief* 43; *Reasonable Apprehensions and Reassuring Hints* 48
Ford, Sheridan 30, 31
Formerly the Mansion of Sir Joshua Reynolds (Messrs. Puttick & Simpson) 110
Forster, Joseph: *Tricks and Tricksters* 88
Forsyth, Evelyn: *Ye Gestes of Ye Ladye Anne* 59
Fortnight in a Waggonette, A 62
Foster, Birket 18
Foster-Brother and The Creoles, The (Still) 71, 120
4 Cards Illustrating Horn-Books (Tuer) 107, 116
Fowl Deceiver, The ("POOF") 65
France, Georgie. *See* Gaskin, Georgie Evelyn Cave
Fred. James under a Spell! (James) 87
French, American and English Confectionery [price list] (Clark, Nickolls, Coombs, Ltd.) 115
Froggy; or, My Lord Mayor (Scotter) 97
From a Yacht. King Arthur & Morgan le Fay (Sargant) 91
From the Bull's Point of View (Corbet) 90
Fuchs, Carl Wilhelm C.: *Practical Guide to the Determination of Minerals by the Blowpipe* 40
Fulham, Old and New (Fèret) 100
Fuller, James Franklin: *Billy. A Sketch for "the New Boy" by an Old Boy* 100; *Doctor Quodlibet. A Study in Ethics* 93
Funnynym Series 94, 121
Furlong, Atherton: *Echoes of Memory* 25, 61

Fusion of Parties in France, A.D. 1872, A (van Laun) 39
"Grasshopper" in Lombard Street, The (Martin) 87
Galsworthy, John: *The Slaughter of Animals for Food* 104
Gaping, Wide-mouthed, Waddling Frog, The 74, 106, 121
Gaskin, Arthur 3, 28
Gaskin, Georgie Evelyn Cave (Mrs. Arthur) 3, 28, 116; bookplate design for Andrew Tuer 28, 107; *History of the Horn-Book* (illust.) 24, 95; *Horn-Book Jingles* 28, 96, 108, 116; possible illust. of Stickphast Paste ad 116*n*
Gatherings (Woods) 82
Gay, James: *Canada's Poet* 57
Gay, John, F.R.C.S.: *On Varicose Disease of the Extremities and its Allied Disorder* 37
Gazder, N. B.: *Streamlets from the Fount of Poesy* 102
Gedde, Walter: *A Booke of Sundry Draughtes* 97
General History of the Kemp and Kempe Families, A (Hitchen-Kemp) 102
Geordie: The Adventures of a North-Country Waif and Stray ("A North-Countrywoman") 83
George Barnewel (Crawhall) 47, 50, 120
Gere, Charles March: *History of the Horn-Boo*k (illust.) 24, 95
Gessner, Solomon: *Solomon Gessner: "The Swiss Theocritus"* 69, 121
"Gibbon, Edwarda." *See* Stone, Charles J.
"Gil": *The Fowl Deceiver* (illust.) 65
Gilbert-Smith, J. W. *See* Denham-Smith, Sir James
Gilpin, W. B.: *Love, Sport, and a Double Event* 100; *Ranch-Land* 82; *A Set of Four Hunting and Racing Stories* 72
Gladstone, William 6, 19, 24, 68, 79
Gladstone Government: a Chapter of Contemporary History (Parry) 19, 68
Glass in the Old World (Wallace-Dunlop) 46
Glimpses of the Great Jacobins (A. Taylor) 46
Gloamin' Buchte, The (Crawhall) 47, 54, 55, 120
Goddard & Son (publishers): *Clayton's Annual Register of Shipping* 7, 37
Godlee, Sir Rickman John: *Introductory Address in the Faculty of Medicine at University College, London. October 1889* 80
"Goosestep" 19; *Bric-à-Brac Ballads* 88; Funnynym Series 121; *Rustling Reeds* 94; *Splay-Feet Splashings in Divers Places* 87
Gosse, Edmund 3, 19, 94*n*; *The Grievances between Authors & Publishers* (contr.) 73
Gotham and the Gothamites (Karlstein) 72
Grain, Mrs. (pseud. Stephen Syeds); *Mohammed Aben Alamar* 103
Graphic, The (newspaper) 7, 40*n*, 44
Gray, Thomas: *Gray's Elegy in a Country Churchyard* 71
Great Drama, and Other Poems, The (Lascelles) 96, 121

Green, Evelyn Everett: *Six Stories* (contr.) 100
Green, John. *See* Townsend, George Henry
Green, Samuel Gosnell: *The Christmas Box, or New Year's Gift* (introd.) 77
Greenaway, Kate 14, 29, 29*n*
Greet, Dora Victoire: *Mrs. Greet's Story of the Golden Owl* 21, 88
Gresswell, Albert and George: *The Wonderland of Evolution* 58
Gresswell, Henry William and George: *How to Play the Fiddle* 68
Grievances between Authors & Publishers, The (Society of Authors) 73, 106
Griffith, Francis Llewellyn: *A Season in Egypt 1877* (illust.) 76; *Hawara, Biahmu, and Arsinoe* (contr.) 79
Griffiths, Emily W. (the Hon.): *Through England on a Side Saddle* (introd.) 77
Gueraut, R.: *Histoire du Bonhomme Misère* 12, 40
Guercino Etchings Dispute, The [scrapbook] 14, 14*n*
Guess the Title of This Story! (Tuer) 26, 86, 86*n*, 106
Guide to the River Thames, A (Salter) 57
Gülich, John: *Novel Notes* (illust.) 90
Haight, Andreas Valette (printer) 10
Hailing's Circular 9, 9*n*
Hailing, Thomas 9, 58
Halkett, George R.: *Our Grandmothers' Gowns* (illust.) 60
Hamilton, Islay: *A Splendid Rally: A Story of a Love Set* 72
Hammond, Gertrude: *Novel Notes* (illust.) 90
Handbook of Freight Tables and Tonnage Schedules, A (Angier) 41
Handbook of London Bankers, A (Price) 82
Handsome Examiner, The (Corbet) 81
Hanworth Park, April 25th 1882. Programme [of an Amateur Concert] and Analytical Remarks 110
Happy Blend; or, How John Bull Was Suited to a T, The [handbill] 113
Harford, Rev. Frederick K.: *Ballads of Schiller No. 1. The Diver* 12, 41
Harris's Cabinet. Numbers One to Four (Welsh) 51
Hartley, Walter Noel: *Index to the Published Researches and Original Papers* 98
Hatton, Joseph: *In Jest and Earnest. A Book of Gossip* 91
"Have Ye Read It?" Look Sharp! (Woods) 93
Hawara, Biahmu, and Arsinoe (Petrie) 27, 78–79
Haweis, Mrs. (Mary Eliza Joy): *Rus in Urbe* 21, 69
Hazlitt, William Carew: *Joe Miller in Motley* 88–89
Heath, Francis George: *Tree Gossip* 20, 27, 61
Heckford, Sarah Maud 26*n*; *The Life of Christ, and Its Bearing on the Doctrines of Communism* 26, 39
Hieroglyphic Bible, The 76–77
Henry Irving, Actor and Manager (Archer) 48*n*, 49, 119

Henry Irving Dream of Eugene Aram, The (Hood, Niblett) 21, 76
Herbert, George, Earl of Carnarvon: *Catalogue of Books Selected from the Library of an English Amateur* 92
"Hercules": *British Railways and Canals* 63
Herkomer, Sir Hubert von 29
Herrick, Robert: *Selections from the Hesperides* 46
Hill, Alonza F.: *Secrets of the Sanctum: An Inside View of an Editor's Life* 40
Hilton, Robert 11
Histoire du Bonhomme Misère (Legros) 12, 40
Historical Sporting Series 62, 120
History of English Lotteries, A (Ashton) 16, 27, 91
History of Little Goody Two Shoes, The 99, 121
History of St. Conan 60
History of the Decline and Fall of the British Empire (Stone) 18, 19, 55, 120
History of the Horn-Book (Tuer) 24, 28, 31, 32, 33, 95-96, 106, 107n, 116n
History of the Worshipful Company of Gold and Silver Wyre-Drawers (Stewart) 86
Hitchen-Kemp, Frederick: *A General History of the Kemp and Kempe Families* 102; *Ye Legende of Ye Kempes* 102
Hitchman, Francis: *Lord Beaconsfield on the Constitution* (preface) 57
Holyoake, John J.: *Isola, or the Disinherited* (contr.) 102
Hollingshead, John: *The Grievances between Authors & Publishers* (contr.) 73
Holt, Vincent M.: *Why Not Eat Insects?* 64
Holy Blue! (de Florian) 25, 56
Hood, Thomas: *The Henry Irving Dream of Eugene Aram* 76
Hooper, Albert E.: *Up the Moonstair* 83
Hooper, Jane Margaret Winnard (Mrs. George): *Prince Pertinax* 27, 50, 108
Hooper, Margaret L. (illustrator): *The Story of a Nursery Rhyme* 44; *Prince Pertinax* 27, 50
Hooper, William Harcourt: bookplate designs for Andrew Tuer 3, 106-107
Hopkins, Everard: *History of the Horn-Book* (illust.) 95
Hopkins, Manley: *Spicilegium Poeticum* 25, 89
Hoppner, John: *Bygone Beauties* 51-52, 106
Horn-Book Jingles (G. E. C. Gaskin) 28, 96, 108, 116
Horrocks, William H.: *The Life of Sir Astley Cooper* 101
Hounsell, George C.: *Flags and Signals of All Nations* 39
Housekeeping Made Easy ("A Lady") 37
How Is the Gospel to Be Preached to the Poor? (Blomfield) 39
How the World Came to an End in 1881 (Kingsford, E. Maitland) 54, 120
How to Fail in Literature (Lang) 18, 25, 81
How to Play the Fiddle (Gresswell) 68
How We Went to Rome in 1857 (C. F. Maitland) 89

Hudson, Graham: "Artistic Printing: a Re-evaluation" in the *Journal of the Printing Historical Society* 11n
Humours and Oddities of the London Police Courts ("Dogberry") 19, 93
Hunt, Mrs. Alfred W. (Margaret): *Our Grandmothers' Gowns* 21, 60
Hunter, Colin: *Songs of the North* (illust.) 64
Hurst, Hal: *Novel Notes* (illust.) 90
Hutchinson, George: *Novel Notes* (illust.) 28, 90
Idle Thoughts of an Idle Fellow, The (Jerome) 19, 69
I Know What I Know (Crawhall) 47, 50, 120
Illustrated London News 20, 46
Illustrated Shilling Series of Forgotten Children's Books 99n, 121
Illustrations of the Author of Waverley (Chambers) 56
Imaginary Conversations of Three White-Letter Days in the Anglo-Saxon Cloisters (Wood) 103
In Chains of Fate (Max) 80
Index to the Paper & Printing Trades Journal (Pearce) 39
Index to the Published Researches and Original Papers (Hartley) 98
India General Steam Navigation Company (Brame) 100
Ingold, John: *Roughly Told Stories* 94
In Jest and Earnest. A Book of Gossip (Hatton) 91
International Health Exhibition 15, 58, 58n, 112
Introductory Address in the Faculty of Medicine at University College, London. October 1889 (Godlee) 80
Inventions Exhibition, 1885 15, 113
Isola, or the Disinherited (Dixie) 26, 102
Is There Any Resemblance between Shakespeare & Bacon? (Steel) 77
Izaak Walton: His Wallet Booke (Crawhall) 17, 66
Jackson, Holbrook 2
Jamaica under the New Form of Government ("A West Indian") 37-38
James, Fred.: *Fred. James under a Spell!* 87
James, Harry A.: *A Professional Pugilist* 92
Jemmy & Nancy of Yarmouth (Crawhall) 47, 50, 120
Jerome, Jerome Klapka 19; *On the Stage—and Off* 19, 28, 36, 64, 87; *The Idle Thoughts of an Idle Fellow* 19, 69; *Told after Supper* 83, 83n; *Novel Notes* 28, 90
Joe Miller in Motley (Hazlitt) 88-89
John & Joan (Crawhall) 47, 50, 120
John Bull's Womankind (O'Rell) 18, 58, 59, 105
John Bull's Womankind (Suggestions for an Alteration in the Law of Copyright) (Tuer) 18, 58-59, 105
John Bull and His Daughters (piracy of *Les filles de John Bull*) 58n
John Bull and His Island (O'Rell) 18, 52
John Bull Junior or French as She Is Traduced (O'Rell) 79-80
John Cunningham, the Pastoral Poet (Crawhall) 47, 55, 120

John Oldcastle's Guide for Literary Beginners (W. Meynell) 42, 48*n*, 55–56, 120
Johnson, Alfred Forbes: "Old-Face Types in the Victorian Age" in *The Monotype Recorder* 1, 1*n*
Johnson, John de Monins 5, 34; "The Development of Printing, other than Book-Printing" 5*n*; "The Printers, His Customers and His Men" 34*n*
Jones, George W. 11
Joseph Crawhall, The Newcastle Wood Engraver (Felver) 48
Journalistic Jumbles; or, Trippings in Type (Williams) 48*n*, 56, 120
Journals and Journalism: With a Guide for Literary Beginners (W. Meynell) 13, 36, 42, 56
Karlstein, Heinrich Oscar von (pseud.): *Gotham and the Gothamites* 72
Karuth, F.: *King Solomon's Golden Ophir* (trans.) 98
Katalog der auf Hamburger Bibliotheken vorhandenen Litteratur... (1890) 44*n*
Kaukneigh Awlminek, 1883, The (Tuer) 19, 20, 46, 105
Keene, Charles 11, 16, 18, 33, *Songs of the North* (illust.) 65
Kelly & Co. 32
Kelmscott Press 2, 3, 20
Kelmscott Press, a History of William Morris's Typographical Adventure, The (Peterson) 2
Kelvin, Norman: *The Collected Letters of William Morris, Vol. 3, 1889–1892* 3*n*
Kempis, Thomas à: *One Hundred and Forty-Two Selected Texts from The Imitation of Christ* 48*n*, 54
Kendrew, James 109
Kensington Picturesque & Historical (W. J. Loftie) 29, 78
Kent, Edward: *A Lawful Crime* 99; *That Headstrong Boy* 97
Kerr, Charles H. M.: *History of the Horn-Book* (illust.) 24, 95
Kerr, F. A.: *The Marriage Ring* (introd.) 49
Keys 'at Home': A New Year's-Eve Entertainment, The (Lowry) 59
King, J. Percy: *As the Wind Blows. Stray Songs in Many Moods* 86
King, Jonathan 109
Kinglake, Edward: *The Australian at Home* 85
Kingsford, Anna Bonus: *The Perfect Way; or, The Finding of Christ* 26, 45, 54, 76; *How the World Came to an End in 1881* 54; *Chapters from "The Perfect Way." The Nature and Constitution of the Ego* 76; mistaken authorship attribution for *The Mother: The Woman Clothed with the Sun* 62*n*
King Solomon's Golden Ophir (Peters) 98
King Squash of Toadyland 80–81
Kitten's Goblins (Davidson) 26, 78
Kuzmanovic, N. Natasha: *John Paul Cooper, Designer and Craftsman of the Arts and Crafts Movement* 32*n*

Lacouperie, Terrien de: *Amongst the Shans* (introd.) 61; *The Cradle of the Shan Race* 61
Laffan, Robert Stuart de Courcy: *Aspects of Fiction* 62
Lamb, Charles: *Beauty and the Beast* 25, 73; *Poetry for Children* 89; *Prince Dorus* 79, 106
Lambert, George: *St. Dunstan: A Paper Written to Be Read at Goldsmiths' Hall* 48
Lane, John 32
Lang, Andrew 11; *Beauty and the Beast* (introd.) 25, 73; *How to Fail in Literature* 18, 25, 81
Langtry, Lilly: *Antony & Cleopatra* (actress) 83
Lansdowne, Andrew: *A Life's Reminiscences of Scotland Yard* 82
Lascelles, John: Sun and Serpent Series 20, 94, 96; *The Great Drama, and Other Poems* 96; *.X.Y.Z. and Other Poems* 94
Laurence Oliphant: Supplementary Contributions to His Biography (Scott) 94–95
Laveleye, Émile de: *The Socialism of To-day* 62
Lawful Crime, A (Kent) 99
Lawson, Cecil: *Songs of the North* (illust.) 65
Lawson, Lizzie: *The Bairns' Annual* (illust.) 67
Lawson, Malcolm Leonard: *Seven Songs to Sing* (contr.) 90; *Songs of the North* (arr.) 64–65
Lays of a Lazy Lawyer (Somers) 84–85, 85*n*
Lays of the Bards. I.-the Holy Isle 96
Leadenhall Press, E.C., The. *See* Field & Tuer, The Leadenhall Press, E.C. (1879-1892)
Leadenhall Press, Ltd., The (1892-1927): incorporation 31; imprint 35, 76*n*; directors, subscribers 7, 31; decline in output 32; end of publishing 35; move to Southwark 33; dissolution, 1927 34; archives destroyed 2
Leadenhall Press Series of Forgotten Picture Books for Children 14, 74, 76, 121
Leadenhall Press Sixteenpenny Series: Illustrated Gleanings from the Classics 13, 69, 70, 75
Ledger (Field & Tuer) 37
Legros, Alphonse: *Histoire du Bonhomme Misère* 12, 40
Leighton, John: *History of the Horn-Book* (illust.) 24, 95
Les filles de John Bull (O'Rell) 58, 59
Levetus, Celia: *History of the Horn-Book* (illust.) 24, 95
Levey, Andrew: *The Winter's Tale* (music) 78
Life's Reminiscences of Scotland Yard, A (Lansdowne) 82
Life and Poetical Works of James Woodhouse, The (J. Woodhouse, R. I. Woodhouse) 96
Life and Times of Colonel Fred Burnaby, The (Ware, Mann) 65
Life of Christ, and Its Bearing on the Doctrines of Communism, The (Heckford) 26, 39
Life of Sir Astley Cooper, The (Horrocks) 101
Light, Kate: *History of the Horn-Book* (illust.) 24, 95
Lily, of the Valley, A Play (Moore) 101
Lines Grave and Gay (Warde) 68

Lion's Masquerade, The (Dorset) 51
List of the Works of Bartolozzi (Tuer) 45
Literary World, The (periodical) 26, 82*n*
Little, R.: *Songs of the North* (illust.) 65
Littlechild, John George: *The Reminiscences of Chief-Inspector Littlechild* 93
Liverpool Mercury (newspaper) 24*n*
Loan Exhibition of the Worshipful Company of Horners 24
"Lochnell": *Saxon Lyrics and Legends after Aldhelm* 68
Lockhart, William Ewart: *Songs of the North* (illust.) 65
Loftie, Martha Jane (Mrs.): *Comfort in the Home* 94
Loftie, William John: *An Essay of Scarabs* 60; *Kensington Picturesque & Historical* 29, 78; *London City* 29, 84, 115
Log Book, Containing a Record . . . (Field & Tuer) 37
London City (W. J. Loftie) 29, 84, 115
London City [copyright pamphlet] (Tuer) 81–82, 105
"London City" by W. J. Loftie [Advertisement] 115
London City subscription receipt 115
London City Suburbs (Fitzgerald) 29, 90, 115
London Cries: with Six Charming Children (Tuer) 15, 52–53, 105
London Life Seen with German Eyes (Brand) 72
Long Pack: a Northumbrian Tale, The (Crawhall) 47, 54, 120
Look Here!: A Book for the Rail (Searle) 65
Lord Beaconsfield on the Constitution (Disraeli) 25, 57
Lorello. A Play (Cartwright) 64
Lorimer, John Henry: *Songs of the North* (illust.) 65
Lorraine, Lewis: *The Corpse in the Copse or the Perils of Love* 68
Lost! A Day (Milford) 69
Lost in a Bucket-Shop. A Story of Stock Exchange Speculation (Scotter) 80
Louttit, Duncan 7, 31
Louttit, Samuel 7, 31
Louttit, Thomasine Louisa. *See* Tuer, Thomasine Louisa Louttit
Love, Sport, and a Double Event (Gilpin) 100
Love Letters by a Violinist (G. E. Mackay) 60
Lover's Litanies, A (G. E. Mackay) 75
Lovering, Ida: *History of the Horn-Hook* (illust.) 95
Lowry, James Moody: *A Book of Jousts* 25, 75; *The Dolls' Garden Party* 87; *The Keys 'at Home': A New Year's-Eve Entertainment* 59
Lubbock, Nevile: *British Sugar and French Bounties* 40
Luker, William, Jr. (illustrator) 28: *The Bairns' Annual 1885-6* 67; *Kensington Picturesque and Historical* 29, 78; *London City* 29, 84, 115; *A Successful Picture!* 87;*London City* receipt 115; *London City Suburbs* 29, 90; *History of the Horn-Book* 24, 95; *The Children's London* 101
Luxurious Bathing: A Sketch (Tuer) 12, 13, 15, 29, 36, 41, 42, 105
Lyon, William and Walter F. K.: *Lyon of Ogil* 37
Lyon of Ogil (W. Lyon, W. F. K. Lyon) 37
Lytton, Lord (Robert Bulwer-Lytton): *The Grievances between Authors & Publishers* (contr.) 73
"M. H.": *Socialism or Protection? Which Is to Be?* 93
"Mabel": *Views of English Society: by a Little Girl of Eleven* 21, 22, 70
Macbeth, R. W.: *Songs of the North* (illust.) 65
Mackay, George Eric 30; *Love Letters by a Violinist* 60; *A Lover's Litanies* 75
Mackay, W. D.: *Songs of the North* (illust.) 65
MacLeod, Anne Campbell: *Songs of the North* (ed.) 64–65
MacWhirter, John: *Songs of the North* (illust.) 65
Madame de Maintenon; an Etude (Morison) 64
Madame Marie, Singer (Dale) 101
Maitland, Edward: *The Perfect Way; or, The Finding of Christ* 45, 54; *How the World Came to an End in 1881* 54
Maitland, Hon. Caroline Fuller: *How We Went to Rome in 1857* 89
Maitland, John Alexander Fuller: *English Carols of the Fifteenth Century* (ed.) 85; *English County Songs* (ed.) 90
Manifold Papers [Leadenhall Press samples] 117
Mann, R. K.: *The Life and Times of Colonel Fred Burnaby* 65
Manners & Customs of the French (Sotheran, Rotch) 91
Manners, Millwood: *Three Beauties; or, the Idols of the Village* 82
Marah. A Prose Idyll (Marsh) 67
Marriage Ring, The (J. Taylor) 49
Marsh, Eleanor Mary: *Marah. A Prose Idyll* 67
Marshall, Herbert: *Eton Songs* (illust.) 87
Marshall, Julian 57*n*; *Tennis Cuts and Quips* 57
Martin, John Biddulph: *"The Grasshopper" in Lombard Street* 87
Marzials, Theo: *Seven Songs to Sing* (contr.) 90
Master Jimmy's Fables (Browne) 94
Masters of Raffaello, The (Minghetti) 46
Matabeleland: the War, and Our Position in South Africa (Colquhoun) 27, 92
Mathews, Elkin 32
Mawley, R.: *Pottery and Porcelain in 1876* 41
Max, John: *In Chains of Fate* 80
May, Margery: *Prince Pertinax* (illust.) 27, 50
May, Philip William 11, 28, 29; *Fifty Hitherto Unpublished Pen-and-Ink Sketches* 98; *History of the Horn-Book* (illust.) 24, 95; *Phil May's ABC* 29, 97; *Phil May's Gutter-snipes* 29, 96; *Stickphast Paste Sticks* [advertising insert] (illust.) 117
McLean, Ruari 16; *Victorian Book Design and Colour Printing* 16*n*

McQuoid, Percy: *History of the Horn-Book* (illust.) 24, 95
Memento: Inventions Exhibition, South Kensington, 1885 113
Memento Imprynted yn Ye Olde Streete of London Towne ye Greate Attraction yn Ye Health Exhibition 112
Memoranda of Art & Artists (Sandell) 38
Memories of a Life of Toil (Turnerelli) 59
Men, Maidens and Manners a Hundred Years Ago (Ashton) 27, 77
Meredith, George: *The Child Set in the Midst: by Modern Poets* 25, 88
Methuen, Sir Algernon 32
Mew, James: *Drinks of the World* 87
Meynell, Alice (pseud. Francis Phillimore) 11; *Dickens Memento* 13, 63
Meynell, Francis: *Modern Books and Writers: Catalogue of an Exhibition* 1, 1*n*
Meynell, Wilfrid, (pseud. John Oldcastle) 11, 13, 21; *Journals and Journalism: With a Guide for Literary Beginners* 36, 42, 56; *John Oldcastle's Guide for Literary Beginners* 42, 48, 55, 120; *Sir Charles Grandison* (preface) 69; *Solomon Gessner: "The Swiss Theocritus"* (preface) 70; *The Seasons* (preface) 75; *Tristram Shandy* (introd.) 75; *The Child Set in the Midst: by Modern Poets* (ed.) 13, 25, 88
Michael's Crag (Allen) 25, 26, 91
Milford, Fred C.: *55 Guineas Reward* 70; *Lost! A Day* 69
Millington, James 31; *English as She Is Spoke: or, a Jest in Sober Earnest* (introd.) 48; *English as She Is Spoke...Her Seconds Part* (introd.) 52; *'Are We to Read ?SDRAWKCAB* 16, 53, 119; *Holy Blue!* (introd.) 56; *'Fining Down' on Natural Principles without Banting* 57; *Canada's Poet* (introd.) 57; *The True Story of Mazeppa* (trans.) 60; *The Chinese Painted by Themselves* (trans.) 63
Mind or the Spiritual Part of Life, The (Brooks) 96–97
Minghetti, Marco: *The Masters of Raffaello* 46
Miss Spinney (Mostyn) 101
Modern Men. By a Modern Maid (Eccles) 73
Mohammed Aben Alamar (Grain) 103
Monkhouse, Cosmo: *The Child Set in the Midst: by Modern Poets* 88
Monselet, Charles: *A Fusion of Parties in France, A.D. 1872* 39
Monsieur at Home (Rhodes) 59
Monthly Musical Record, The 7
Moore, Albert: *Songs of the North* (illust.) 65
Moore, Francis W.: *Lily, of the Valley: A Play* 101
Morison, James Cotter: *Madame de Maintenon* 64
Morison, Stanley 15; "Decorative Types" in *The Fleuron* 15*n*

Morris, William 2–3, 3*n*, 16, 20, 28, 29
Mostyn, Rev. Sydney Gwenffrwd: *Miss Spinney* 101; *My First Curacy* 84, 84*n*
Mother: The Woman Clothed with the Sun, The 62
Mother Darling! (Bewicke) 64
Mowbray & Son (printers) 10
Moxon, Edward: *Contemporary Notices of Charles Lamb* 85
Mrs. Greet's Story of the Golden Owl (Greet) 21, 88
Muir, Jessie A. H.: *Diary J.A.H.M.* 21, 71–72
Mundy, Mark: *The Vagaries of To-day* 97
Muntz, V. Gertrude: *Eight Tales of Fairyland* (illust.) 73
Myers, S.: *Ye Foure Etchynges By Maister S. Myers* 66
My First Curacy (Mostyn) 84, 84*n*, 121
My Ladye and Others: Poems (Denham-Smith) 43–44
Nash, E. Barrington: *Catalogue of the Second Exhibition ... of Engravings & Etchings by Francesco Bartolozzi* (foreword) 47
Nature and Prevalence of Modern Unbelief, The (Footman) 43
"*Never Hit a Man Named Sullivan!*" (Willock) 18, 82
Newberry, Percy Edward: *A Pearl of English Rhetoric. Thomas Carlyle on the Repeal of the Union* (pref.) 78; *Hawara, Biahmu, and Arsinoe* (contr.) 79; *Rescued Essays of Thomas Carlyle* (ed.) 87
New Catalogue of British Literature for 1896 36
Newman, A. K., and the Minerva Press 14*n*, 74, 76
Newman, J. T. (architect) 11
New Shilling Book of Alphabets, A 16, 78, 116
Next Ninety-Three, or Crown, Commune and Colony, The (Watlock) 68
Niblett, F. Drummond: *The Henry Irving Dream of Eugene Aram* 21, 76
No Actress. A Stage Door-keeper's Story (Besemeres) 38
Noel, Maurice: "*Evidence*" 69
"North-Countrywoman": *Geordie: The Adventures of a North-Country Waif and Stray* 83
North Wales Chronicle 6*n*
Notes and Queries (perodical) 32, 48
Notions of a Nobody, The (Dahle) 88, 90–91
Novel Notes (Jerome) 28, 90
Ohlson, James L.: *British Sugar Industries and Foreign Export Bounties* 42
Old Aunt Elspa's ABC (Crawhall) 17, 57–58, 112
Old Aunt Elspa's Spelling Bee (Crawhall) 17, 60–61
Oldcastle, John. *See* Meynell, Wilfrid
Olde ffrendes wyth newe Faces (Crawhall) 1, 17, 47, 47*n*, 50, 54–55, 120
Olde Tayles Newlye Relayted (Crawhall) 16, 17, 47–48
Old London Street Cries and the Cries of To-day (Tuer) 15, 19, 53, 65, 105
Ω [Omega]: *Facta Non Verba. An Examination of the Figures and Statements Published as the Result of the Analyses ... on the London Water Supply* 41

On a Raft, and Through the Desert (T. Ellis) 13, 15, 29, 43
One Hundred and Forty-Two Selected Texts from The Imitation of Christ (Kempis) 54
1,000 Quaint Cuts from Books of Other Days 15, 66, 71, 105
On the Stage–and Off (Jerome) 19, 28, 36, 64, 87
On Varicose Disease of the Extremities and its Allied Disorder (Gay) 37
Opening of China, The (Colquhoun) 60
Oracles of Nostradamus (Ward) 85
O'Rell, Max (Leon-Paul Blouët) 18, 52*n*, 58; *John Bull and His Island* 18, 52; *John Bull's Womankind* 18, 59; *The Dear Neighbours!* 67; *Drat the Boys!* 71; *John Bull Junior* 79
Orpen, Goddard H.: *The Socialism of To-day* (trans.) 62
Our Grandmothers' Gowns (Hunt) 21, 60
Our Sea-Fish and Sea-Food (Davies) 73
Owls of Olynn Belfry, The (A. Y. D.) 28, 67
Oxford to Palestine, Being Notes of a Tour in 1889 (Rev. J. L Thomson) 83–84
Oxley & Son (printers) 10
Pages and Pictures from Forgotten Children's Books (Tuer) 98, 106, 117
Palaver; or, the Fairy Genius of Atlantis ("B.") 81
Pall Mall Gazette 20, 25, 30, 32, 32*n*, 33, 72
Palmer, Samuel: *St. Pancras: Being Antiquarian, Topographical, and Biographical Memoranda* 8, 38
Paper & Printing Trades Journal, The 2, 8, 9, 11, 23, 31, 39, 42
Paris Exhibition, 1878 (Taylor Brothers) 110
Parker, John Alfred: *Ernest England; or, a Soul Laid Bare* 94
Parkes, Harry (illustrator): *People We Meet* 77; *The Rogues' Gallery* 81; *Up the Moonstair* 83
Parodies & Satires ("Flammam") 94
Parry, Edward Abbot (pseud. "Teufelsdröckk Junior"): *Gladstone Government: a Chapter of Contemporary History* 19, 68
Patmore, Coventry: *The Child Set in the Midst: by Modern Poets* 25, 88
Paton, Noel: *Songs of the North* (illust.) 65
Peacock at Home, The (Dorset) 51
Pearce, Edwin R.: *Index to the Paper & Printing Trades Journal* 39
Pearl of English Rhetoric. Thomas Carlyle on the Repeal of the Union, A (Carlyle) 78
Pears' Soap [advertisements] 113–114, 115
Pearson, Mrs.: *Dame Wiggins of Lee* 74
People We Meet (Ridcal) 77
"Perfect Way" Shilling Series, The 54, 120
Perfect Way; or, The Finding of Christ, The (Kingsford, E. Maitland) 26, 45
Peters, Karl: *King Solomon's Golden Ophir* 98

Petersen, Marie: *The Princess Ilse: A Legend of the Harz Mountains* 98
Peterson, William: *The Kelmscott Press, a History of William Morris's Typographical Adventure* 2
Petrie, William Matthew Flinders: *The Arts of Ancient Egypt* 60; *An Essay of Scarabs* (illust.) 60; *Hawara, Biahmu, and Arsinoe* 27, 78; *The Pyramids and Temples of Gizeh* 27, 49; *A Season in Egypt 1887* 27, 76
Pettie, John: *Songs of the North* (illust.) 65
Pfeiffer, Emily Jane: *Flying Leaves from East and West* 26, 67; *Sonnets. Revised and Enlarged Edition* 26, 71
Pfieffer, J. E.: *Sonnets. Revised and Enlarged Edition* (ed.) 71
Pfungst, Henry: *Descriptive Catalogue of a Small Collection Principally of Xvth and Xvith Century Bronzes* 100
Phillimore, Francis. *See* Meynell, Alice
Phil May's ABC (May) 29, 97
Phil May's Gutter-snipes (May) 29, 96
Pickering, William 2, 15
Pilley, John James: *The Progress Book* 104
Plays for Young People (Still) 71, 73, 120
Pochhammer, Max von: *Six Stories* 100
Poems: and Other Pieces (M. Bell) 93
Poetry for Children (Lamb) 89
Poirez, Louise Blennerhassett: *Eight Tales of Fairyland* 26, 73
Police! (Clarkson, Richardson) 79
Political Catechism, A ("B.") 78
Political Wit and Humour in Our Own Times (Williams) 79
Pollack, Frederick: *The Grievances between Authors & Publishers* (contr.) 73
"POOF" 19; *The Fowl Deceiver* 65
Porritt, Norman: *"Cornered"* 84
Port of Gibraltar, The 41
Pottery and Porcelain in 1876 (Mawley) 41
Powell, Frederick York 1
Practical Guide to the Determination of Minerals by the Blowpipe (Fuchs) 40
Prescott, Norman: *The Vicar's Pups* 98
Prescott-Davies, Norman: *The Vicar's Pups* (illust.) 98
Price, Frederick George Hilton: *A Handbook of London Bankers* 82; *The Signs of Old Lombard Street* 74
Price List of Ladies' under Clothing, India Outfits, and Wedding Outfits from Whitelock & Son, India 109
Prime Minister and Tom, The (Still) 73, 120
Prince Bismarck's Map of Europe ("Cylinder") 76
Prince Dorus (Lamb) 79, 106
Prince Pertinax (J. M. W. Hooper) 27, 50, 108
Princess Ilse: A Legend of the Harz Mountains, The (Petersen) 98
Principles of Warfare, The (Blaker) 100

Printer's International Specimen Exchange, The 2, 9–10, 9*n*, 10, 10*n*, 15, 42–43, 106, 109
Printers' Universal Book of Reference and Every-hour Office Companion, The 39*n*
Prize Specimens of Handwriting (*Tit-Bits*) 77
Proceedings of the Fortnightly Club, The 68
Professional Pugilist, A (James) 92
Progress Book, The (Pilley) 104
Prospectus: *Bartolozzi and His Works* 110; *Crawhall's Chap-book Chaplets* 112; *Olde ffrendes wyth newe Faces* 112; *Izaak Walton: His Wallet Booke* 113; *Quads; Quads (enlarged edition); Quads within Quads* 112; *London City* 115; *London City Suburbs* 115; *History of the Horn-Book* 116; *Horn-Book Jingles* 116; *Pages and Pictures from Forgotten Children's Books* 117
Publishers's Circular 17, 21, 36, 48, 53*n*, 72*n*, 83*n*, 87*n*
Publishers's Weekly 9, 33
"Puck" 19; *This Year, Next Year, Some Time, Never* 59
Punch 6, 11, 18, 19, 33, 81*n*
Putnam, George Haven: *The Grievances between Authors & Publishers* (contr.) 73
Pyramids and Temples of Gizeh, The (Petrie) 27, 49
Quads for Authors, Editors, & Devils (Tuer) 58, 105
Quads within Quads (Tuer) 23, 48*n*, 58, 105, 112
Quaritch, Bernard 29, 33
Queensberry, Marquess of 26
Quilter, Harry: *Sententiae Artis* 29–30
Radical Nightmare, A (an Ex-M.P.) 67
Raithby, Lawrence & Co. 11
Ranch-Land (Gilpin) 82
Rawnsley, Hardwicke Drummond: *The Undoing of De Harcla* 89
Real Sailor-Songs (Ashton) 27, 85–86
Reasonable Apprehensions and Reassuring Hints (Footman) 48, 48*n*, 119
Recent Books and Something About Them (Field & Tuer) 48*n*, 58, 60, 119
Reid, George: *Songs of the North* (illust.) 65
Reminiscences of Chief-Inspector Littlechild, The (Littlechild) 93
Report of Mr. John H. Darby, M.Inst.C.E., on the Blythe River Iron Mines (Darby) 100–101
Report of the Committee to the Half-Yearly Meeting of . . . West India Planters and Merchants 40
Rescued Essays of Thomas Carlyle (Carlyle) 87
Respectfully Inscribed to Mr. G. Ridler (Cole) 36
Revelation of Jesus Christ, with Notes for the 144,000, The (Bible) 61
Review of Reviews 87*n*
Rhodes, Albert: *Monsieur at Home* 59
Rhymers' Club 29
Richardson, Joseph Hall: *Police!* 79; *The Rogues' Gallery* 81

Richardson, Samuel: *Sir Charles Grandison* 69, 121
Richardson, William Lambert: *The Duties and Conduct of Nurses in Private Nursing* 74
Rideal, Charles F.: *People We Meet* 77
Ridge, William Pett (pseud. Warwick Simpson): *Eighteen of Them. Singular Stories* 92
righte Merrie Christmasse!!!, A (Ashton) 27, 93
Rimington, Alexander Wallace: *Colour Music* 95*n*
Robinson, Robert: *Bewick Memento* 62
Rockstro, William Smith: *English Carols of the Fifteenth Century* 85
Roeckel, Joseph Leopold: *Seven Songs to Sing* (contr.) 90
Rogues' Gallery, The (Clarkson, Richardson) 81
Roscoe, William: *The Butterfly's Ball and the Grasshopper's Feast* 51
Ross, William Stewart: *The Story of Ijain* (contr.) 102
Rossetti, Dante Gabriel: *The Child Set in the Midst: by Modern Poets* 25, 88
Rotch, Benjamin: *Manners & Customs of the French* 91
Rothwell, Charles C.: *The Stolen Bishop* 95
Rougement, Herbert de: *A Century of Lloyd's Patriotic Fund* 103
Roughly Told Stories (Ingold) 94
Rowlandson, Thomas 15, 52
Rus in Urbe (Haweis) 21, 69
Ruskin, John: and Andrew Tuer 10, 14; support for *Printers' International Specimen Exchange* 10, 10*n*; *Dame Wiggins of Lee* 14; Guercino Etchings Dispute 14; and J. M. Whistler 30
Russell, Thomas 6; "Commercial Advertising. Six Lectures at the London School of Economics" 6*n*
Rustling Reeds ("Goosestep") 94
Sala, George Augustus 14, review of *The Kaukneigh Awlminek* 20, 20*n*, 46*n*; *Living London: Being Echoes Re-echoed* 20*n*, 46*n*
"Saladin." *See* Ross, William Stewart
Salter, John Henry: *A Guide to the River Thames* 57
Sambourne, Linley 11; *History of the Horn-Book* (illust.) 24, 95
Sambourne, Maud: *History of the Horn-Book* (illust.) 95
Sampson Low, Son & Marston 7, 19
Sandell, Joseph: *Memoranda of Art & Artists* 38
Sandys, Frederick: *Songs of the North* (illust.) 28, 65
Sargant, Alice B. 91*n*; *From a Yacht. King Arthur & Morgan le Fay* 91
Savage Club 25th Anniversary Dinner [menu] 110
Sayce, Archibald Henry: *Hawara, Biahmu, and Arsinoe* (contr.) 79
Saxon Lyrics and Legends after Aldhelm ("Lochnell") 68
Scent of the Heather, The (Tupper) 95
Scott, Charles Newton: *Laurence Oliphant: Supplementary Contributions to His Biography* 94; *The Age of Marie Antoinette* 80

140

Scotter, Charles James: *Froggy; or, My Lord Mayor* 97; *Lost in a Bucket-Shop. A Story of Stock Exchange Speculation* 80; *Who Is His Father?* 70
Scribner & Welford 12, 85*n*
Searle, Charles: *Look Here!: A Book for the Rail* 65
Season in Egypt 1887, A (Petrie) 27, 76
Seasons, The (J. Thomson) 75, 121
Secrets of the Sanctum: An Inside View of an Editor's Life (Hill) 40
Selection of Sketches and Letters on Sport and Life in Morocco, A (Wake) 80
Selections from the Hesperides (Herrick) 46
Sellers, Charles: *Tales from the Lands of Nuts and Grapes* 76
Selous, Millie: *The Stage in the Drawing-Room: Short One-Act Sketches* 90
"Senex": *Counsel to Ladies and Easy-Going Men on their Business Investments* 88
Sermons in Sentences (Brownrig) 25, 58
Set of Four Hunting and Racing Stories, A (Gilpin) 72
Seven Songs to Sing (H. Boulton) 90
Shadow of Death, The (Stenbock) 25, 92
Shakespeare, William: *Antony & Cleopatra* 29, 83; *The Winter's Tale* 29, 78
Sharpe, Richard Scrafton: *Dame Wiggins of Lee* 74, 106
Sharpe, Sutton: *Luxurious Bathing* (illust.) 12, 41–42, 105
Shaw, George Bernard: on Tuer's representation of cockney 20; Leadenhall Press vs. Kelmscott Press 20; "The Author's View" in *Caxton Magazine* and *Bernard Shaw on Modern Typography* 20*n*; review of *A Song of Love and Liberty* in *The Pall Mall Gazette* 72, 72*n*
Shaw, Henry: *A Booke of Sundry Draughtes* (ed.) 97
Shearman, Sir Montague: *Foot-Ball: Its History for Five Centuries* 62
Shepard, Leslie: *The History of the Horn-Book: a Bibliographical Essay* 24*n*
Short, F. Golden: *Some Reminiscences of Thomas Francis and Mary Adams* (illust.) 94
Short History of St. George's Chapter, A (Taylor) 92
Short Poems in Sunlight and Shade (Ffoulkes) 72
Sidney, Philip: *Abou-Hamed: Being Some Account of Its Battle and Its Ghost Story* 102
Signs of Old Lombard Street, The (Price) 74
Silver-Voice: A Fairy Tale 75
Simpkin, Marshall & Co. 7
Simpson, Warwick. *See* Ridge, William Pett
Sir Charles Grandison (Richardson) 69, 121
Six Etchings of Well-Known Views in Kensington Gardens (T. Ellis) 29, 45
Six Stories (Pochhammer) 100
Skeaping, Kenneth (illustrator): *Told After Supper* 28, 83; *The Devil's Acres* 84; *On the Stage–and Off* 28, 87; *A Professional Pugilist* 92; *Rustling Reeds* 94
Slaughter of Animals for Food, The (Galsworthy) 104
Slip-shod English in Polite Society 18, 63
Smith & Ritchie (printers) 10
Smith, Cecil: *Hawara, Biahmu, and Arsinoe* (contr.) 79
Smith, Colin: *Bridge Condensed* 102
Smith, George M.: *The Grievances between Authors & Publishers* (contr.) 73
Smith, W. H.: *British Sugar and French Bounties* 40
Socialism of To-day, The (Laveleye) 62
Socialism or Protection? Which Is to Be? ("M. H.") 93
Society of Antiquaries 24, 32
Society of Authors 32; *The Grievances between Authors & Publishers* 73, 106
Solomon Gessner: "The Swiss Theocritus" (Gessner) 69–70, 121
"Somebody's" Story (Fargus) 68
Some Reminiscences of Thomas Francis and Mary Adams (W. Q. Warren) 94
Somers, Alexander (pseud. Al-So): *Lays of a Lazy Lawyer* 84
Somerset, Lord Henry: *Seven Songs to Sing* (contr.) 90
Some Rules for the Conduct of Life 8, 8*n*, 40, 40*n*
Some Well-known "Sugar'd Sonnets" by William Shakespeare (E. Ellis, T. Ellis) 29, 45–46
Song of Love and Liberty, A (Addy) 72
Song of the Wind, A (Stout) 38
Songs of a Child, Part I, The (Dixie) 101, 103
Songs of a Child, Part II, The (Dixie) 103
Songs of the Morning. Lyrics for Music (Teschemacher) 102
Songs of the North (MacLeod, Boulton) 3, 28, 64–65
Songs Sung and Unsung (H. Boulton) 21, 92–93
Sonnenschein, William Swan: *A Bibliography of Literature* 72*n*
Sonnets. Revised and Enlarged Edition (E. Pfeiffer) 26, 71
Sotheby auctions of Tuer estate: 1900, Sotheby, Wilkinson & Hodge 33, 33*n*, 108; 1927, Sotheby & Co. 34, 108
Sotheran, Henry: *Manners & Customs of the French* 91
Southward, John 8, 31, 39*n*; *Practical Printing* 8*n*
Specimens of Types from the Leadenhall Press 114–115
Spicilegium Poeticum (Hopkins) 25, 89
Spielman, M. H.: *The History of "Punch"* 18*n*
Splay-Feet Splashings in Divers Places ("Goosestep") 87
Splendid Rally: A Story of a Love Set, A (Hamilton) 72
Springer, John (printer) 10
St. Dunstan: A Paper Written to Be Read at Goldsmiths' Hall (Lambert) 48
St. Pancras: Being Antiquarian, Topographical, and Biographical Memoranda (Palmer) 8, 38
Stables, W. Gordon: *Tea: The Drink of Pleasure and of Health* 47

Staff, Frank: *The Valentine & Its Origins* 109n
Stage in the Drawing-Room: Short One-Act Sketches, The (Selous) 90
Standring, Benjamin: *Epigrams: Original and Selected* 41
Staples, Robert, Jr.: *Business and Pleasure in Brazil* 55
Steel, Charles F.: *Is There Any Resemblance between Shakespeare & Bacon?* 77
Stenbock, Eric Stanislaus: *The Shadow of Death* 25
Sterne, Laurence: *Tristram Shandy* 75
Stevens, James: *Ye Perfecte Historie Offe Ye Antiente Fraternitie Offe Ye Rahere Almoners* 46
Stevens, R. T., Capt.: *A Table of Distances in Nautical Miles between the Principal Ports of the United Kingdom, and Ports in the North Sea* 39; *Table of Distances, to and from the Principal Commercial Seaports of the World* 44; *The A B C Mariners' Guide* 39, 44, 46, 53
Stewart, Horace: *History of the Worshipful Company of Gold and Silver Wyre-Drawers* 86
Stickphast Paste 6, 33, 86, 107, 112, 116–118
Still, Elizabeth, Dowager Countess of Harrington: *The Foster-Brother and The Creoles* 71; *The Prime Minister and Tom* 73
Stinks in Leadenhall Street, The (Tuer) 116
Stone, Charles J. (pseud. "Edwarda Gibbon"): *History of the Decline and Fall of the British Empire* 18, 19, 55, 120
Stolen Bishop, The (Rothwell) 95
Stories from Old-Fashioned Children's Books (Tuer) 99, 106
Story of "Bradshaw's Guide," The (Fitzgerald) 81
Story of a London Clerk, The 95
Story of a Nursery Rhyme, The ("C. B.") 21, 29, 36, 44, 49, 119
Story of Ijain, or, the Evolution of a Mind, The (Dixie) 26, 102
Story of Stops, A (Davidson) 26, 83
Stout, William M.: *A Song of the Wind* 38
Stray Minutes: . . . Proceedings of the Literary Club at St. Mungo-by-the-Sea (E. Watson) 91
Streamlets from the Fount of Poesy (Gazder) 102
Studio, The (periodical) 11, 24
Successful Picture!, A! (Luker) 87
Sugar Bounties: Deputation of Proprietors and Merchants Interested in the Sugar Colonies 41
Summer Exhibition, 1885: Catalogue of the Collection of Water Colour Drawings, Paintings, Choice Modern Etchings and Bartolozzi Prints 65
Sun and Serpent Series 20, 94, 96, 121
Sword-Dancers, The (Crawhall) 47, 54, 120
Sybil's Dutch Dolls (Burne) 73
Syeds, Stephen. *See* Grain, Mrs.
Symons, Arthur: *Shakespeare's Antony & Cleopatra* (introd.) 83

Table of Distances, to and from the Principal Commercial Seaports of the World (R. T. Stevens) 44
Table of Distances in Nautical Miles between the Principal Ports of the United Kingdom, and Ports in the North Sea, A (R. T. Stevens) 39
Tales from the Lands of Nuts and Grapes (Sellers) 76
Tales of the "Wild and Woolly West" (Welcker) 85
Taming of a Shrew, The (Crawhall) 47, 50, 120
Taylor, Aeleanor: *Glimpses of the Great Jacobins* 46
Taylor, G. W.: *A Short History of St. George's Chapter* 92
Taylor, Jeremy: *The Marriage Ring* 49
Tcheng-Ki-Tong, Colonel: *The Chinese Painted by Themselves* 63
Tea: The Drink of Pleasure and of Health (Stables) 47
Tennis Cuts and Quips (J. Marshall) 18, 57
Teschemacher, Edward: *Songs of the Morning. Lyrics for Music* 102
"Teufelsdröckh Junior." *See* Parry, Edward Abbot
That Headstrong Boy (Kent) 97
The New River: Unique Auction, May, 1890 115
"Thenks Awf'lly!" Sketched in Cockney and Hung on Twelve Pegs (Tuer) 19, 81, 105
The Stinks in Leadenhall Street (Tuer) 116
This Year, Next Year, Some Time, Never ("Puck") 59
Thompson, Francis: *The Child Set in the Midst: by Modern Poets* 25, 88
Thompson, Silvanus P. 114
Thomson, James: *The Seasons* 75
Thomson, Rev. Joseph Llewelyn: *Oxford to Palestine, Being Notes of a Tour in 1889* 83
Thorpe, Charlotte: *The Children's London* 101
"Those Foreign Devils!" (Yüan) 86, 88
Thought-Reading or Modern Mysteries Explained (Blackburn) 57
Three Beauties; or, the Idols of the Village (Manners) 82
Through England on a Side Saddle (Fiennes) 26, 77
Tit-Bits: Prize Specimens of Handwriting 77
Todhunter, John: *A Book of Jousts* 75
Told after Supper (Jerome) 83, 83n
Told After Supper [copyright pamphlet] (Tuer) 83, 106
Tomlinson, Lizzie Joyce: *A Bit of Humanity* 96
Torch & Colonial Book Circular 86n
Torkington, Sir Richard: *Ye Oldest Diarie of Englysshe Travell* 54
Townsend, George Henry: *Evans's Music and Supper Rooms* 38
Tree Gossip (Heath) 20, 27, 61
Tricks and Tricksters (Forster) 88
Tristram Shandy (Sterne) 75, 121
Trübner & Co 7
True Relation of the Apparition of Mrs. Veal to Mrs. Bargrave, A (Crawhall) 47, 54
True Story of Mazeppa, The (Vogüé) 59–60
Truth About Democracy, The ("B.") 84

Truth about Tonquin, The (Colquhoun) 27, 48*n*, 55
Tuer, Andrew White: early years 5, 7; Field & Tuer partnership 5; inventions 6, 7, 33; marketing ideas 6, 19, 26; marriage and home life 7, 11, 11*n*; collections and interests 8, 11, 14, 19, 32; bookplates 106–108; sense of humor 2, 18, 19; book design 3, 5, 20; publisher and printer 1, 3, 8, 15, 19; Caxton Celebration 9; *Guercino Etchings Dispute* 14, 125; jokes for *Punch* 18, 33; Leadenhall Press, Ltd. Managing Director, 31; interest in shagreen 32; correspondent to periodicals 32; memberships 32; Kelly & Co. director 32; death, obituaries 32–33; Sotheby auctions 33–34, 108

Tuer, Andrew White, works of: *The Paper & Printing Trades Journal* (ed.) 8, 10, 39; *Luxurious Bathing* 12, 13, 15, 29, 36, 41, 42, 105; *The Printers' International Specimen Exchange* (ed.) 10, 11, 42; *Bartolozzi and His Works* 14, 33, 36, 44, 66, 105; *List of the Works of Bartolozzi* 45; *The Kaukneigh Awlminek, 1883* 19, 20, 46, 105; *Catalogue of a Loan Collection of Engravings & Etchings by Francesco Bartolozzi* (introd.) 47, 106; *Bygone Beauties* (annot.) 51–52, 106; *London Cries: with Six Charming Children* 15, 52–53, 105; *Quads for Authors, Editors, & Devils* 58, 105; *Quads within Quads* 23, 48, 58, 105; *John Bull's Womankind (Suggestions for an Alteration in the Law of Copyright)* 18, 58, 105; *Old London Street Cries and the Cries of To-day* 15, 19, 53, 65, 105; *The Follies & Fashions of Our Grandfathers* 22, 70, 105; *1,000 Quaint Cuts from Books of Other Days* 15, 66, 71, 105; *The First Year of a Silken Reign* 72, 105; *The Grievances between Authors & Publishers* (appendix) 73, 106; "*Thenks Awf'lly!*" *Sketched in Cockney and Hung on Twelve Pegs* 19, 81, 105; "The Art of Silhouetting" 12, 105; *Dame Wiggins of Lee* (introd.) 74, 106; *The Gaping, Wide-mouthed, Waddling Frog* (introd.) 74, 106; *Deborah Dent and Her Donkey* 74, 106; *Prince Dorus* (introd.) 79, 106; *London City* (copyright pamphlet) 81, 105; *Told After Supper* (copyright pamphlet) 83, 105; *Guess the Title of This Story!* 26, 86, 106; *The Book of Delightful and Strange Designs* 1, 31, 89; *History of the Horn-Book* 24, 28, 31, 32, 33, 95, 106, 107, 116; *Pages and Pictures from Forgotten Children's Books* 98, 106, 117; *Stories from Old-Fashioned Children's Books* 99, 106

Tuer, Joseph (grandfather) 5
Tuer, Joseph Robertson and Jane Taft (parents) 5
Tuer, Thomasine Louisa Louttit: marriage to Andrew Tuer 7; amateur contralto 7; interest in bridge 7; and Leadenhall Press, Ltd. 26, 33; husband's estate 33; death 34

Tuke, Henry Scott: *History of the Horn-Book* (illust.) 95
Tupper, Margaret Elenora: *The Scent of the Heather* 95
Turner, Mrs. Elizabeth: *The Cowslip* 99; *The Daisy* 99
Turnerelli, Edward Tracy: *Memories of a Life of Toil* 59
12 New Songs by Some of the Best-Known British Composers (H. Boulton) 86
Tynan, Katherine: *The Child Set in the Midst: by Modern Poets* 25, 88
Types and Types of Beauty from the Leadenhall Press 103
Typographic Printing Company 3*n*
Twelvetrees, W. H.: *Report of Mr. John H. Darby, M.Inst.C.E., on the Blythe River Iron Mines* 101
Uncle, Can You Find a Rhyme for Orange? 7, 37
Undoing of De Harcla, The (Rawnsley) 89
University Magazine, a Literary and Philosophic Review: review of *Luxurious Bathing* 12, 12*n*
Unwin Bros., the Gresham Press 10
Up the Moonstair (A. Hooper) 83
Vagaries of To-day, The (Mundy) 97
Valentine, Ferdinand Charles: *Gotham and the Gothamites* (trans.) 72
Valentines (Kendrew, King) 109
van Laun, Henri: *A Fusion of Parties in France, A.D. 1872* 39
Vellum-Parchment Shilling Series of Miscellaneous Literature 21, 48, 49, 51, 52, 53, 54, 55, 56, 59, 119
Vicar's Pups. In a Few Yelps and a Couple of Growls, The (Davies, Prescott) 98
Victoria, Queen: accepts copy of Printers' International Specimen Exchange 10; Bartolozzi Exhibition patronage 111; books dedicated to by command 24, 29, 45, 70, 84, 87, 90, 95; subject of *The First Year of a Silken Reign* 72
Views of English Society: by a Little Girl of Eleven ("Mabel") 21, 70
Vigne: *Fred. James under a Spell!* (illust.) 87
Vincent, James E.: *Foot-Ball: Its History for Five Centuries* 62
Visible to-Be. A Story of Hand-Reading, The 88, 91
Vogüé, E. Melchior de, Viscount: *The True Story of Mazeppa* 59; *Le Fils de Pierre le Grand* 60
"W": *Can Parliament Break Faith* 55
Wain, Louis: *Novel Notes* (illust.) 28, 90
Wake, Richard: *A Selection of Sketches and Letters on Sport and Life in Morocco* 80
Walker, Emery 3*n*
Wallace-Dunlop, Madeline Anne: *Glass in the Old World* 46
"Wandering Jew, The": *The First Century and the Nineteenth* 88
Ward, Chas. (Charles) A.: *Oracles of Nostradamus* 85
Warde, Walter, Eldred: *Lines Grave and Gay* 68
Ware, J. Redding: *The Life and Times of Colonel Fred Burnaby* 65

Warren, Walter: *Master Jimmy's Fables* (illust.) 94
Warren, William Quinn: *Some Reminiscences of Thomas Francis and Mary Adams* (ed.) 94
Watkins-Pitchford, Walter M. (pseud. Samuel Bagshaw): *Amateur Tommy Atkins* 63
Watlock, W. A.: *The Next Ninety-Three, or Crown, Commune and Colony* 68
Watson, Edmund Henry Lacon: *Ephemera: Essays* 82; *Stray Minutes: . . . Proceedings of the Literary Club at St. Mungo-by-the-Sea* 91
Watson, John: *The Confessions of a Poacher* 84
Weather Wisdom (Allan) 80
Week in a Wherry on the Norfolk Broads, A ("Blue Peter") 83
Welcker, Adair: *Tales of the "Wild and Woolly West"* 85
Welsh, Charles: *Harris's Cabinet. Numbers One to Four* 51
West, James (illustrator): *The Confessions of a Poacher* 84; *The Signs of Old Lombard Street* 84
West, Walter J.: *History of the Horn-Book* (illust.) 24, 95
West India Committee: *West India Mails* 40
West India Mails 40
Westward Hoe for Avalon in the New-Found-Land (Whitbourne) 38
What Grade to Use? [price list] 117
What Is the Church? (R. I. Woodhouse) 70
When Is Your Birthday? (E. Ellis) 49
Whistler, James McNeill: *Songs of the North* (illust.) 28, 65; *The Gentle Art of Making Enemies*, Sheridan Ford, and Field & Tuer 30–31
Whitbourne, Captain Richard: *Westward Hoe for Avalon in the New-Found-Land* 38
Whitburn, Thomas: *Westward Hoe for Avalon in the New-Found-Land* (illust.) 38
White, Andrew and Ophelia: guardians of Andrew Tuer 5
White, Gleeson 1, 11; "The Sampler, an appreciation and a plea for its revival" in *The Studio* 11*n*
Whittingham, Charles 15
Who Is His Father? (Scotter) 70
Why Not Eat Insects? (Holt) 64
Wilde, Lady Jane: "The Child's Dream" in *The Bairns' Annual 1885-6* 26, 67
Wilde, Oscar: *A Book of Jousts* 25; review of *Echoes of Memory* 25
Wilde, William C. K.: *A Book of Jousts* 75
Wilkin, Charles: *Bygone Beauties* 51–52, 106
Wilkinson, W. H.: *"Those Foreign Devils!"* (trans.) 86
William Heinemann & Co. 30, 32
Williams, Frederick Condé: *Journalistic Jumbles; or, Trippings in Type* 56, 120
Williams, R. I.: *History of the Horn-Book* (illust.) 24, 95; possible illust. of Stickphast Paste ad 116*n*
Williams, T.: *Political Wit and Humour in Our Own Times* 79
Willock, A. Dewar: *"Never Hit a Man Named Sullivan!"* 18, 82
Windsor Gallery: *Catalogue of a Loan Collection of Engravings & Etchings by Francesco Bartolozzi* 46; *Catalogue of the Second Exhibition . . . of Engravings & Etchings by Francesco Bartolozzi* 47
Windt, Harry de: *Ennui De Voyage* 80
Wingfield, Lewis: *Antony & Cleopatra* (prod.) 83
Winter's Tale, The (Shakespeare) 29, 78
Wonderland of Evolution, The (Gresswell) 58
Woodehouse, James: *The Life and Poetical Works of James Woodhouse* 96
Woodhouse, Rev. Reginald Illingworth: *What Is the Church?* 70; *Baby's Record* 79; *The Life and Poetical Works of James Woodhouse* (ed.) 96; *A Brief Guide to Merstham Parish Church, Surrey* 103
Wood J.: *Imaginary Conversations of Three White-Letter Days in the Anglo-Saxon Cloisters* 103
Woods, Charlotte Elizabeth (Mrs. R. W.): *Gatherings* 82; *"Have Ye Read It?" Look Sharp!* 93; *An Every-Day Life* 95
.X.Y.Z. and Other Poems (Lascelles) 94, 121
Ye antiente fraternitie of ye Rahere Almoners 43
Yeats, John Butler 29
Yeats, William Butler 29
Ye Foure Etchynges By Maister H. Crickmore 66
Ye Foure Etchynges By Maister S. Myers 66
Ye Gestes of Ye Ladye Anne (Forsyth) 59
Ye Leadenhalle Presse Oblong Shilling-Series 42, 120
Ye Leadenhalle Presse Pamphlets 55, 120
Ye Leadenhalle Workes 8, 39*n*
Ye legende of ye anciente fraternitie of ye Rahere Almoners 43
Ye Legende of Ye Kempes (Hitchen-Kemp) 102
Ye Loving Ballad of Lorde Bateman (Crawhall) 47, 54, 120
Ye Oldest Diarie of Englysshe Travell (Torkington) 40, 48*n*, 54, 119
Ye Openynge of ye Reading Room atte ye Halsteade Brewehouse [handbill] 111
Ye Perfecte Historie Offe Ye Antiente Fraternitie Offe Ye Rahere Almoners (J. Stevens) 46
You Shouldn't ("Brother Bob") 19, 48*n*, 53*n*, 55, 119
Yüan Hsiang-fu: *"Those Foreign Devils!"* 86
Yuletide at the Scala Theatre [playbill] 117